HATCHET

GARY PAULSEN

WORKBOOK

HATCHET

1판 1쇄   2018년   3월 16일
2판 3쇄   2024년   4월 22일

지은이   GARY PAULSEN
기획   김승규
책임편집   김보경 정소이
콘텐츠제작및감수   롱테일 교육 연구소
저작권   명채린
마케팅   두잉글 사업 본부

펴낸이   이수영
펴낸곳   롱테일북스
출판등록   제2015-000191호
주소   04033 서울특별시 마포구 양화로 113, 3층(서교동, 순흥빌딩)
전자메일   help@ltinc.net

ISBN 979-11-91343-93-9 14740

Contents

아동 도서계의 노벨상!' 미국 최고 권위의 아동 문학상

뉴베리 상(Newbery Award)은 미국 도서관 협회에서 해마다 미국 아동 문학 발전에 가장 크게 이바지한 작가에게 수여하는 아동 문학상입니다. 1922년에 시작된 이 상은 미국에서 가장 오랜 역사를 지닌 아동 문학상이자, '아동 도서계의 노벨상'이라 불릴 만큼 높은 권위를 자랑하는 상입니다.

뉴베리 상은 그 역사와 권위만큼이나 심사 기준이 까다롭기로 유명한데, 심사단은 책의 주제 의식은 물론 정보의 깊이와 스토리의 정교함, 캐릭터와 문체의 적정성 등을 꼼꼼히 평가하여 수상작을 결정합니다.

그해 최고의 작품으로 선정된 도서에게는 '뉴베리 메달(Newbery Medal)'이라고 부르는 금색 메달을 수여하며, 최종 후보에 올랐던 주목할 만한 작품들에게는 '뉴베리 아너(Newbery Honor)'라는 이름의 은색 마크를 수여합니다.

뉴베리 상을 받은 도서는 미국의 모든 도서관에 비치되어 더 많은 독자들을 만나게 되며, 대부분 수십에서 수백만 부가 판매되는 베스트셀러가 됩니다. 뉴베리 상을 수상한 작가는 그만큼 필력과 작품성을 인정받게 되어, 수상 작가의 다른 작품들 또한 수상작 못지않게 커다란 주목과 사랑을 받습니다.

왜 뉴베리 수상작인가?
쉬운 어휘로 쓰인 '검증된' 영어원서!

뉴베리 수상작들은 '검증된 원서'로 국내 영어 학습자들에게 큰 사랑을 받고 있습니다. 뉴베리 수상작이 원서 읽기에 좋은 교재인 이유는 무엇일까요?

1. 아동 문학인 만큼 어휘가 어렵지 않습니다.
2. 어렵지 않은 어휘를 사용하면서도 '문학상'을 수상한 만큼 문장의 깊이가 상당합니다.
3. 적당한 난이도의 어휘와 깊이 있는 문장으로 구성되어 있기 때문에 초등 고학년부터 성인까지, 영어 초보자부터 실력자까지 모든 영어 학습자들이 읽기에 좋습니다.

실제로 뉴베리 수상작은 국제중·특목고에서는 입시 필독서로, 대학교에서는 영어 강독 교재로 다양하고 폭넓게 활용되고 있습니다. 이런 이유로 뉴베리 수상작은 한국어 번역서보다 오히려 원서가 훨씬 많이 판매되는 기현상을 보이고 있습니다.

'베스트 오브 베스트'만을 엄선한 「뉴베리 컬렉션」

「뉴베리 컬렉션」은 뉴베리 메달 및 아너 수상작, 그리고 뉴베리 수상 작가의 유명 작품들을 엄선하여 한국 영어 학습자들을 위한 최적의 교재로 재탄생시킨 영어 원서 시리즈입니다.

1. 어휘 수준과 문장의 난이도, 분량 등 국내 영어 학습자들에게 적합한 정도를 종합적으로 검토하여 선정하였습니다.
2. 기존 원서 독자층 사이의 인기도까지 감안하여 최적의 작품들을 선별하였습니다.
3. 판형이 좁고 글씨가 작아 읽기 힘들었던 원서 디자인을 대폭 수정하여, 판형을 시원하게 키우고 읽기에 최적화된 영문 서체를 사용하여 가독성을 극대화하였습니다.
4. 함께 제공되는 워크북은 어려운 어휘를 완벽하게 정리하고 이해력을 점검하는 퀴즈를 덧붙여 독자들이 원서를 보다 쉽고 재미있게 읽을 수 있도록 구성하였습니다.
5. 기존에 높은 가격에 판매되어 구입이 부담스러웠던 오디오북을 부록으로 제공하여 리스닝과 소리 내어 읽기에까지 원서를 두루 활용할 수 있도록 했습니다.

게리 폴슨(Gary Paulsen)은 미국의 유명한 아동 문학 작가입니다. 그는 어린 시절을 필리핀에서 보냈고 작가가 되기 전에 선원, 사냥꾼, 양궁 선수, 엔지니어, 배우 등 다양한 직업을 가졌습니다. 또한 알래스카에서 개 썰매 경주에 참여하기도 했습니다. 이런 다양한 경험이 녹아든 그의 이야기는 독자들의 큰 사랑을 받았고, 그는 『Dogsong』, 『The Winter Room』 그리고 『Hatchet』을 통해 뉴베리 아너를 세 번이나 수상했습니다.

「Hatchet」은 경비행기를 타고 캐나다에 사는 아버지를 만나러 가는 길에 조종사의 심장마비로 비행기 추락사고를 겪게 된 열세 살 소년 브라이언(Brian)의 이야기입니다. 갑자기 캐나다의 삼림지대에 홀로 남겨진 브라이언은 막막하기만 합니다. 끊임없이 그를 괴롭히는 모기, 배고픔, 그리고 두렵게만 여겨지는 대자연에 맞서야 하는 브라이언이 가지고 있는 것은 그의 어머니가 선물한 손도끼뿐입니다. 그에게는 부모님의 이혼으로 이어진 그 끔찍한 비밀에 대해 분노하거나, 자기 연민을 하거나, 절망을 할 시간이 없습니다. 브라이언은 이제 자신이 가진 모든 기지와 용기를 끌어내서 생존해야만 합니다.
오랜 세월 많은 독자들의 마음을 사로잡은 이 책은 한 소년의 모험을 통해 성장과 생존의 진정한 의미에 대해 따뜻한 울림을 선사하고 있습니다.

원서 본문

내용이 담긴 원서 본문입니다.
원어민이 읽는 일반 원서와 같은 텍스트지만,
암기해야 할 중요 어휘들은 볼드체로 표시되
어 있습니다. 이 어휘들은 지금 들고 계신 워
크북에 챕터별로 정리되어 있습니다.

학습 심리학 연구 결과에 따르면, 한 단어씩
따로 외우는 단어 암기는 거의 효과가 없다고
합니다. 단어를 제대로 외우기 위해서는 문맥
(context) 속에서 단어를 암기해야 하며, 한 단
어당 문맥 속에서 15번 이상 마주칠 때 완벽하
게 암기할 수 있다고 합니다.

이 책의 본문에서는 중요 어휘를 볼드체로 강조하여, 문맥 속의 단어들을 더 확
실히 인지(word cognition in context)하도록 돕고 있습니다. 또한 대부분의 중요 단
어들은 다른 챕터에서도 반복해서 등장하기 때문에 이 책을 읽는 것만으로도 자
연스럽게 어휘력을 향상시킬 수 있습니다.

또한 본문 하단에는 내용 이해를 돕기 위한
'각주'가 첨가되어 있습니다. 각주는 굳이 암기
할 필요는 없지만, 알아 두면 도움이 될 만한
정보를 설명하고 있습니다. 각주를 참고하면
스토리를 더 깊이 있게 이해할 수 있어 원서를
읽는 재미가 배가됩니다.

워크북(Workbook)

Check Your Reading Speed
해당 챕터의 단어 수가 기록되어 있어, 리딩 속도를 측정할 수 있습니다. 특히 리딩 속도를 중시하는 독자들이 유용하게 사용할 수 있습니다.

Build Your Vocabulary
본문에 볼드 표시되어 있던 단어들이 정리되어 있습니다. 리딩 전, 후에 반복해서 보면 원서를 더욱 쉽게 읽을 수 있고, 어휘력도 빠르게 향상될 것입니다.

단어는 〈스펠링 – 빈도 – 발음기호 – 품사 – 한글 뜻 – 영문 뜻〉 순서로 표기되어 있으며 빈도 표시(★)가 많을수록 필수 어휘입니다. 반복해서 등장하는 단어는 빈도 대신 '복습'으로 표기되어 있습니다. 품사는 아래와 같이 표기했습니다.

n. 명사 | a. 형용사 | ad. 부사 | v. 동사

conj. 접속사 | prep. 전치사 | int. 감탄사 | idiom 숙어 및 관용구

Comprehension Quiz
간단한 퀴즈를 통해 읽은 내용에 대한 이해력을 점검해 볼 수 있습니다.

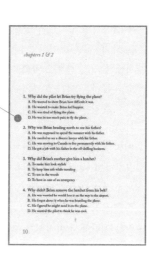

「뉴베리 컬렉션」 이렇게 읽어 보세요!

아래와 같이 프리뷰(Preview) → 리딩(Reading) → 리뷰(Review) 세 단계를 거치면서 읽으면, 더욱 효과적으로 영어실력을 향상할 수 있습니다!

1. 프리뷰(Preview) : 오늘 읽을 내용을 먼저 점검하자!

- 워크북을 통해 오늘 읽을 챕터에 나와 있는 단어들을 쭉 훑어봅니다. 어떤 단어들이 나오는지, 내가 아는 단어와 모르는 단어가 어떤 것들이 있는지 가벼운 마음으로 살펴봅니다.
- 평소처럼 하나하나 쓰면서 암기하려고 하지는 마세요! 익숙하지 않은 단어들을 주의 깊게 보되, 어차피 리딩을 하면서 점차 익숙해질 단어라는 것을 기억하며 빠르게 훑어봅니다.
- 뒤 챕터로 갈수록 '복습'이라고 표시된 단어들이 늘어나는 것을 알 수 있습니다. '복습' 단어인데도 여전히 익숙하지 않다면 더욱 신경을 써서 봐야겠죠? 매일매일 꾸준히 읽는다면, 익숙한 단어들이 점점 많아진다는 것을 몸으로 느낄 수 있습니다.

2. 리딩(Reading) : 내용에 집중하며 빠르게 읽어 나가자!

- 프리뷰를 마친 후 바로 리딩을 시작합니다. 방금 살펴봤던 어휘들을 문장 속에서 다시 만나게 되는데 이 과정에서 단어의 쓰임새와 어감을 자연스럽게 익히게 됩니다.
- 모르는 단어나 이해되지 않는 문장이 나오더라도 멈추지 말고 전체적인 맥락을 잡아가면서 속도감 있게 읽어 나가세요. 이해되지 않는 문장들은 따로 표시를 하되, 일단 넘어가고 계속 읽는 것이 좋습니다. 뒷부분을 읽다 보면 자연히 이해가 되는 경우도 있고, 정 이해가 되지 않는 부분은 리딩을 마친 이후에 따로 리뷰하는 시간을 가지면 됩니다. 문제집을 풀듯이 모든 문장을 분석하면서 원서를 읽는 것이 아니라, 리딩을 할 때는 리딩에만, 리뷰를 할 때는 리뷰에만 집중하는 것이 필요합니다.
- 볼드 처리된 단어의 의미가 궁금하더라도 워크북을 바로 펼치지 마세요. 정 궁금하다면 한 번씩 참고하는 것도 나쁘진 않지만, 워크북과 원서를 번갈아 보면서 읽는 것은 리딩의 흐름을 끊고 단어 하나하나에 집착하는 좋지 않은 리딩 습관을 심어 줄 수 있습니다.
- 같은 맥락에서 번역서를 구해 원서와 동시에 번갈아 보는 것도 좋은 방법이 아닙니다. 한글 번역을 가지고 있다고 해도 일단 영어로 읽을 때는 영어에만 집중하고 어느 정도 분량을 읽은 후에 번역서와 비교하도록 하세요. 모든 문장을 일일이 번역해서 완벽하게 이해하려는 것은 오히려 좋지 않은 리딩 습관을 심

어 주어 장기적으로는 바람직하지 않은 결과를 얻을 수 있습니다. 처음부터 완벽하게 이해하려고 하는 것보다는 빠른 속도로 2~3회 반복해서 읽는 방식이 실력 향상에 더 도움이 됩니다. 만일 반복해서 읽어도 내용이 전혀 이해되지 않아 곤란하다면 책 선정에 문제가 있다고 할 수 있습니다. 그럴 때는 좀 더 쉬운 책을 골라 실력을 다진 뒤 다시 도전하는 것이 좋습니다.

- 초보자라면 분당 150단어의 리딩 속도를 목표로 잡고 리딩을 합니다. 분당 150단어는 원어민이 말하는 속도로, 영어 학습자들이 리스닝과 스피킹으로 넘어가기 위해 가장 기초적으로 달성해야 하는 단계입니다. 분당 50~80단어 정도의 낮은 리딩 속도를 가지고 있는 경우는 대부분 영어 실력이 부족해서라기보다 '잘못된 리딩 습관'을 가지고 있어서 그렇습니다. 이해력이 조금 떨어진다고 하더라도 분당 150단어까지는 속도에 대한 긴장감을 놓치지 말고 속도감 있게 읽어 나가도록 하세요.

3. 리뷰(Review) : 이해력을 점검하고 꼼꼼하게 다시 살펴보자!

- 해당 챕터의 Comprehension Quiz를 통해 이해력을 점검해 봅니다.
- 오늘 만난 어휘들을 다시 한번 복습합니다. 이때는 읽으면서 중요하다고 생각했던 단어를 연습장에 써 보면서 꼼꼼하게 외우는 것도 좋습니다.
- 이해가 되지 않는다고 표시해 두었던 부분도 주의 깊게 분석해 봅니다. 다시 한번 문장을 꼼꼼히 읽고, 어떤 이유에서 이해가 되지 않았는지 생각해 봅니다. 따로 메모를 남기거나 노트를 작성하는 것도 좋은 방법입니다.
- 사실 꼼꼼히 리뷰하는 것은 매우 고된 과정입니다. 원서를 읽고 리뷰하는 시간을 가지는 것이 영어 실력 향상에 많은 도움이 되기는 하지만, 이 과정을 철저히 지키려다가 원서 읽기의 재미를 반감시키는 것은 바람직하지 않습니다. 그럴 때는 차라리 리뷰를 가볍게 하는 것이 좋을 수 있습니다. '내용에 빠져서 재미있게', 문제집에서는 상상도 못할 '많은 양'을 읽으면서, 매일매일 조금씩 꾸준히 실력을 키워가는 것이 원서를 활용하는 기본적인 방법이며, 영어 공부의 왕도입니다. 문제집 풀듯이 원서 읽기를 시도하고 접근해서는 실패할 수밖에 없습니다.
- 이런 방식으로 원서를 끝까지 다 읽었다면, 다시 반복해서 읽거나 오디오북을 활용하는 등 다양한 방식으로 원서 읽기를 확장해 나갈 수 있습니다. 이에 대한 자세한 안내가 워크북 말미에 실려 있습니다.

1. Why did the pilot let Brian try flying the plane?
   A. He wanted to show Brian how difficult it was.
   B. He wanted to make Brian feel happier.
   C. He was tired of flying the plane.
   D. He was in too much pain to fly the plane.

2. Why was Brian heading north to see his father?
   A. He was supposed to spend the summer with his father.
   B. He needed to see a divorce lawyer with his father.
   C. He was moving to Canada to live permanently with his father.
   D. He got a job with his father in the oil-drilling business.

3. Why did Brian's mother give him a hatchet?
   A. To make him look stylish
   B. To keep him safe while traveling
   C. To use in the woods
   D. To have in case of an emergency

4. Why didn't Brian remove the hatchet from his belt?
   A. He was worried he would lose it on the way to the airport.
   B. He forgot about it when he was boarding the plane.
   C. He figured he might need it on the plane.
   D. He wanted the pilot to think he was cool.

5. What happened when Brian used the radio?

    A. He was able to inform the other person of his exact location.

    B. The person on the other end told him to keep flying.

    C. The headset got damaged when the nose of the plane dropped.

    D. The signal broke up and was eventually lost.

6. What two options did Brian have?

    A. He could keep flying onward or turn back to the airport in New York.

    B. He could stay on the original course or search for a quicker route to Canada.

    C. He could wait for the plane to run out of gas or make the plane go down sooner.

    D. He could find more fuel for the engine or jump out of the plane with a parachute.

7. What was NOT part of Brian's plan for landing?

    A. To fly into trees

    B. To head toward a lake

    C. To land kind of on water

    D. To reduce the impact

1분에 몇 단어를 읽는지 리딩 속도를 측정해보세요.

$$\frac{2{,}606 \text{ words}}{\text{reading time ( ) sec}} \times 60 = (\quad\quad) \text{ WPM}$$

Build Your Vocabulary

stare*
[stɛər]
v. 빤히 쳐다보다, 응시하다; n. 빤히 쳐다보기, 응시
If you stare at someone or something, you look at them for a long time.

endless*
[éndlis]
a. 끝없는; 무한한, 한없는
If you say that something is endless, you mean that it is very large or lasts for a very long time, and it seems as if it will never stop.

wilderness*
[wíldərnis]
n. 황야, 황무지; 버려진 땅
A wilderness is a desert or other area of natural land which is not used by people.

roar*
[rɔ:r]
v. 웅웅거리다; 고함치다; 굉음을 내며 질주하다; n. 함성; 울부짖는 듯한 소리
If something roars, it makes a very loud noise.

consume*
[kənsú:m]
v. (강렬한 감정이) 사로잡다; 먹다; 소모하다 (consuming a. 엄청나게 강렬한)
If a feeling or idea consumes you, it affects you very strongly indeed.

ruin
[ru:in]
v. 엉망으로 만들다; 폐허로 만들다; n. 붕괴, 몰락; 파멸
To ruin something means to severely harm, damage, or spoil it.

passenger
[pǽsəndʒər]
n. 승객
A passenger in a vehicle such as a bus, boat, or plane is a person who is traveling in it, but who is not driving it or working on it.

pilot
[páilət]
n. 조종사, 비행사 (copilot n. 부조종사)
A pilot is a person who is trained to fly an aircraft.

take off
idiom 날아오르다; (서둘러) 떠나다 (take-off n. (항공기의) 이륙)
If an aircraft takes off, it leaves the ground and starts flying.

drive*
[draiv]
v. (drove–driven) 운전하다; 만들다; 박아 넣다; 몰아가다; n. 드라이브; 충동, 욕구
When you drive somewhere, you operate a car or other vehicle and control its movement and direction.

initial*
[iníʃəl]
a. 처음의, 초기의; n. 이름의 첫 글자
You use initial to describe something that happens at the beginning of a process.

control
[kəntróul]
n. (기계·차량의) 제어 장치; 통제, 제어; v. 지배하다; 조정하다
A control is a device such as a switch or lever which you use in order to operate a machine or other piece of equipment.

instrument[**] [ínstrəmənt]
n. (차량 · 기계에서) 계기; 악기; 수단
An instrument is a device that is used for making measurements of something such as speed, height, or sound, for example on a ship or plane or in a car.

claw[*] [klɔ:]
v. 헤치며 나아가다; (손톱 · 발톱으로) 할퀴다; n. (동물 · 새의) 발톱
If you claw your way somewhere, you move there with great difficulty, trying desperately to find things to hold on to.

altitude[*] [ǽltətjù:d]
n. (해발) 고도; 고도가 높은 곳, 고지
If something is at a particular altitude, it is at that height above sea level.

jerk[*] [dʒə:rk]
v. 홱 움직이다; n. 얼간이; 홱 움직임
If you jerk something or someone in a particular direction, or they jerk in a particular direction, they move a short distance very suddenly and quickly.

slide[*] [slaid]
v. 미끄러지듯이 움직이다; 슬며시 넣다; n. 떨어짐; 미끄러짐
When something slides somewhere or when you slide it there, it moves there smoothly over or against something.

current[**] [kə́:rənt]
n. (물 · 공기의) 흐름; 해류; 전류; a. 현재의, 지금의
A current is a steady and continuous flowing movement of some of the water in a river, lake, or sea.

level off
idiom 수평을 유지하다
If an aircraft levels off, it starts to travel horizontally rather than going up or down.

drone [droun]
n. (낮게) 웅웅거리는 소리; 저음; v. 웅얼거리는 소리를 내다
A drone is a continuous low humming sound.

nose[***] [nouz]
n. (항공기 · 우주선 등의) 앞부분; 코; v. 천천히 조심스럽게 나아가다
The nose of a vehicle such as a car or airplane is the front part of it.

flow[***] [flou]
v. 계속 흘러가다; (액체 · 기체가) 흐르다; n. 흐름
If a number of people or things flow from one place to another, they move there steadily in large groups, usually without stopping.

horizon[**] [həráizn]
n. 지평선, 수평선
The horizon is the line in the far distance where the sky seems to meet the land or the sea.

spread[***] [spred]
v. (spread–spread) (넓은 범위에 걸쳐) 펼쳐지다; 펴다; 퍼지다, 확산되다;
n. 확산, 전파
If something spreads out or is spread, it covers or exists across a large area.

swamp[*] [swamp]
n. 늪, 습지; v. (일 등이) 쇄도하다
A swamp is an area of very wet land with wild plants growing in it.

wander[*] [wándər]
v. (이리저리 천천히) 돌아다니다; (일행들로부터) 떨어져 나가다;
n. (잠깐 동안 이리저리) 거닐기
If you wander in a place, you walk around there in a casual way, often without intending to go in any particular direction.

stream^{**} [striːm]	n. 개울, 시내; (액체·기체의) 줄기; v. (액체·기체가) 줄줄 흐르다; 줄을 지어 이어지다 A stream is a small narrow river.
thunder[*] [θʌ́ndər]	v. 우르릉거리다; 천둥이 치다; 쏜살같이 보내다; n. 천둥; 천둥 같은 소리 If something thunders, it makes a very loud noise, usually continuously.
catalog[*] [kǽtəlɔ̀ːg]	v. 목록을 만들다; 일련의 것들을 보여 주다; n. (상품 · 자료의) 목록 To catalog things means to make a list of them.
lead up to	idiom ~에 이르다; ~로 향하게 하다 If events, problems, or actions lead up to an important event, they happen one after another in a way that makes it possible for the event to happen.
flight^{**} [flait]	n. 비행; 항공기; 계단, 층계; 탈출, 도피 A flight is a journey made by flying, usually in an airplane.
divorce[*] [divɔ́ːrs]	n. 이혼; v. 이혼하다 A divorce is the formal ending of a marriage by law.
tear^{**} [tɛər]	① v. 찢다, 뜯다; 뜯어 내다; n. 찢어진 곳, 구멍 (tearing a. 괴로운) ② n. 눈물 Tearing means causing continued or repeated pain or distress.
yell[*] [jel]	v. 고함치다, 소리 지르다; n. 고함, 외침 If you yell, you shout loudly, usually because you are excited, angry, or in pain.
lawyer^{**} [lɔ́ːjər]	n. 변호사 A lawyer is a person who is qualified to advise people about the law and represent them in court.
legal^{**} [líːgəl]	a. 법률과 관련된; 법이 허용하는, 합법적인 Legal is used to describe things that relate to the law.
term^{**} [təːrm]	n. 용어, 말; 기간; v. (이름 · 용어로) 칭하다 A term is a word or expression with a specific meaning, especially one which is used in relation to a particular subject.
come apart	idiom 끝장나다; 부서지다, 흩어지다 To come apart means to begin to fail.
shatter[*] [ʃǽtər]	v. 산산이 부수다, 산산조각 내다; 엄청난 충격을 주다 If something shatters your dreams, hopes, or beliefs, it completely destroys them.
solid^{**} [sálid]	a. 확실한; 단단한; 견고한, 속이 꽉 찬; 완전한; n. 고체, 고형물 Solid evidence or information is reliable because it is based on facts.
burn^{***} [bəːrn]	v. 화끈거리다; 불에 타다, 데다, (햇볕 등에) 타다; (마음 등에) 새겨지다; n. 화상 If a part of your body burns or if something burns it, it has a painful, hot or stinging feeling.
seep [siːp]	v. 스미다, 배다 If something such as liquid or gas seeps somewhere, it flows slowly and in small amounts into a place where it should not go.

14

wipe*
[waip]

v. (먼지 · 물기 등을) 닦다; 지우다; n. 닦기
If you wipe something, you rub its surface to remove dirt or liquid from it.

out of the corner of one's eye

idiom 곁눈질로; 흘깃 보고
If you see something out of the corner of your eye, you see it but not clearly because it happens to the side of you.

notice***
[nóutis]

v. 알아채다, 인지하다; 주의하다; n. 신경 씀, 주목, 알아챔
If you notice something or someone, you become aware of them.

wheel**
[hwi:l]

n. (자동차 등의) 핸들; 바퀴; v. (반대 방향으로) 휙 돌다; (바퀴 달린 것을) 밀다
The wheel of a car or other vehicle is the circular object that is used to steer it.

rudder**
[rʌ́dər]

n. (항공기의) 방향타; (배의) 키
An airplane's rudder is a vertical piece of metal at the back which is used to make the plane turn to the right or to the left.

pedal*
[pedl]

n. 페달, 발판; v. 페달을 밟다; (자전거를) 타고 가다
A pedal in a car or on a machine is a lever that you press with your foot in order to control the car or machine.

extend**
[iksténd]

v. 관련시키다, 포함하다; (거리 · 기간을) 포괄하다; (팔 · 다리를) 뻗다
(extension n. 연장, 확대)
Something that is an extension of something else is a development of it that includes or affects more people, things, or activities.

dashboard
[dǽʃbɔ:rd]

n. (승용차의) 계기판
The dashboard in a car is the panel facing the driver's seat where most of the instruments and switches are.

dial*
[dáiəl]

n. (시계 · 계기 등의) 문자반; v. 다이얼을 돌리다, 전화를 걸다
A dial is a control on a device or piece of equipment which you can move in order to adjust the setting, for example to select or change the frequency on a radio or the temperature of a heater.

switch*
[swiʧ]

n. 스위치; 전환; v. 전환하다, 바꾸다
A switch is a small control for an electrical device which you use to turn the device on or off.

meter*
[mí:tər]

n. 계량 장치; 계량기; v. 계량기로 재다
A meter is a device that measures and records something such as the amount of gas or electricity that you have used.

knob*
[nab]

n. (동그란) 손잡이; 혹, 마디
A knob is a round switch on a piece of machinery or equipment.

lever*
[lévər]

n. (기계 · 차량 조작용) 레버; 지레; 수단; v. 지렛대로 움직이다
A lever is a handle or bar that is attached to a piece of machinery and which you push or pull in order to operate the machinery.

crank
[kræŋk]

n. (기계의) 크랭크; v. 크랭크로 돌리다
A crank is a device that you turn in order to make something move.

wiggle
[wigl]

v. 꿈틀꿈틀 움직이다; n. 꿈틀꿈틀 움직이기
If you wiggle something or if it wiggles, it moves up and down or from side to side in small quick movements.

flicker
[flíkər]

v. (불 · 빛 등이) 깜박거리다; 움직거리다; n. (빛의) 깜박거림; 움직거림
If a light or flame flickers, it shines unsteadily.

indicate[*]
[índikèit]

v. (계기가) 가리키다; 보여 주다; (손가락이나 고갯짓으로) 가리키다
If a technical instrument indicates something, it shows a measurement or reading.

open up

idiom 마음을 터놓다
If you open up, you talk more about your personal feelings and experiences.

lean[**]
[li:n]

v. 기울이다, (몸을) 숙이다; ~에 기대다; a. 군살이 없는, 호리호리한
When you lean in a particular direction, you bend your body in that direction.

temple[*]
[templ]

n. 관자놀이; 신전, 사원, 절
Your temples are the flat parts on each side of the front part of your head, near your forehead.

overcome[*]
[ouvərkám]

v. 극복하다; 꼼짝 못하게 되다, 압도당하다
If you overcome a problem or a feeling, you successfully deal with it and control it.

cockpit
[kákpit]

n. (항공기 · 보트 · 경주용 자동차의) 조종석
In an airplane or racing car, the cockpit is the part where the pilot or driver sits.

confuse[**]
[kənfjú:z]

v. (사람을) 혼란시키다; 혼동하다 (confusing a. 혼란스러운)
Something that is confusing makes it difficult for people to know exactly what is happening or what to do.

complicated[**]
[kámpləkèitid]

a. 복잡한
If you say that something is complicated, you mean it has so many parts or aspects that it is difficult to understand or deal with.

shrug[*]
[ʃrʌg]

v. (어깨를) 으쓱하다; n. 어깨를 으쓱하기
If you shrug, you raise your shoulders to show that you are not interested in something or that you do not know or care about something.

grip[**]
[grip]

n. 꽉 붙잡음, 움켜쥠; 통제, 지배; v. 꽉 잡다, 움켜잡다; (마음 · 흥미 · 시선을) 끌다
A grip is a firm, strong hold on something.

knuckle
[nʌkl]

n. 손가락 관절; v. 주먹으로 치다
Your knuckles are the rounded pieces of bone that form lumps on your hands where your fingers join your hands, and where your fingers bend.

slew
[slu:]

v. 휙 돌다, 미끄러지다; n. 많음, 다수, 대량
If a vehicle slews or is slewed across a road, it slides across it.

momentary[*]
[móuməntèri]

a. 순간적인, 잠깐의 (momentarily ad. 잠깐)
Momentarily means for a short time.

vibrate[*]
[váibreit]

v. (가늘게) 떨다, 진동하다 (vibration n. 떨림, 진동)
If something vibrates or if you vibrate it, it shakes with repeated small, quick movements.

16

slight**
[slait]

a. 약간의, 조금의; 작고 여윈 (slightly ad. 약간, 조금)
Slightly means to some degree but not to a very large degree.

immediate**
[imíːdiət]

a. 즉각적인; 당면한; 아주 가까이에 있는 (immediately ad. 즉시, 즉각)
If something happens immediately, it happens without any delay.

bank**
[bæŋk]

v. (비행기 · 차를) 좌우로 기울이다; 땔감을 쌓아 올리다; n. 은행; 둑
If you bank an aircraft or vehicle, you tilt it or cause it to tilt sideways in making a turn.

press**
[pres]

v. 누르다; (무엇에) 바짝 대다; 꾹 밀어 넣다; n. 언론
If you press something or press down on it, you push hard against it with your foot or hand.

leave off

idiom 중단하다; ~을 제외하다
To leave off something or doing something means to stop it or stop doing it.

pressure**
[préʃər]

n. 압박, 압력; 스트레스; v. 강요하다; 압력을 가하다
Pressure is force that you produce when you press hard on something.

straighten*
[streitn]

v. 똑바르게 하다; (자세를) 바로 하다; 해결하다
If you straighten something, you make it tidy or put it in its proper position.

nod**
[nad]

v. (고개를) 끄덕이다, 까딱하다; n. (고개를) 끄덕임
If you nod, you move your head downward and upward to show that you are answering 'yes' to a question, or to show agreement, understanding, or approval.

rub**
[rʌb]

v. (손 · 손수건 등을 대고) 문지르다; (두 손 등을) 맞비비다; n. 문지르기, 비비기
If you rub a part of your body, you move your hand or fingers backward and forward over it while pressing firmly.

ache*
[eik]

n. (계속적인) 아픔; v. (계속) 아프다
An ache is a steady, fairly strong pain in a part of your body.

gratitude**
[grǽtətjùːd]

n. 고마움, 감사
Gratitude is the state of feeling grateful.

ocean**
[óuʃən]

n. (광활하게) 펼쳐짐; 바다
If you say that there is an ocean of something, you are emphasizing that there is a very large amount of it.

flood**
[flʌd]

v. (감정 · 생각이) 밀려들다; 물에 잠기다; n. 홍수; 쇄도, 폭주
If an emotion, feeling, or thought floods you, you suddenly feel it very intensely. If feelings or memories flood back, you suddenly remember them very clearly.

split**
[split]

n. 분열; (길게 찢어진) 틈; v. 나뉘다; 찢어지다, 쪼개지다; 분열되다
A split in an organization is a disagreement between its members.

court**
[kɔːrt]

n. 법정, 법원; (테니스 등을 하는) 코트
A court is a place where legal matters are decided by a judge and jury or by a magistrate.

judge[***]
[dʒʌdʒ]

n. 판사; 심판, 심사위원; v. 판단하다; 심판을 보다; 짐작하다
A judge is the person in a court of law who decides how the law should be applied, for example how criminals should be punished.

visitation
[vìzətéiʃən]

n. (전남편 · 전처와 살고 있는 자녀에 대한) 방문권; 시찰, 감찰
Visitation is the right of a divorced parent to visit children who live with the other parent.

bench[**]
[bentʃ]

n. 판사석; 벤치
In a court of law, the bench is the judge or magistrates.

phrase[**]
[freiz]

n. 구절, 관용구; v. (말 · 글을) 표현하다
A phrase is a small group of words which forms a unit, either on its own or within a sentence.

lurch
[ləːrtʃ]

v. (갑자기) 휘청하다; (공포 · 흥분으로) 떨리다; n. 휘청함; 요동침
To lurch means to make a sudden movement, especially forward, in an uncontrolled way.

embarrass[**]
[imbǽrəs]

v. 당황스럽게 하다, 어색하게 하다; 곤란하게 하다
If something or someone embarrasses you, they make you feel shy or ashamed.

obvious[**]
[ábviəs]

a. 분명한, 확실한; 너무 빤한; 명백한 (obviously ad. 분명히)
You use obviously to indicate that something is easily noticed, seen, or recognized.

discomfort
[diskʌ́mfərt]

n. (신체적인) 불편; v. (마음을) 불편하게 하다
Discomfort is a painful feeling in part of your body when you have been hurt slightly or when you have been uncomfortable for a long time.

stomach[**]
[stʌ́mək]

n. 위(胃), 복부, 배
Your stomach is the organ inside your body where food is digested before it moves into the intestines.

mechanical[*]
[məkǽnikəl]

a. 기계와 관련된; (행동이) 기계적인
Mechanical means relating to machines and engines and the way they work.

engineer[*]
[endʒiníər]

n. 기사, 엔지니어; 기술자, 수리공; v. 수작을 부리다
An engineer is a person who uses scientific knowledge to design, construct, and maintain engines and machines or structures such as roads, railways, and bridges.

design[**]
[dizáin]

v. 설계하다; 만들다; n. 디자인; 설계도, 도안
When someone designs a garment, building, machine, or other object, they plan it and make a detailed drawing of it from which it can be built or made.

invent[**]
[invént]

v. 발명하다; (사실이 아닌 것을) 지어내다
If you invent something such as a machine or process, you are the first person to think of it or make it.

drill[*]
[dril]

n. 드릴; 반복 연습; v. 훈련시키다; (드릴로) 구멍을 뚫다
A drill is a tool or machine that you use for making holes.

18

sharpen[*]
[ʃɑ́ːrpən]

v. (날카롭게) 갈다; (기량 등을) 갈고 닦다; 더 강렬해지다
If you sharpen an object, you make its edge very thin or you make its end pointed.

equipment[**]
[ikwípmənt]

n. 장비, 용품; 준비, 채비
Equipment consists of the things which are used for a particular purpose, for example a hobby or job.

lash
[læʃ]

v. (밧줄로) 단단히 묶다; 후려치다, 휘갈기다; n. 채찍질
If you lash two or more things together, you tie one of them firmly to the other.

rear[*]
[riər]

n. 뒤쪽; 궁둥이; a. 뒤쪽의; v. 앞다리를 들어올리며 서다
The rear of something such as a building or vehicle is the back part of it.

fabric[*]
[fǽbrik]

n. 직물, 천
Fabric is cloth or other material produced by weaving together cotton, nylon, wool, silk, or other threads.

survive[**]
[sərváiv]

v. 살아남다, 생존하다 (survival n. 생존)
If you refer to the survival of something or someone, you mean that they manage to continue or exist in spite of difficult circumstances.

pack[*]
[pæk]

n. 꾸러미; 무리; v. (짐을) 싸다; (사람 · 물건으로) 가득 채우다
A pack of things is a collection of them that is sold or given together in a box or bag.

emergency[**]
[imə́ːrdʒənsi]

n. 비상
An emergency is an unexpected and difficult or dangerous situation, especially an accident, which happens suddenly and which requires quick action to deal with it.

supply[**]
[səplái]

n. (pl.) 용품, 비품; 비축(량); 공급; v. 공급하다, 제공하다
You can use supplies to refer to food, equipment, and other essential things that people need, especially when these are provided in large quantities.

in case

idiom (~할) 경우에 대비해서
If you do something in case or just in case a particular thing happens, you do it because that thing might happen.

land[***]
[lænd]

v. (땅 · 표면에) 내려앉다, 착륙하다; 놓다, 두다; n. 육지, 땅; 지역
(emergency landing n. 비상 착륙)
When someone or something lands, they come down to the ground after moving through the air or falling.

turn out

idiom ~인 것으로 드러나다; 되어 가다; 나타나다
If things turn out, they are discovered or they prove to be the case finally and surprisingly.

constant[*]
[kánstənt]

a. 끊임없는; 거듭되는; 변함없는
You use constant to describe something that happens all the time or is always there.

odor[*]
[óudər]

n. (불쾌한) 냄새, 악취
An odor is a particular and distinctive smell.

wince
[wins]

v. (통증 · 당혹감으로) 움찔하고 놀라다
If you wince, the muscles of your face tighten suddenly because you have felt a pain or because you have just seen, heard, or remembered something unpleasant.

bother
[báðər]

v. 신경 쓰이게 하다; 귀찮게 하다, 귀찮게 말을 걸다; 신경 쓰다; n. 성가심
If something bothers you, or if you bother about it, it worries, annoys, or upsets you.

unseeing
[ʌnsíːiŋ]

a. 주의 깊게 보지 않는; 눈이 보이지 않는
If you describe a person or their eyes as unseeing, you mean that they are not looking at anything, or not noticing something, although their eyes are open.

sack
[sæk]

n. (종이) 봉지, 부대
A sack is a paper or plastic bag, which is used to carry things bought in a food shop.

hatchet
[hǽtʃit]

n. 손도끼
A hatchet is a small ax that you can hold in one hand.

handgrip
[hǽndgrip]

n. 손잡이; 악수
A handgrip is a handle for holding something by.

stout
[staut]

a. 튼튼한; 통통한
Stout shoes, branches, or other objects are thick and strong.

brass
[bræs]

n. 놋쇠, 황동
Brass is a yellow-colored metal made from copper and zinc.

rivet
[rívit]

v. 대갈못으로 고정하다; (흥미 · 관심을) 고정시키다; n. 대갈못, 리벳
To rivet means to fasten parts together with a rivet.

loop
[luːp]

n. 고리; v. 고리 모양을 만들다
A loop is a curved or circular shape in something long, for example in a piece of string.

weave
[wiːv]

v. 이리저리 빠져 나가다; (옷감 등을) 짜다; n. 엮어서 만든 것; (직물을) 짜는 법
If you weave your way somewhere, you move between and around things as you go there.

traffic
[trǽfik]

n. 차량들, 교통; 수송
Traffic refers to all the vehicles that are moving along the roads in a particular area.

hollow
[hálou]

a. 공허한; (속이) 빈; n. 움푹 꺼진 곳; v. 우묵하게 만들다
A hollow sound is dull and echoing.

hokey
[hóuki]

a. 감상적인
If you describe something as hokey, you mean that it is too emotional or artificial and therefore difficult to believe.

humor
[hjúːmər]

v. 비위를 맞춰 주다; n. 유머, (재치 있는) 농담
If you humor someone who is behaving strangely, you try to please them or pretend to agree with them, so that they will not become upset.

loosen[*]
[lu:sn]

v. 풀다; 느슨하게 하다; (통제 · 구속 등을) 완화하다
If you loosen your clothing or something that is tied or fastened or if it loosens, you undo it slightly so that it is less tight or less firmly held in place.

thread^{**}
[θred]

v. (실 등을) 꿰다; n. 실; (가느다란) 줄기
If you thread a long thin object through something, you pass it through one or more holes or narrow spaces.

scootch
[sku:tʃ]

v. 약간 옮기다, 살짝 움직이다
To scootch means to slide as with short, jerky movements.

ridiculous^{**}
[ridíkjuləs]

a. 웃기는, 말도 안 되는, 터무니없는
If you say that something or someone is ridiculous, you mean that they are very foolish.

scout[*]
[skaut]

n. 스카우트 (단원); 정찰병; v. 돌아다니다, 정찰하다
A Scout is a member of the Scouts which is an organization for children and young people which teaches them to be practical, sensible, and helpful.

tender[*]
[téndər]

a. 상냥한, 다정한; 따가운; 연한 (tenderness n. 부드러움, 상냥함)
Someone or something that is tender expresses gentle and caring feelings.

forehead[*]
[fɔ́:rhèd]

n. 이마
Your forehead is the area at the front of your head between your eyebrows and your hair.

security[*]
[sikjúərəti]

n. 경비 담당 부서; 보안, 경비; 안도감, 안심
Security refers to all the measures that are taken to protect a place, or to ensure that only people with permission enter it or leave it.

grab[*]
[græb]

v. (와락 · 단단히) 붙잡다; 급히 ~하다; n. 와락 잡아채려고 함
If you grab something, you take it or pick it up suddenly and roughly.

remove^{**}
[rimú:v]

v. (옷 등을) 벗다; 없애다, 제거하다; 치우다, 내보내다
If you remove something from a place, you take it away.

glance[*]
[glæns]

v. 흘낏 보다; 대충 훑어보다; 비스듬히 맞다; n. 흘낏 봄
If you glance at something or someone, you look at them very quickly and then look away again immediately.

grimace
[gríməs]

v. 얼굴을 찡그리다; n. 찡그린 표정
If you grimace, you twist your face in an ugly way because you are annoyed, disgusted, or in pain.

hiss[*]
[his]

n. 쉭쉭거리는 소리; v. 쉿 하는 소리를 내다; (화난 어조로) 낮게 말하다
A hiss is a long 's' sound like the sound that a snake makes.

barely[*]
[béərli]

ad. 거의 ~아니게; 간신히, 가까스로
You use barely to say that something is only just true or only just the case.

audible
[ɔ́:dəbl]

a. 들리는, 들을 수 있는
A sound that is audible is loud enough to be heard.

spasm
[spǽzm]

n. 발작; 경련
A spasm is a sudden strong pain or unpleasant emotion which lasts for a short period of time.

cord*
[kɔːrd]

n. 전선; 끈, 줄
Cord is wire covered in rubber or plastic which connects electrical equipment to an electricity supply.

arc*
[aːrk]

n. 둥근 (활) 모양; 호, 원호; v. 활 모양을 그리다
An arc is a smoothly curving line or movement.

flip*
[flip]

v. 홱 뒤집다, 휙 젖히다; 툭 던지다; n. 회전; 툭 던지기
If you flip a device on or off, or if you flip a switch, you turn it on or off by pressing the switch quickly.

jolt
[dʒoult]

n. 덜컥 하고 움직임; 충격; v. 갑자기 거칠게 움직이다; (~하도록) 충격을 주다
A jolt is a sudden violent movement.

hammer**
[hǽmər]

n. 망치, 해머; v. 망치로 치다; 쿵쿵 치다
A hammer is a tool that consists of a heavy piece of metal at the end of a handle. It is used, for example, to hit nails into a piece of wood or a wall, or to break things into pieces.

blow**
[blou]

n. 세게 때림, 강타; 충격; v. (입으로) 불다; (바람·입김에) 날리다; 폭파하다
If someone receives a blow, they are hit with a fist or weapon.

forceful*
[fɔ́ːrsfəl]

a. 강력한; 단호한; 강압적인 (forcefully ad. 강력하게; 강압적으로)
Something that is forceful has a very powerful effect and causes you to think or feel something very strongly.

crush**
[krʌʃ]

v. 으스러뜨리다; 밀어 넣다; n. 홀딱 반함
If you are crushed against someone or something, you are pushed or pressed against them.

rigid*
[rídʒid]

a. 뻣뻣한, 단단한; 엄격한, 융통성 없는
A rigid substance or object is stiff and does not bend, stretch, or twist easily.

swear**
[swear]

v. (swore-sworn) 욕을 하다; 맹세하다
If someone swears, they use language that is considered to be rude or offensive, usually because they are angry.

slam*
[slæm]

n. 쾅 하고 놓기; 탕 하는 소리; v. 세게 치다, 놓다; 쾅 닫다
A slam is an instance of something slamming down or slamming shut, or the noise made by this.

heart attack
[háːrt ətæk]

n. 심근 경색, 심장마비
If someone has a heart attack, their heart begins to beat very irregularly or stops completely.

awful**
[ɔ́ːfəl]

a. 끔찍한, 지독한; (정도가) 대단한, 아주 심한
If you say that something is awful, you mean that it is extremely unpleasant, shocking, or bad.

twist**
[twist]

n. 돌리기; (고개·몸 등을) 돌리기; v. (고개·몸 등을) 돌리다; 휘다, 구부리다
A twist is the action of turning or rotating on an axis.

22

spit*
[spit]

n. 침; (침 등을) 뱉기; v. (침 · 음식 등을) 뱉다
Spit is the watery liquid produced in your mouth.

contract**
[kántrækt]

v. 줄어들다, 수축하다; 계약하다; n. 계약
When something contracts or when something contracts it, it becomes smaller or shorter.

incredible*
[inkrédəbl]

a. 믿을 수 없는, 믿기 힘든 (incredibly ad. 믿을 수 없을 정도로, 엄청나게)
If you say that something is incredible, you mean that it is very unusual or surprising, and you cannot believe it is really true, although it may be.

take in

idiom 이해하다; ~을 눈여겨보다
If you take in something, you understand and remember something that you hear or read.

thrum
[θrʌm]

v. 계속해서 낮은 소리를 내다; (현악기를) 통기다
When something such as a machine or engine thrums, it makes a low beating sound.

core*
[kɔːr]

n. 핵심; (사물의) 중심부; a. 핵심적인, 가장 중요한
A core is the part of something that is central to its existence or character.

strike***
[straik]

v. (struck-struck/stricken) (생각 등이) 갑자기 떠오르다; (세게) 치다, 부딪치다; n. 공격; 치기, 때리기
If an idea or thought strikes you, it suddenly comes into your mind.

flash**
[flæʃ]

n. 갑자기 떠오름; (잠깐) 반짝임; v. (잠깐) 비치다; 휙 내보이다; 휙 움직이다
You talk about a flash of something when you are saying that it happens very suddenly and unexpectedly.

horror*
[hɔ́ːrər]

n. 공포, 경악; ~의 참상
Horror is a feeling of great shock, fear, and worry caused by something extremely unpleasant.

terror*
[térər]

n. 두려움, 공포; 공포의 대상
Terror is very great fear.

intense*
[inténs]

a. 극심한, 강렬한; 치열한; 진지한
Intense is used to describe something that is very great or extreme in strength or degree.

freeze**
[friːz]

v. (두려움 등으로 몸이) 얼어붙다; 얼다; n. 얼어붙음; 동결; 한파
If someone who is moving freezes, they suddenly stop and become completely still and quiet.

massive*
[mǽsiv]

a. 엄청나게 심각한; (육중하면서) 거대한
If you describe a medical condition as massive, you mean that it is extremely serious.

coma
[kóumə]

n. 혼수상태, 코마
Someone who is in a coma is in a state of deep unconsciousness.

1분에 몇 단어를 읽는지 리딩 속도를 측정해보세요.

$$\frac{2,813 \text{ words}}{\text{reading time ( ) sec}} \times 60 = (\quad) \text{ WPM}$$

Build Your Vocabulary

lead**
[led]
① n. 납; (연필)심 ② v. 안내하다; 이어지다; n. 선두
Lead is a soft, gray, heavy metal.

pilot복습
[páilət]
n. 조종사, 비행사
A pilot is a person who is trained to fly an aircraft.

control복습
[kəntróul]
n. (기계 · 차량의) 제어 장치; 통제, 제어; v. 지배하다; 조정하다
A control is a device such as a switch or lever which you use in order to operate a machine or other piece of equipment.

pedal복습
[pedl]
n. 페달, 발판; v. 페달을 밟다; (자전거를) 타고 가다
A pedal in a car or on a machine is a lever that you press with your foot in order to control the car or machine.

turbulence
[tə́:rbjuləns]
n. 난기류; 격동, 격변
Turbulence is violent and uneven movement within a particular area of air, liquid, or gas.

stretch**
[stretʃ]
v. (팔 · 다리를) 뻗다; 기지개를 켜다; 펼쳐지다; n. (길게) 뻗은 구간; 기간
If you stretch your arm or leg, you move it away from your body in order to reach something.

tremble*
[trembl]
v. (몸을) 떨다; (가볍게) 흔들리다; n. 떨림, 전율
If you tremble, you shake slightly because you are frightened or cold.

procedure*
[prəsí:dʒər]
n. 절차, 방법; 수술
A procedure is a way of doing something, especially the usual or correct way.

victim*
[víktim]
n. (범죄 · 질병 · 사고 등의) 피해자
A victim is someone who has been hurt or killed.

heart attack복습
[há:rt ətæk]
n. 심근 경색, 심장마비
If someone has a heart attack, their heart begins to beat very irregularly or stops completely.

strap*
[stræp]
v. 끈으로 묶다; 붕대를 감다; n. 끈, 줄, 띠
If you strap something somewhere, you fasten it there with a strap.

tip*
[tip]
n. (뾰족한) 끝; v. 기울어지다; 젖혀지다; 살짝 건드리다
The tip of something long and narrow is the end of it.

24

beat
[bi:t]

n. 고동, 맥박; 리듬; v. (게임 · 시합에서) 이기다; 때리다; (심장이) 고동치다
(heartbeat n. 심장 박동)
Your heartbeat is the regular movement of your heart as it pumps blood around your body.

lurch
[ləːrtʃ]

v. (갑자기) 휘청하다; (공포 · 흥분으로) 떨리다; n. 휘청함; 요동침
To lurch means to make a sudden movement, especially forward, in an uncontrolled way.

nose
[nouz]

n. (항공기 · 우주선 등의) 앞부분; 코; v. 천천히 조심스럽게 나아가다
The nose of a vehicle such as a car or airplane is the front part of it.

dive
[daiv]

v. 급강하하다; 급히 움직이다; (물 속으로) 뛰어들다; n. (물 속으로) 뛰어들기
If an airplane dives, it flies or drops down quickly and suddenly.

slight
[slait]

a. 약간의, 조금의; 작고 여윈 (slightly ad. 약간, 조금)
Slightly means to some degree but not to a very large degree.

angle
[ǽŋgl]

n. 기울기; 각도, 각; 관점; v. 비스듬히 움직이다
An angle is the difference in direction between two lines or surfaces. Angles are measured in degrees.

increase
[inkríːs]

v. (양 · 수 · 가치 등이) 증가하다, 인상되다, 늘다; n. 증가
If something increases or you increase it, it becomes greater in number, level, or amount.

ultimate
[ʌ́ltəmət]

a. 궁극적인, 최종적인; 최고의, 최상의; n. 극치 (ultimately ad. 궁극적으로, 결국)
Ultimately means finally, after a long and often complicated series of events.

horizon
[həráizn]

n. 지평선, 수평선
The horizon is the line in the far distance where the sky seems to meet the land or the sea.

wheel
[hwiːl]

n. (자동차 등의) 핸들; 바퀴; v. (반대 방향으로) 홱 돌다; (바퀴 달린 것을) 밀다
The wheel of a car or other vehicle is the circular object that is used to steer it.

rudder
[rʌ́dər]

n. (항공기의) 방향타; (배의) 키
An airplane's rudder is a vertical piece of metal at the back which is used to make the plane turn to the right or to the left.

tug
[tʌg]

n. (갑자기 세게) 잡아당김; v. (세게) 잡아당기다
A tug is a short strong pull.

slide
[slaid]

v. (slid-slid/slidden) 미끄러지듯이 움직이다; 슬며시 넣다; n. 떨어짐; 미끄러짐
When something slides somewhere or when you slide it there, it moves there smoothly over or against something.

tilt
[tilt]

n. 기울어짐, 젖혀짐; v. 기울이다, (뒤로) 젖히다; (의견 · 상황 등이) 기울어지다
The tilt of something is the fact that it tilts or slopes, or the angle at which it tilts or slopes.

swoop
[swuːp]

v. 급강하하다, 위에서 덮치다; 급습하다; n. 급강하; 급습
When a bird or airplane swoops, it suddenly moves downward through the air in a smooth curving movement.

eager***
[íːgər]

a. 열렬한, 간절히 바라는, 열심인 (eagerly ad. 열심히; 몹시)
If you are eager to do or have something, you want to do or have it very much.

drive*복습
[draiv]

v. (drove–driven) 만들다; 운전하다; 박아 넣다; 몰아가다; n. 드라이브; 충동, 욕
To drive someone into a particular state or situation means to force them into that state or situation.

stomach*복습
[stʌ́mək]

n. 복부, 배, 위(胃)
You can refer to the front part of your body below your waist as your stomach.

shallow*
[ʃǽlou]

a. 얕은; 피상적인; n. (pl.) (강ㆍ바다의) 얕은 곳
A shallow container, hole, or area of water measures only a short distance from the top to the bottom.

float**
[flout]

v. (물 위나 공중에서) 떠가다; (물에) 뜨다; n. 부표
Something that floats in or through the air hangs in it or moves slowly and gently through it.

violent**
[váiələnt]

a. 격렬한, 맹렬한; 폭력적인; 지독한 (violently ad. 격렬하게, 맹렬히)
A violent event happens suddenly and with great force.

settle***
[setl]

v. 자리를 잡다; 진정되다; (서서히) 가라앉다; 결정하다
If something settles or if you settle it, it sinks slowly down and becomes still.

aim***
[eim]

v. 겨누다; 목표하다; n. 겨냥, 조준; 목적
If you aim a weapon or object at something or someone, you point it toward them before firing or throwing it.

steady**
[stédi]

a. 흔들림 없는, 안정된; 꾸준한; v. 진정되다; 가라앉히다
If an object is steady, it is firm and does not shake or move about.

fluff
[flʌf]

n. (동물이나 새의) 솜털; 보풀; v. 망치다; 부풀리다
(fluffy a. 푹신해 보이는, 솜털 같은)
If you describe something such as a towel or a toy animal as fluffy, you mean that it is very soft.

endless*복습
[éndlis]

a. 끝없는; 무한한, 한없는
If you say that something is endless, you mean that it is very large or lasts for a very long time, and it seems as if it will never stop.

scatter**
[skǽtər]

v. 흩뿌리다; 황급히 흩어지다; n. 흩뿌리기; 소수, 소량
If you scatter things over an area, you throw or drop them so that they spread all over the area.

dashboard*복습
[dǽʃbɔːrd]

n. (승용차의) 계기판
The dashboard in a car is the panel facing the driver's seat where most of the instruments and switches are.

dial*복습
[dáiəl]

n. (시계ㆍ계기 등의) 문자반; v. 다이얼을 돌리다, 전화를 걸다
A dial is a control on a device or piece of equipment which you can move in order to adjust the setting, for example to select or change the frequency on a radio or the temperature of a heater.

compass*
[kʌ́mpəs]

n. 나침반; (pl.) (제도용) 컴퍼스; (도달 가능한) 범위
A compass is an instrument that you use for finding directions.

26

confuse
[kənfjúːz]

v. (사람을) 혼란시키다; 혼동하다 (confusing a. 혼란스러운)
Something that is confusing makes it difficult for people to know exactly what is happening or what to do.

jumble
[dʒʌmbl]

n. 뒤죽박죽 뒤섞인 것; v. (마구) 뒤섞다
A jumble of things is a lot of different things that are all mixed together in a disorganized or confused way.

display [*]
[displéi]

n. 표시 장치; 전시, 진열; 표현; v. (정보를) 보여주다; 전시하다; 내보이다
The display on a computer screen is the information that is shown there. The screen itself can also be referred to as the display.

indicate
[índikèit]

v. (계기가) 가리키다; 보여 주다; (손가락이나 고갯짓으로) 가리키다
If a technical instrument indicates something, it shows a measurement or reading.

needle ^{**}
[niːdl]

n. (계기의) 바늘, 지침; 바늘, 침; (pl.) 솔잎
On an instrument which measures something such as speed or weight, the needle is the long strip of metal or plastic on the dial that moves backward and forward, showing the measurement.

altimeter
[æltímətər]

n. (항공기 등의) 고도계
An altimeter is an instrument in an aircraft that shows the height of the aircraft above the ground.

device [*]
[diváis]

n. 장치, 기구; 폭발물; 방법
A device is an object that has been invented for a particular purpose, for example for recording or measuring something.

rectangle [*]
[réktæŋgl]

n. 직사각형 (rectanular a. 직사각형의; 직각의)
A rectangle is a four-sided shape whose corners are all ninety degree angles. Each side of a rectangle is the same length as the one opposite to it.

panel [*]
[pǽnl]

n. (자동차 등의) 계기판; 판, 패널; 자문단
A control panel or instrument panel is a board or surface which contains switches and controls to operate a machine or piece of equipment.

knob
[nab]

n. (동그란) 손잡이; 혹, 마디
A knob is a round switch on a piece of machinery or equipment.

tiny ^{**}
[táini]

a. 아주 작은
Something or someone that is tiny is extremely small.

transmitter
[trænsmítər]

n. 전송기, 송신기
A transmitter is a piece of equipment that is used for broadcasting television or radio programs.

stamp ^{**}
[stæmp]

v. (도장·스탬프 등을) 찍다; 밟다; n. 도장; (발을) 쿵쿵거리기
If you stamp a mark or word on an object, you press the mark or word onto the object using a stamp or other device.

sideways [*]
[sáidwèiz]

ad. 옆으로; 옆에서
Sideways means in a direction to the left or right, not forward or backward.

jam[**]
[dʒæm]

v. 밀어 넣다; 움직이지 못하게 되다; n. 교통 체증; 혼잡; 잼
If you jam something somewhere, you push or put it there roughly.

switch[복습]
[swiʧ]

n. 스위치; 전환; v. 전환하다, 바꾸다
A switch is a small control for an electrical device which you use to
turn the device on or off.

clip[*]
[klip]

v. 핀으로 고정하다; 깎다, 자르다; n. 핀, 클립; 장전된 총알 한 세트
When you clip things together or when things clip together, you fasten
them together using a small metal device.

smooth[**]
[smuːð]

a. 부드러운; (소리가) 감미로운; 매끈한; v. 매끈하게 하다 (smoothly ad. 부드럽게)
A smooth ride, flight, or sea crossing is very comfortable because there
are no unpleasant movements.

elbow[**]
[élbou]

n. 팔꿈치; v. (팔꿈치로) 밀치다
Your elbow is the part of your arm where the upper and lower halves
of the arm are joined.

bump[*]
[bʌmp]

v. (~에) 부딪치다; 덜컹거리며 가다; n. 쿵, 탁 (하는 소리)
If you bump into something or someone, you accidentally hit them
while you are moving.

grab[복습]
[græb]

v. (와락 · 단단히) 붙잡다; 급히 ~하다; n. 와락 잡아채려고 함
If you grab something, you take it or pick it up suddenly and roughly.

go through

idiom 거치다; ~을 겪다; ~을 살펴보다
If you go through something, you perform a set of actions.

wrench[*]
[renʧ]

v. (가슴을) 쓰라리게 하다; 확 비틀다; (발목 · 어깨를) 삐다; n. 확 비틂
(stomach-wrenching a. 속이 뒤틀리는)
Stomach-wrenching events or experiences make you feel extremely
shocked or upset.

cord[복습]
[kɔːrd]

n. 전선; 끈, 줄
Cord is wire covered in rubber or plastic which connects electrical
equipment to an electricity supply.

jerk[복습]
[dʒəːrk]

v. 홱 움직이다; n. 얼간이; 홱 움직임
If you jerk something or someone in a particular direction, or they jerk
in a particular direction, they move a short distance very suddenly and
quickly.

tube[**]
[tjuːb]

n. 관; 튜브; 통
A tube is a long hollow object that is usually round, like a pipe.

depress[*]
[diprés]

v. (기계의 어느 부분을) 누르다; 우울하게 하다
If you depress something, you press it down.

blow[복습]
[blou]

v. (blew-blown) (입으로) 불다; (바람 · 입김에) 날리다; 폭파하다;
n. 세게 때림, 강타; 충격
If you blow, you send out a stream of air from your mouth.

panic[*]
[pǽnik]

n. 극심한 공포, 공황; 허둥지둥함; v. 어쩔 줄 모르다, 공황 상태에 빠지다
Panic is a very strong feeling of anxiety or fear, which makes you act
without thinking carefully.

terror ^{복습}
[térər]

n. 두려움, 공포; 공포의 대상
Terror is very great fear.

slam ^{복습}
[slæm]

v. 세게 치다, 놓다; 쾅 닫다; n. 쾅 하고 놓기; 탕 하는 소리
If you slam something down, you put it there quickly and with great force.

sob[*]
[sab]

n. 흐느껴 울기, 흐느낌; v. (흑흑) 흐느끼다, 흐느껴 울다
A sob is one of the noises that you make when you are crying.

mock[*]
[mak]

v. 놀리다, 조롱하다; 무시하다; a. 거짓된, 가짜의
If someone mocks you, they show or pretend that they think you are foolish or inferior, for example by saying something funny about you, or by imitating your behavior.

aware^{**}
[əwéər]

a. 알고 있는, 자각하고 있는; 눈치 채고 있는 (awareness n. 의식, 관심)
If you are aware of something, you know about it.

release[*]
[rilíːs]

v. 풀다; 놓아 주다; (감정을) 발산하다; n. 풀어 줌; 발표, 공개
If you release a device, you move it so that it stops holding something.

wave^{**}
[weiv]

n. (열·소리·빛 등의) –파; 물결; (감정·움직임의) 파도; (팔·손·몸을) 흔들기;
v. (손·팔을) 흔들다; 손짓하다
Waves are the form in which things such as sound, light, and radio signals travel.

static[*]
[stǽtik]

n. (수신기의) 잡음; 정전기; a. 고정된, 정지 상태의
If there is static on the radio or television, you hear a series of loud noises which spoils the sound.

net^{**}
[net]

n. 통신망; 그물, 망; v. 그물로 잡다; (무엇을) 획득하다
The net is a communications or broadcasting network, especially of maritime radio.

roger
[rádʒər]

int. 알았다(무선 교신에서 상대방의 말을 알아들었다는 뜻으로 하는 말)
You can say 'Roger' or 'Roger that' to show your acknowledgement or understanding of the received message in radio communications.

faint[*]
[feint]

a. 희미한, 약한; v. 실신하다, 기절하다; n. 실신, 기절
A faint sound, color, mark, feeling, or quality has very little strength or intensity.

break up

idiom (휴대전화의 통화가) 끊기다; 헤어지다
If the connection between two telephones, or two radios that are used for sending and receiving messages, is breaking up, the people speaking can no longer hear each other clearly.

state^{***}
[steit]

v. 말하다, 진술하다; n. 상태; 국가, 나라; 주(州)
If you state something, you say or write it in a formal or definite way.

location[*]
[loukéiʃən]

n. 위치, 소재
The location of someone or something is their exact position.

signal^{**}
[sígnəl]

v. 암시하다; (동작·소리로) 신호를 보내다; n. 신호; 징조
If someone or something signals an event, they suggest that the event is happening or likely to happen.

transmit[*]
[trænsmít]

v. 전송하다, 송신하다; 전염시키다; 전도하다 (transmission n. 전송, 송신)
The transmission of television or radio programs is the broadcasting of them.

proper[**]
[prápər]

a. 적절한, 제대로 된; 올바른, 정당한 (properly ad. 제대로, 적절히)
The proper thing is the one that is correct or most suitable.

hesitate[***]
[hézətèit]

v. 망설이다, 주저하다; 거리끼다 (hesitation n. 주저, 망설임)
Hesitation is an unwillingness to do something, or a delay in doing it, because you are uncertain, worried, or embarrassed about it.

barely[복습]
[béərli]

ad. 거의 ~아니게; 간신히, 가까스로
You use barely to say that something is only just true or only just the case.

flight[복습]
[flait]

n. 항공기; 비행; 계단, 층계; 탈출, 도피
You can refer to an airplane carrying passengers on a particular journey as a particular flight.

roar[복습]
[rɔːr]

v. 웅웅거리다; 고함치다; 굉음을 내며 질주하다; n. 함성; 울부짖는 듯한 소리
If something roars, it makes a very loud noise.

rattle[*]
[rætl]

v. 덜거덕거리다; 당황하게 하다; n. 덜컹거리는 소리
When something rattles or when you rattle it, it makes short sharp knocking sounds because it is being shaken or it keeps hitting against something hard.

hiss[복습]
[his]

v. 쉿 하는 소리를 내다; (화난 어조로) 낮게 말하다; n. 쉭쉭거리는 소리
To hiss means to make a sound like a long 's.'

tear[복습]
[tɛər]

① v. (tore–torn) 찢다, 뜯다; 뜯어 내다; n. 찢어진 곳, 구멍 ② n. 눈물
To tear something from somewhere means to remove it roughly and violently.

frustrate[*]
[frʌ́streit]

v. 좌절감을 주다, 불만스럽게 하다; 방해하다 (frustration n. 불만, 좌절감)
If something frustrates you, it upsets or angers you because you are unable to do anything about the problems it creates.

hopeless[*]
[hóuplis]

a. 가망 없는, 절망적인; 엉망인
If you feel hopeless, you feel very unhappy because there seems to be no possibility of a better situation or success.

figure out

idiom ~을 이해하다, 알아내다; 계산하다, 산출하다
If you figure out someone or something, you come to understand them by thinking carefully.

airspeed
[ɛ́ərspiːd]

n. (항공기의) 대기 속도
An aircraft's airspeed is the speed at which it travels through the air.

groundspeed
[gráundspiːd]

n. (항공기의) 대지 속도
An aircraft's ground speed is its speed when measured against the ground rather than the air through which it moves.

propeller[*]
[prəpélər]

n. 프로펠러
A propeller is a device with blades which is attached to a boat or aircraft.

prisoner[**]
[prízənər]

n. 죄수, 포로
A prisoner is a person who is kept in a prison as a punishment for a crime that they have committed.

cell[**]
[sel]

n. 감방; (작은) 칸
A cell is a small room in which a prisoner is locked.

hurtle
[hə:rtl]

v. 돌진하다
If someone or something hurtles somewhere, they move there very quickly, often in a rough or violent way.

run out of

idiom ~을 다 써버리다; ~이 없어지다
If you run out of something like money or time, you use up all of them.

fuel[*]
[fjú:əl]

n. 연료; v. (감정 등을) 부채질하다; 연료를 공급하다
Fuel is a substance such as coal, oil, or petrol that is burned to provide heat or power.

period[**]
[pí:əriəd]

int. 끝, 이상이다; n. 기간, 시기; 시대; 끝
You can say 'period' at the end of a statement to show that you believe you have said all there is to say on a subject and you are not going to discuss it any more.

rebel[*]
[ribél]

v. 저항하다; 반란을 일으키다; n. 반역자; 반항적인 사람
When someone rebels, they start to behave differently from other people and reject the values of society or of their parents.

vague[*]
[veig]

a. 희미한, 어렴풋한; 모호한, 애매한
If you have a vague memory or idea of something, the memory or idea is not clear.

altitude[복습]
[ǽltətjù:d]

n. (해발) 고도; 고도가 높은 곳, 고지
If something is at a particular altitude, it is at that height above sea level.

make sense

idiom 이해가 되다; 타당하다; 이해하기 쉽다
If something makes sense, you can understand it.

glide[*]
[glaid]

v. 활공하다; 미끄러지듯 움직이다; n. 미끄러지는 듯한 움직임
When birds or airplanes glide, they float on air currents.

clearing[*]
[klíəriŋ]

n. (숲 속의) 빈터
A clearing is a small area in a forest where there are no trees or bushes.

swamp[복습]
[swamp]

n. 늪, 습지; v. (일 등이) 쇄도하다
A swamp is an area of very wet land with wild plants growing in it.

trail[*]
[treil]

n. 시골길, 산길; 자국, 흔적; 자취; v. 끌다; 뒤쫓다, 추적하다
A trail is a rough path across open country or through forests.

land[복습]
[lænd]

v. (땅·표면에) 내려앉다, 착륙하다; 놓다, 두다; n. 육지, 땅; 지역
When someone or something lands, they come down to the ground after moving through the air or falling.

edge**
[edʒ]

n. 끝, 가장자리; 우위; v. 조금씩 움직이다; 테두리를 두르다
The edge of something is the place or line where it stops, or the part of it that is furthest from the middle.

chant*
[ʧænt]

n. (연이어 외치는) 구호; v. 되풀이하여 말하다; 구호를 외치다, 연호하다
A chant is a word or group of words that is repeated over and over again.

interval*
[íntərvəl]

n. (두 사건 사이의) 간격; 잠깐
If something happens at intervals, it happens several times with gaps or pauses in between.

skin**
[skin]

n. 피부; (동물의) 껍질; 거죽, 외피; v. (동물의) 가죽을 벗기다; (피부가) 까지다
Your skin is the natural covering of your body.

tighten*
[taitn]

v. (더) 팽팽해지다; (더 단단히) 조이다; 더 엄격하게 하다
If you tighten a rope or chain, or if it tightens, it is stretched or pulled hard until it is straight.

rehearse
[rihə́ːrs]

v. 연습하다; 예행연습을 하다
If you rehearse something that you are going to say or do, you silently practise it by imagining that you are saying or doing it.

mental**
[mentl]

a. 마음의, 정신의; 정신병의 (mentally ad. 마음속으로)
Mental means relating to the process of thinking.

reduce**
[ridjúːs]

v. (규모 · 크기 · 양 등을) 줄이다
If you reduce something, you make it smaller in size or amount, or less in degree.

impact*
[ímpækt]

n. 충돌, 충격; (강력한) 영향; v. 영향을 주다; 충돌하다
An impact is the action of one object hitting another, or the force with which one object hits another.

crash**
[kræʃ]

n. (자동차 · 항공기) 사고; 요란한 소리; v. 충돌하다; 부딪치다; 굉음을 내다
A crash is an accident in which a moving vehicle hits something and is damaged or destroyed.

visualize
[víʒuəlàiz]

v. 마음속에 그려 보다, 상상하다
If you visualize something, you imagine what it is like by forming a mental picture of it.

cough**
[kɔːf]

v. 털털거리다; 기침하다; (기침을 하여 무엇을) 토하다; n. 기침
If something coughs, it makes a short, loud sound like a cough.

wind mill
[wínd mìl]

v. (풍차처럼) 회전시키다; n. 풍차
If you windmill your arms, you move or be moved round in a circle in a manner suggestive of the rotating sails or vanes of a windmill.

cockpit**
[kákpit]

n. (항공기 · 보트 · 경주용 자동차의) 조종석
In an airplane or racing car, the cockpit is the part where the pilot or driver sits.

throw up

idiom ~을 토하다; ~을 두드러지게 하다
If you throw up, you bring food you have eaten back out of your mouth.

32

1. What happened to the plane?
   A. It got caught in the trees.
   B. It crashed through the trees and landed on the ground.
   C. It hit the lake and sank.
   D. It floated to the edge of the lake.

2. What was the Secret?
   A. Brian's father driving an unfamiliar car
   B. Brian's mother sitting with another man
   C. Brian's friend Terry sharing a private story
   D. Brian going to the mall when he wasn't allowed to

3. What did Brian NOT notice when he first woke up?
   A. The weather was extremely hot.
   B. It was painful to move.
   C. His legs were in the water.
   D. His surroundings were quiet.

4. In what condition was his body?
   A. His legs were steady and strong.
   B. His arms felt absolutely shattered.
   C. His ankle seemed to be broken.
   D. His head was badly aching.

5. How did he feel about the plane crash?
   A. It was both real and unreal.
   B. It happened just like he thought it would.
   C. Every moment of the crash was clear in his mind.
   D. He had experienced a similar accident before.

6. Why did the mosquitoes and flies disappear so abruptly?
   A. They were done attacking Brian.
   B. They could not handle strong sunlight.
   C. They found something more appealing to bite.
   D. They were scared of the steam coming off of Brian's clothes.

7. What did he think about his luck?
   A. He felt completely lucky about all the recent events in his life.
   B. He felt like he had had good luck until the plane crashed.
   C. He felt unlucky to be alone but lucky to be in a calm and comfortable place.
   D. He felt lucky to have survived but unlucky about everything else that had happened.

1분에 몇 단어를 읽는지 리딩 속도를 측정해보세요.

$$\frac{925 \text{ words}}{\text{reading time (} \quad \text{) sec}} \times 60 = (\quad) \text{ WPM}$$

Build Your Vocabulary

wipe[복습]
[waip]

v. (먼지 · 물기 등을) 닦다; 지우다; n. 닦기
If you wipe something, you rub its surface to remove dirt or liquid from it.

glide[복습]
[glaid]

n. 미끄러지는 듯한 움직임; v. 활공하다; 미끄러지듯 움직이다
When birds or airplanes glide, they float on air currents.

altitude[복습]
[ǽltətjùːd]

n. (해발) 고도; 고도가 높은 곳, 고지
If something is at a particular altitude, it is at that height above sea level.

horizon[복습]
[həráizn]

n. 지평선, 수평선
The horizon is the line in the far distance where the sky seems to meet the land or the sea.

glitter*
[glítər]

v. 반짝반짝 빛나다; (눈이) 번득이다; n. 반짝반짝 하는 빛; (눈의) 번득임; 화려함
If something glitters, light comes from or is reflected off different parts of it.

desperate[**]
[déspərət]

a. 필사적인; 간절히 원하는; 자포자기한 (desperately ad. 필사적으로)
If you are desperate for something or desperate to do something, you want or need it very much indeed.

windshield
[wíndʃìːld]

n. (자동차 등의) 앞유리
The windshield of a car or other vehicle is the glass window at the front through which the driver looks.

tighten[복습]
[taitn]

v. (더 단단히) 조이다; (더) 팽팽해지다; 더 엄격하게 하다
If a part of your body tightens, the muscles in it become tense and stiff, for example because you are angry or afraid.

knot[**]
[nat]

n. (긴장 · 화 등으로) 뻣뻣한 느낌; 매듭; v. 매듭을 묶다
If you feel a knot in your stomach, you get an uncomfortable tight feeling in your stomach, usually because you are afraid or excited.

burst[**]
[bəːrst]

n. (갑자기) ~을 함; 파열, 폭발; v. 갑자기 ~하다; 불쑥 움직이다; 터지다
A burst is a sudden increase in something, especially for a short period.

rounded
[ráundid]

a. (모양이) 둥근; (여러 가지를 균형 있게) 아우르는
Something that is rounded is curved in shape, without any points or sharp edges.

36

aim 복습
[eim]

v. 겨누다; 목표하다; n. 겨냥, 조준; 목적
If you aim a weapon or object at something or someone, you point it toward them before firing or throwing it.

tiny 복습
[táini]

a. 아주 작은
Something or someone that is tiny is extremely small.

cost***
[kɔːst]

v. (cost/costed–cost/costed) 잃게 하다; (값 · 비용이) ~이다; n. 값, 비용
If an event or mistake costs you something, you lose that thing as the result of it.

dramatic*
[drəmǽtik]

a. 극적인; 감격적인, 인상적인; 과장된 (dramatically ad. 극적으로)
A dramatic change or event happens suddenly and is very noticeable and surprising.

wallow
[wálou]

v. 뒹굴다; (쾌락을 주는 것에) 빠져 있다; n. 뒹굴기
If a person or animal wallows in water or mud, they lie or roll about in it slowly for pleasure.

frighten***
[fraitn]

v. 겁먹게 하다, 놀라게 하다
If something or someone frightens you, they cause you to suddenly feel afraid, anxious, or nervous.

increase 복습
[inkríːs]

v. (양 · 수 · 가치 등이) 증가하다, 인상되다, 늘다; n. 증가
If something increases or you increase it, it becomes greater in number, level, or amount.

pond*
[pand]

n. 연못
A pond is a small area of water that is smaller than a lake.

edge 복습
[edʒ]

n. 끝, 가장자리; 우위; v. 조금씩 움직이다; 테두리를 두르다
The edge of something is the place or line where it stops, or the part of it that is furthest from the middle.

at once

idiom 동시에; 즉시
If a number of different things happen at once or all at once, they all happen at the same time.

vision*
[víʒən]

n. 보이는 것, 광경; 상상력; 시력, 통찰력
Your vision is everything that you can see from a particular place or position.

lane*
[lein]

n. (배 · 비행기의) 항로; (도로의) 차선; 좁은 길
A lane is a course that a ship or aircraft follows.

channel*
[ʧænl]

n. 물길; 수로; (텔레비전 · 라디오의) 채널; v. (돈 · 감정 · 생각 등을) (~에) 쏟다
A channel is a passage along which water flows.

commit***
[kəmít]

v. 전념하다; 약속하다; (범죄를) 저지르다
To commit means to promise or give your loyalty, time, or money to a particular principle, person, or plan of action.

crash 복습
[kræʃ]

v. 충돌하다; 부딪치다; 굉음을 내다; n. (자동차 · 항공기) 사고; 요란한 소리
If a moving vehicle crashes or if the driver crashes it, it hits something and is damaged or destroyed.

brace *
[breis]

v. (스스로) 대비를 하다; (몸에) 단단히 힘을 주다; n. 버팀대; 치아 교정기
If you brace yourself for something unpleasant or difficult, you prepare yourself for it.

instant *
[ínstənt]

n. 순간, 아주 짧은 동안; a. 즉각적인
An instant is an extremely short period of time.

wrench ᵇᵉ
[renʃ]

v. 확 비틀다; (가슴을) 쓰라리게 하다; (발목·어깨를) 삐다; n. 확 비틂
If you wrench something that is fixed in a particular position, you pull or twist it violently, in order to move or remove it.

pine *
[pain]

n. 소나무
A pine tree or a pine is a tall tree which has very thin, sharp leaves and a fresh smell. Pine trees have leaves all year round.

clearing ᵇᵉ
[klíəriŋ]

n. (숲 속의) 빈터
A clearing is a small area in a forest where there are no trees or bushes.

rip *
[rip]

v. (재빨리·거칠게) 떼어 내다, 뜯어 내다; (갑자기) 찢다; n. (길게) 찢어진 곳
When something rips or when you rip it, you tear it forcefully with your hands or with a tool such as a knife.

explode *
[iksplóud]

v. 폭발하다; 갑자기 ~하다; (강한 감정을) 터뜨리다 (explosion n. 폭발, 폭파)
An explosion is a sudden, violent burst of energy, for example one caused by a bomb.

momentary ᵇᵉ
[móuməntèri]

a. 순간적인, 잠깐의 (momentarily ad. 잠깐)
Momentarily means for a short time.

blind **
[blaind]

v. (잠시) 앞이 안 보이게 하다; 눈이 멀게 하다; a. 눈이 먼; 눈치 채지 못하는
If something blinds you, it makes you unable to see, either for a short time or permanently.

smash *
[smæʃ]

v. (세게) 부딪치다; 박살내다; 부서지다; n. 박살내기; 요란한 소리
If something smashes or is smashed against something solid, it moves very fast and with great force against it.

skip *
[skip]

v. 표면을 스치며 날다; (일을) 거르다; 생략하다; n. 깡충깡충 뛰기
To skip means to move quickly over the surface of something, or to make something do this.

shatter ᵇᵉ
[ʃǽtər]

v. 산산이 부수다, 산산조각 내다; 엄청난 충격을 주다
If something shatters or is shattered, it breaks into a lot of small pieces.

rake *
[reik]

v. (손톱으로) 긁다; 갈퀴질을 하다; n. 갈퀴
To rake means to pull your fingers through or along something, for example your hair or skin.

nail **
[neil]

n. 손톱; 발톱; 못; v. (못 같은 것으로) 고정시키다
Your nails are the thin hard parts that grow at the ends of your fingers and toes.

release ᵇᵉ
[rilíːs]

v. 풀다; 놓아 주다; (감정을) 발산하다; n. 풀어 줌; 발표, 공개
If you release a device, you move it so that it stops holding something.

38

claw ^{복습}
[klɔː]

v. 헤치며 나아가다; (손톱 · 발톱으로) 할퀴다; n. (동물 · 새의) 발톱
If you claw your way somewhere, you move there with great difficulty, trying desperately to find things to hold on to.

surface **
[sə́ːrfis]

n. 표면, 지면, 수면; 외관; v. 수면으로 올라오다; (갑자기) 나타나다
The surface of something is the flat top part of it or the outside of it.

lung **
[lʌŋ]

n. 폐, 허파
Your lungs are the two organs inside your chest which fill with air when you breathe in.

suck **
[sʌk]

v. (특정한 방향으로) 빨아들이다; 빨아 먹다; n. 빨기, 빨아 먹기
If you suck something, you hold it in your mouth and pull at it with the muscles in your cheeks and tongue, for example in order to get liquid out of it.

vomit
[vámit]

v. 토하다, 게우다; n. 토함, 게움
If you vomit, food and drink comes back up from your stomach and out through your mouth.

weed *
[wiːd]

n. 잡초; v. 잡초를 뽑다
A weed is a wild plant that grows in gardens or fields of crops and prevents the plants that you want from growing properly.

muck
[mʌk]

n. 진흙, 진창; 배설물
Muck is dirt or some other unpleasant substance.

brush **
[brʌʃ]

n. 덤불, 잡목 숲; 붓; 솔; v. (솔이나 손으로) 털다; 솔질을 하다; ~을 스치다
Brush is an area of rough open land covered with small bushes and trees. You also use brush to refer to the bushes and trees on this land.

coarse *
[kɔːrs]

a. 거친; 굵은
Coarse things have a rough texture because they consist of thick threads or large pieces.

blade *
[bleid]

n. 풀잎; (칼 · 도구 등의) 날
A blade of grass is a single piece of grass.

spiral *
[spáiərəl]

v. 나선형으로 움직이다, 나선형을 그리다; n. 나선, 나선형
If something spirals or is spiralled somewhere, it grows or moves in a spiral curve.

1분에 몇 단어를 읽는지 리딩 속도를 측정해보세요.

$$\frac{2{,}539 \text{ words}}{\text{reading time ( ) sec}} \times 60 = (\qquad) \text{ WPM}$$

Build Your Vocabulary

slice[*]
[slais]

v. 베다; 자르다; n. (얇게 썬) 조각; 부분, 몫
If something slices through a substance, it moves through it quickly, like a knife.

trail[복습]
[treil]

n. 시골길, 산길; 자국, 흔적; 자취; v. 끌다; 뒤쫓다, 추적하다
A trail is a rough path across open country or through forests.

incredible[복습]
[inkrédəbl]

a. 믿을 수 없는, 믿기 힘든
If you describe something or someone as incredible, you like them very much or are impressed by them, because they are extremely or unusually good.

flash[복습]
[flæʃ]

v. (잠깐) 비치다; 휙 내보이다; 휙 움직이다; n. 갑자기 떠오름; (잠깐) 반짝임
If a light flashes or if you flash a light, it shines with a sudden bright light, especially as quick, regular flashes of light.

temperature[**]
[témpərətʃər]

n. 온도, 기온; 체온
The temperature of something is a measure of how hot or cold it is.

wave[복습]
[weiv]

v. (손 · 팔을) 흔들다; 손짓하다;
n. (열 · 소리 · 빛 등의) −파; 물결; (감정 · 움직임의) 파도; (팔 · 손 · 몸을) 흔들기
If you wave or wave your hand, you move your hand from side to side in the air, usually in order to say hello or goodbye to someone.

blond[*]
[bland]

a. 금발의
If you describe someone's hair as blond, you mean that it is pale yellow or golden.

scene[**]
[si:n]

n. 장면, 광경; 현장; 풍경
You can describe an event that you see, or that is broadcast or shown in a picture, as a scene of a particular kind.

exact[***]
[igzǽkt]

a. 정확한; 꼼꼼한, 빈틈없는
Exact means correct in every detail.

sob[복습]
[sab]

n. 흐느껴 울기, 흐느낌; v. (흑흑) 흐느끼다, 흐느껴 울다
A sob is one of the noises that you make when you are crying.

hammer[복습]
[hǽmər]

v. 쿵쿵 치다; 망치로 치다; n. 망치, 해머
If you hammer something, you hit or kick it very hard.

shorten[*]
[ʃɔ:rtn]

v. 짧아지다; 짧게 하다, 단축하다
If you shorten an object or if it shortens, it becomes smaller in length.

40

gasp[*]
[gæsp]

n. 헉 하는 소리를 냄; v. 헉 하고 숨을 쉬다; 숨을 제대로 못 쉬다
A gasp is a short quick breath of air that you take in through your mouth, especially when you are surprised, shocked, or in pain.

abate
[əbéit]

v. (강도가) 약해지다
If something bad or undesirable abates, it becomes much less strong or severe.

dull^{**}
[dʌl]

a. (고통이) 둔하게 아픈; 따분한, 재미없는; 흐릿한, 칙칙한
Dull feelings are weak and not intense.

ache^{복습}
[eik]

n. (계속적인) 아픔; v. (계속) 아프다
An ache is a steady, fairly strong pain in a part of your body.

sink^{***}
[siŋk]

v. (sank-sunk) 가라앉다, 빠지다; 박다; (구멍을) 파다; n. (부엌의) 개수대
If a boat sinks or if someone or something sinks it, it disappears below the surface of a mass of water.

crawl^{**}
[krɔːl]

v. 기어가다; 우글거리다; n. 기어가기
When you crawl, you move forward on your hands and knees.

grunt[*]
[grʌnt]

v. 끙 앓는 소리를 내다; (돼지가) 꿀꿀거리다; n. (사람이) 끙 하는 소리
If you grunt, you make a low sound, especially because you are annoyed or not interested in something.

on fire

idiom (몸의 일부가) 화끈거리는; 열중하여, 흥분하여
If a part of your body is on fire, it is giving you a painful burning feeling.

forehead^{복습}
[fɔ́ːrhèd]

n. 이마
Your forehead is the area at the front of your head between your eyebrows and your hair.

pound[*]
[paund]

v. (여러 차례) 두드리다; (가슴이) 쿵쿵 뛰다; 쿵쾅거리며 걷다
If you pound something or pound on it, you hit it with great force, usually loudly and repeatedly.

knee^{**}
[niː]

n. 무릎; v. 무릎으로 치다
Your knee is the place where your leg bends.

shore^{**}
[ʃɔːr]

n. 기슭, 해안, 호숫가
The shores or the shore of a sea, lake, or wide river is the land along the edge of it.

stand^{***}
[stænd]

n. 수목, 관목; 가판대, 좌판; v. 서다; (어떤 위치에) 세우다
A stand is a group of growing plants of a specified kind, especially trees.

brush^{복습}
[brʌʃ]

n. 덤불, 잡목 숲; 붓; 솔; v. (솔이나 손으로) 털다; 솔질을 하다; ~을 스치다
Brush is an area of rough open land covered with small bushes and trees. You also use brush to refer to the bushes and trees on this land.

dreamless
[dríːmlis]

a. 꿈도 꾸지 않고 자는, 깊고 평안한
A dreamless sleep is very deep and peaceful, and without dreams.

panic^{복습}
[pǽnik]

v. 어쩔 줄 모르다, 공황 상태에 빠지다; n. 극심한 공포, 공황; 허둥지둥함
If you panic or if someone panics you, you suddenly feel anxious or afraid, and act quickly and without thinking carefully.

mumble
[mʌmbl]

v. 중얼거리다, 웅얼거리다; n. 중얼거림
If you mumble, you speak very quietly and not at all clearly with the result that the words are difficult to understand.

hoarse
[hɔːrs]

a. 목 쉰, 쉰 목소리의
If your voice is hoarse or if you are hoarse, your voice sounds rough and unclear, for example because your throat is sore.

whisper*
[hwíspər]

n. 속삭임, 소곤거리는 소리; v. 속삭이다, 소곤거리다
A whisper is a very quiet way of saying something so that other people cannot hear you.

cramp
[kræmp]

v. 경련을 일으키다; (비좁은 곳에) 처박아 넣다; n. (근육의) 경련; 꺾쇠
If a part of your body is cramped, it suffers from sudden and painful contractions of a muscle or muscles.

keen*
[kiːn]

v. 애끓는 소리로 울부짖다; a. 간절히 ~하고 싶은, ~을 열망하는; 강한, 깊은
If someone keens, they cry out or make sounds to express their sorrow at someone's death.

throb*
[θrab]

n. 욱신거림; 진동; v. (몸이) 욱신거리다, 지끈거리다; 고동치다, 울리다
A throb is a feeling of pain in a series of regular beats.

pulse*
[pʌls]

v. 맥박 치다, 고동치다; 활기가 넘치다; n. 맥박; (강한) 리듬
If something pulses, it moves, appears, or makes a sound with a strong regular rhythm.

beat ^{복습}
[biːt]

n. 고동, 맥박; 리듬; v. (게임·시합에서) 이기다; 때리다; (심장이) 고동치다
Your heartbeat is the regular movement of your heart as it pumps blood around your body.

rub ^{복습}
[rʌb]

v. (손·손수건 등을 대고) 문지르다; (두 손 등을) 맞비비다; n. 문지르기, 비비기
If you rub a part of your body, you move your hand or fingers backward and forward over it while pressing firmly.

shatter ^{복습}
[ʃǽtər]

v. 산산이 부수다, 산산조각 내다; 엄청난 충격을 주다
If something shatters or is shattered, it breaks into a lot of small pieces.

sprain
[sprein]

v. (팔목·발목을) 삐다, 접지르다
If you sprain a joint such as your ankle or wrist, you accidentally damage it by twisting it or bending it violently.

plow
[plau]

v. 충돌하다, 들이받다; (밭을) 경작하다; 힘들여 나아가다; n. 쟁기
If you plow into someone or something, you crash into them with force, especially because you are moving or driving too quickly or in a careless or uncontrolled way.

ankle*
[ǽŋkl]

n. 발목
Your ankle is the joint where your foot joins your leg.

cast***
[kæst]

n. 깁스 (붕대); 출연자들; v. (시선·미소 등을) 던지다; 내던지다
A cast is a hard cover for protecting a broken or injured part of the body, such as an arm or leg, while it is getting better.

batter*
[bǽtər]

v. 두드리다, 때리다, 구타하다; n. (야구에서) 타자
To batter someone means to hit them many times, using fists or a heavy object.

42

massive 복습
[mǽsiv]

a. (육중하면서) 거대한; 엄청나게 심각한 (massively ad. 크게, 엄청나게)
Something that is massive is very large in size, quantity, or extent.

swell *
[swel]

v. 부풀다; (마음이) 벅차다; (소리가) 더 커지다; n. 증가, 팽창
(swollen a. 부어오른)
If a part of your body is swollen, it is larger and rounder than normal, usually as a result of injury or illness.

mound *
[maund]

n. 언덕; 더미, 무더기
A mound of something is a large rounded pile of it.

tender 복습
[téndər]

a. 따가운; 상냥한, 다정한; 연한
If part of your body is tender, it is sensitive and painful when it is touched.

graze
[greiz]

v. 스치다; (소 · 양 등이) 풀을 뜯다; n. (피부가) 긁힌 상처
If something grazes another thing, it touches that thing lightly as it passes by.

bruise *
[bru:z]

v. 멍이 생기다, 타박상을 입다; 의기소침하게 하다; n. 멍, 타박상
If you bruise a part of your body, a bruise appears on it, for example because something hits you.

strap 복습
[stræp]

v. 끈으로 묶다; 붕대를 감다; n. 끈, 줄, 띠
If you strap something somewhere, you fasten it there with a strap.

scrunch
[skrʌntʃ]

v. 웅크리다; 더 작게 만들다; 찡그리다; 돌돌 구기다
To scrunch means to squeeze a part of your body into a different shape.

sideways 복습
[sáidwèiz]

ad. 옆으로; 옆에서
Sideways means in a direction to the left or right, not forward or backward.

dawn *
[dɔ:n]

n. 새벽, 여명; v. 분명해지다, 이해되기 시작하다; 밝다
Dawn is the time of day when light first appears in the sky, just before the sun rises.

clammy
[klǽmi]

a. (기분 나쁘게) 축축한
Something that is clammy is unpleasantly damp or sticky.

faint 복습
[feint]

a. 희미한, 약한; v. 실신하다, 기절하다; n. 실신, 기절
A faint sound, color, mark, feeling, or quality has very little strength or intensity.

chill *
[tʃil]

n. 냉기, 한기; 오싹한 느낌; v. 아주 춥게 하다; 오싹하게 하다
A chill is a feeling of being cold.

remnant
[rémnənt]

n. 남은 부분, 나머지; 유물, 자취
The remnants of something are small parts of it that are left over when the main part has disappeared or been destroyed.

back and forth

idiom 여기저기에, 왔다갔다; 좌우로; 앞뒤로
If someone moves back and forth, they repeatedly move in one direction and then in the opposite direction.

reality[**]
[riǽləti]

n. 현실; 실제로 존재하는 것
You use reality to refer to real things or the real nature of things rather than imagined, invented, or theoretical ideas.

imagination[**]
[imædʒənéiʃən]

n. 상상력, 상상; 착각; 창의력
Your imagination is the part of your mind which allows you to form pictures or ideas of things that do not necessarily exist in real life.

slash[*]
[slæʃ]

v. 긋다, 베다; 대폭 줄이다; n. (칼 등으로) 긋기
If you slash something, you make a long, deep cut in it.

haze
[heiz]

n. (정신이) 몽롱한 상태; 연무, 실안개; v. 흐릿해지다
A haze can refer to a situation or condition which makes it difficult for you to think clearly.

stare[복습]
[stɛər]

v. 빤히 쳐다보다, 응시하다; n. 빤히 쳐다보기, 응시
If you stare at someone or something, you look at them for a long time.

measure[**]
[méʒər]

v. 측정하다; 판단하다; n. 조치, 정책; 척도
If you measure a quantity that can be expressed in numbers, such as the length of something, you discover it using a particular instrument or device, for example a ruler.

halfway[*]
[hǽfwèi]

ad. (거리 · 시간상으로) 가운데쯤에; 부분적으로, 불완전하게
Halfway means in the middle of a place or between two points, at an equal distance from each of them.

warmth[*]
[wɔːrmθ]

n. 온기; (마음 · 태도 등이) 따뜻함
The warmth of something is the heat that it has or produces.

insect[**]
[ínsekt]

n. 곤충
An insect is a small animal that has six legs. Most insects have wings. Ants, flies, butterflies, and beetles are all insects.

swarm[*]
[swɔːrm]

v. 무리를 지어 다니다; 많이 모여들다; n. (곤충의) 떼, 무리; 군중
When bees or other insects swarm, they move or fly in a large group.

horde
[hɔːrd]

n. (큰) 무리
If you describe a crowd of people as a horde, you mean that the crowd is very large and excited and, often, rather frightening or unpleasant.

mosquito[*]
[məskíːtou]

n. 모기
Mosquitos are small flying insects which bite people and animals in order to suck their blood.

flock[*]
[flɑk]

v. (많은 수가) 모이다; 떼 지어 가다; n. (동물의) 떼; (사람들) 무리
If people flock to a particular place or event, a very large number of them go there, usually because it is pleasant or interesting.

expose[*]
[ikspóuz]

v. 드러내다; 폭로하다; 경험하게 하다
To expose something that is usually hidden means to uncover it so that it can be seen.

skin[복습]
[skin]

n. 피부; (동물의) 껍질; 거죽, 외피; v. (동물의) 가죽을 벗기다; (피부가) 까지다
Your skin is the natural covering of your body.

44

clog
[klag]
v. 막다; 움직임을 방해하다
When something clogs a hole or place, it blocks it so that nothing can pass through.

nostril
[nástrəl]
n. 콧구멍
Your nostrils are the two openings at the end of your nose.

inhale
[inhéil]
v. 숨을 들이마시다, 들이쉬다
When you inhale, you breathe in.

pour**
[pɔːr]
v. 쏟아져 들어오다; 마구 쏟아지다; 붓다, 따르다
If people pour into or out of a place, they go there quickly and in large numbers.

believable
[bilíːvəbl]
a. 그럴듯한
Something that is believable makes you think that it could be true or real.

cough 복습
[kɔːf]
v. (기침을 하여 무엇을) 토하다; 털털거리다; 기침하다; n. 기침
If you cough something up, you make it come out of your throat or lungs when you cough.

spit 복습
[spit]
v. (spit/spat–spit/spat) (침·음식 등을) 뱉다; n. 침; (침 등을) 뱉기
If you spit liquid or food somewhere, you force a small amount of it out of your mouth.

sneeze*
[sniːz]
v. 재채기하다; n. 재채기
When you sneeze, you suddenly take in your breath and then blow it down your nose noisily without being able to stop yourself, for example because you have a cold.

slap*
[slæp]
v. (손바닥으로) 철썩 때리다; 털썩 놓다; n. 철썩 때리기, 치기
If you slap someone, you hit them with the palm of your hand.

crush 복습
[krʌʃ]
v. 으스러뜨리다; 밀어 넣다; n. 홀딱 반함
To crush something means to press it very hard so that its shape is destroyed or so that it breaks into pieces.

dozen**
[dʌzn]
n. (pl.) 다수, 여러 개; 십여 개; 12개
If you refer to dozens of things or people, you are emphasizing that there are very many of them.

whine
[hwain]
v. 윙 소리를 내다; 우는 소리를 하다; 낑낑거리다; n. 윙 하는 소리; 불평
If something or someone whines, they make a long, high-pitched noise, especially one which sounds sad or unpleasant.

buzz*
[bʌz]
v. 윙윙거리다; 부산스럽다, 활기가 넘치다; n. 윙윙거리는 소리
If something buzzes or buzzes somewhere, it makes a long continuous sound, like the noise a bee makes when it is flying.

mass**
[mæs]
n. (pl.) (수·양이) 많은; (많은 사람·사물의) 무리; a. 대량의, 대규모의
Masses of something means a great deal of it.

bite**
[bait]
v. (곤충·뱀 등이) 물다; 베어 물다; n. 한 입; 물기; (짐승·곤충에게) 물린 상처
If a snake or a small insect bites you, it makes a mark or hole in your skin, and often causes the surrounding area of your skin to become painful or itchy.

chew*
[ʧuː]

v. 물어뜯다, 깨물다; 심사숙고하다; (음식을) 씹다; n. 씹기, 깨물기
If a person or animal chews an object, they bite it with their teeth.

puny
[pjúːni]

a. 작고 연약한; 보잘것없는, 별 볼일 없는
Someone or something that is puny is very small or weak.

shelter*
[ʃéltər]

v. 피하다; 막아 주다, 보호하다; n. 대피처, 피신처; 피신
If you shelter in a place, you stay there and are protected from bad weather or danger.

rip^{복습}
[rip]

n. (길게) 찢어진 곳; v. (재빨리 · 거칠게) 떼어 내다, 뜯어 내다; (갑자기) 찢다
A rip is a long cut or split in something made of cloth or paper.

desperate^{복습}
[déspərət]

a. 필사적인; 간절히 원하는; 자포자기한 (desperation n. 필사적임)
Desperation is the feeling that you have when you are in such a bad situation that you will try anything to change it.

flesh**
[fleʃ]

n. (사람의) 피부; (사람 · 동물의) 살
You can use flesh to refer to human skin and the human body, especially when you are considering it in a sexual way.

vicious*
[víʃəs]

a. 사나운, 공격적인; 잔인한, 악랄한; 지독한, 극심한 (viciously ad. 맹렬하게)
A vicious person or a vicious blow is violent and cruel.

frustrate^{복습}
[frʌ́streit]

v. 좌절감을 주다, 불만스럽게 하다; 방해하다 (frustration n. 불만, 좌절감)
If something frustrates you, it upsets or angers you because you are unable to do anything about the problems it creates.

agony*
[ǽgəni]

v. 극도의 (육체적 · 정신적) 고통
Agony is great physical or mental pain.

steam**
[stiːm]

n. 김, 증기; 추진력; v. 김을 내뿜다; 화내다, 발끈하다
Steam is the hot mist that forms when water boils.

bathe***
[beið]

v. (빛으로) 휩싸다; (몸을) 씻다, 세척하다; (강 · 바다 등에서) 멱을 감다
If a place is bathed in light, it is covered with light, especially a gentle, pleasant light.

apparent*
[əpǽrənt]

a. 분명한; ~인 것처럼 보이는 (apparently ad. 보아하니)
You use apparently to refer to something that seems to be true, although you are not sure whether it is or not.

outdoors*
[autdɔ́ːrz]

n. (도시를 벗어난) 전원, 야외; ad. 야외에서
You refer to the outdoors when talking about work or leisure activities which take place outside away from buildings.

naturalist
[nǽʧərəlist]

n. 동식물 연구가, 박물학자
A naturalist is a person who studies plants, animals, insects, and other living things.

scenery*
[síːnəri]

n. 풍경; 배경, 무대 장치
The scenery in a country area is the land, water, or plants that you can see around you.

stretch^{복습}
[streʧ]

v. 기지개를 켜다; (팔 · 다리를) 뻗다; 펼쳐지다; n. (길게) 뻗은 구간; 기간
When you stretch, you put your arms or legs out straight and tighten your muscles.

muscle**
[mʌsl]

n. 근육
A muscle is a piece of tissue inside your body which connects two bones and which you use when you make a movement.

collapse*
[kəlǽps]

v. (의식을 잃고) 쓰러지다; 붕괴되다, 무너지다; n. 실패; (건물의) 붕괴
If you collapse, you suddenly faint or fall down because you are very ill or weak.

puffy
[pʌ́fi]

a. 부어 있는
If a part of someone's body, especially their face, is puffy, it has a round, swollen appearance.

squint
[skwint]

n. 눈을 가늘게 뜨고 보기; 사시; v. 눈을 가늘게 뜨고 보다; 사시이다
If you squint at something, you look at it with your eyes partly closed.

scratch*
[skrætʃ]

v. 긁다; 긁힌 자국을 내다; n. 긁힌 자국; 긁는 소리
If you scratch yourself, you rub your fingernails against your skin because it is itching.

surrounding*
[səráundiŋ]

n. (pl.) 환경, 주위의 상황; a. 인근의, 주위의
When you are describing the place where you are at the moment, or the place where you live, you can refer to it as your surroundings.

absolute*
[ǽbsəlùːt]

a. 완전한, 완벽한 (absolutely ad. 극도로, 굉장히)
Absolute means total and complete.

reflect**
[riflékt]

v. (상을) 비추다; 반사하다; 깊이 생각하다 (reflection n. (거울 등에 비친) 상)
A reflection is an image that you can see in a mirror or in glass or water.

upside down
[ʌ́psàid dáun]

ad. (아래위가) 거꾸로, 뒤집혀 (upside-down a. 거꾸로의)
If something has been moved upside down, it has been turned round so that the part that is usually lowest is above the part that is usually highest.

crow*
[krou]

n. [동물] 까마귀; v. (수탉이) 울다; 마구 자랑하다
A crow is a large black bird which makes a loud, harsh noise.

make up

idiom ~을 이루다; (이야기 등을) 만들어 내다
To make up means to combine together to form something larger.

pine**
[pain]

n. 소나무
A pine tree or a pine is a tall tree which has very thin, sharp leaves and a fresh smell. Pine trees have leaves all year round.

smear
[smiəːr]

v. 마구 바르다; 더럽히다; n. 얼룩, 자국
If you smear a surface with an oily or sticky substance or smear the substance onto the surface, you spread a layer of the substance over the surface.

identify**
[aidéntəfài]

v. (신원 등을) 확인하다; 찾다, 발견하다
If you can identify someone or something, you are able to recognize them or distinguish them from others.

evergreen
[évərgriːn]

n. 상록수, 늘푸른나무
An evergreen is a tree or bush which has green leaves all the year round.

leafy
[líːfi]

a. 잎이 무성한; 나무가 많은
Leafy trees and plants have lots of leaves on them.

moderate*
[mádərət]

a. 보통의, 중간의; 적당한, 적정한; v. 누그러뜨리다, 완화하다
(moderately ad. 중간 정도로, 적당히)
You use moderate to describe something that is neither large nor small in amount or degree.

hilly
[híli]

a. 언덕이 많은
A hilly area has many hills.

hummock
[hʌ́mək]

n. 작은 언덕
A hummock is a small raised area of ground, like a very small hill.

rocky*
[ráki]

a. 바위로 된, 바위투성이의; 고난이 많은, 험난한
A rocky place is covered with rocks or consists of large areas of rock and has nothing growing on it.

ridge*
[ridʒ]

n. 산등성이, 산마루; v. (표면을) 이랑처럼 만들다
A ridge is a long, narrow piece of raised land.

overlook*
[ouvərlúk]

v. 바라보다, 내려다보다; 눈감아주다; n. 전망이 좋은 곳, 높은 곳
If a building or window overlooks a place, you can see the place clearly from the building or window.

smash복습
[smæʃ]

v. (세게) 부딪치다; 박살내다; 부서지다; n. 박살내기; 요란한 소리
If something smashes or is smashed against something solid, it moves very fast and with great force against it.

drive복습
[draiv]

v. 몰아가다; 운전하다; 만들다; 박아 넣다; n. 드라이브, 자동차 여행; 충동, 욕구
If the wind, rain, or snow drives in a particular direction, it moves with great force in that direction.

divorce복습
[divɔ́ːrs]

v. 이혼하다; n. 이혼
If a man and woman divorce or if one of them divorces the other, their marriage is legally ended.

wince복습
[wins]

v. (통증·당혹감으로) 움찔하고 놀라다
If you wince, the muscles of your face tighten suddenly because you have felt a pain or because you have just seen, heard, or remembered something unpleasant.

rounded복습
[ráundid]

a. (모양이) 둥근; (여러 가지를 균형 있게) 아우르는
Something that is rounded is curved in shape, without any points or sharp edges.

layer*
[léiər]

v. 층층이 놓다; n. 층, 막
If you layer something, you arrange it in layers.

mud**
[mʌd]

n. 진흙, 진창
Mud is a sticky mixture of earth and water.

pop*
[pap]

v. 불쑥 나타나다; 펑 하는 소리가 나다; 눈이 휘둥그레지다; n. 펑 (하는 소리); 탄산수
If you pop somewhere, you go there for a short time.

surface복습
[sə́ːrfis]

n. 표면, 지면, 수면; 외관; v. 수면으로 올라오다; (갑자기) 나타나다
The surface of something is the flat top part of it or the outside of it.

48

ripple[*]
[rɪpl]

n. 잔물결, 파문 (모양의 것); v. 잔물결을 이루다; (감정 등이) 파문처럼 번지다
Ripples are little waves on the surface of water caused by the wind or by something moving in or on the water.

lodge[*]
[lɑdʒ]

n. (비버 · 수달의) 굴; 오두막; v. ~에 꽂히다, 박히다; (이의 등을) 제기하다
A lodge can refer to the home that a beaver makes.

channel[복습]
[ʧænl]

n. (텔레비전 · 라디오의) 채널; 물길; 수로; v. (돈 · 감정 · 생각 등을) (~에) 쏟다
A channel is a television station.

splash[*]
[splæʃ]

n. 첨벙 하는 소리; (어디에 떨어지는) 방울; v. 첨벙거리다; (물 등을) 끼얹다
A splash is the sound made when something hits water or falls into it.

signal[복습]
[sígnəl]

n. 신호; 징조; v. 암시하다; (동작 · 소리로) 신호를 보내다
A signal is a gesture, sound, or action which is intended to give a particular message to the person who sees or hears it.

splop
[splɑp]

n. 철퍼덕
A splop is a short sound as of a small, solid object dropping into water without a splash.

daze
[deiz]

n. 멍한 상태; 눈이 부심; v. 멍하게 하다; 눈부시게 하다
If someone is in a daze, they are feeling confused and unable to think clearly, often because they have had a shock or surprise.

blur
[blə:r]

n. 흐릿한 형체; (기억이) 희미한 것; v. 흐릿해지다; 모호해지다
A blur is a shape or area which you cannot see clearly because it has no distinct outline or because it is moving very fast.

traffic[복습]
[trǽfik]

n. 차량들, 교통; 수송
Traffic refers to all the vehicles that are moving along the roads in a particular area.

hum[*]
[hʌm]

n. 윙윙거리는 소리; v. 윙윙거리다; 왁자지껄하다; (노래를) 흥얼거리다
A hum is a low continuous noise made by a machine or a lot of people talking.

awful[복습]
[ɔ́:fəl]

a. (정도가) 대단한, 아주 심한; 끔찍한, 지독한 (awfully ad. 정말, 몹시)
If you say that something is awful, you mean that it is extremely unpleasant, shocking, or bad.

drain[*]
[drein]

v. (힘 · 돈 등을) 빼내 가다; (액체를) 따라 내다; n. 배수관
If something drains you, it leaves you feeling physically and emotionally exhausted.

dizzy[*]
[dízi]

a. 어지러운; (너무 변화가 심해) 아찔한 (dizziness n. 현기증)
If you feel dizzy, you feel that you are losing your balance and are about to fall.

branch[**]
[brænʧ]

n. 나뭇가지; 지사, 분점; v. 갈라지다, 나뉘다
The branches of a tree are the parts that grow out from its trunk and have leaves, flowers, or fruit growing on them.

1. How did Brian feel about drinking the water in the lake?
   A. He was hesitant because he was not sure if the water was safe.
   B. He was concerned because he was not sure if there was water.
   C. He was reluctant because he was disgusted by the color of the water.
   D. He was relieved because he was certain that the water was clean.

2. Why did he try to make his thoughts short and simple?
   A. So that he would not forget important details
   B. So that he would not become distracted
   C. So that he would not make himself tired
   D. So that he would not get overwhelmed

3. What did his English teacher used to say?
   A. To let go of the past and focus on the future
   B. To think creatively and be different
   C. To use motivation to stay positive
   D. To overcome problems through bravery

4. How did he know he had flown off course?
   A. He could sense that he was far from his destination.
   B. He had seen the original flight plan posted in the plane.
   C. He had felt the plane change course because of heavy winds.
   D. He remembered that the pilot had caused the plane to move sideways.

5. Why did he need to find shelter?
   A. There were too many mosquitoes out in the open.
   B. There could be dangerous animals in the woods.
   C. It could rain at any moment.
   D. It was too cold to sleep at the bottom of a tree.

6. What was the main reason he wanted to find shelter near the lake?
   A. There might not be water anywhere else.
   B. Someone flying by might spot the plane in the water.
   C. He did not want to get lost in a strange place.
   D. He wanted to avoid using too much energy.

7. How was he able to find food?
   A. He followed a bunch of birds and discovered they were eating berries.
   B. He saw a trail of berries on the ground and followed it to a berry tree.
   C. He looked for berry bushes that he had seen on TV before and finally found them.
   D. He walked around the lake until he came across the smell of berries nearby.

1분에 몇 단어를 읽는지 리딩 속도를 측정해보세요.

$$\frac{2{,}862 \text{ words}}{\text{reading time ( ) sec}} \times 60 = (\quad) \text{ WPM}$$

Build Your Vocabulary

snap[*]
[snæp]

v. 급히 움직이다; 딱 소리 내다; 딱 부러지다; (동물이) 물려고 하다; n. 탁 하는 소리
If you snap something into a particular position, or if it snaps into that position, it moves quickly into that position, with a sharp sound.

instant^{복습}
[ínstənt]

a. 즉각적인; n. 순간, 아주 짧은 동안 (instantly ad. 즉각, 즉시)
You use instant to describe something that happens immediately.

unbelievable
[ʌnbilíːvəbl]

a. 믿기 어려울 정도인; 믿기 힘든 (unbelievably ad. 믿을 수 없을 정도로)
You can use unbelievable to emphasize that you think something is very bad or shocking.

vicious^{복습}
[víʃəs]

a. 지독한, 극심한; 사나운, 공격적인; 잔인한, 악랄한 (viciously ad. 몹쓸 정도로)
Something that is vicious is very bad or severe.

thirst[*]
[θəːrst]

n. 갈증; 물의 부족; 갈망 (thirsty a. 목이 마른, 갈증이 나는)
If you are thirsty, you feel a need to drink something.

foul[*]
[faul]

a. (성격·맛 등이) 더러운, 아주 안 좋은; 악취 나는; v. 더럽히다
If you describe something as foul, you mean it is dirty and smells or tastes unpleasant.

sticky[*]
[stíki]

a. 끈적거리는, 끈적끈적한; 힘든, 불쾌한
A sticky substance is soft, or thick and liquid, and can stick to other things.

crack^{**}
[kræk]

v. 갈라지다; 깨지다, 부서지다; n. 날카로운 소리; 금; (좁은) 틈
If something hard cracks, or if you crack it, it becomes slightly damaged, with lines appearing on its surface.

bleed[*]
[bliːd]

v. 피를 흘리다, 출혈하다
When you bleed, you lose blood from your body as a result of injury or illness.

wither[*]
[wíðər]

v. 시들다, 말라 죽다; 약해지다, 시들어 가다
If someone or something withers, they become very weak.

burn^{복습}
[bəːrn]

n. 화상; v. 화끈거리다; 불에 타다, 데다; (햇볕 등에) 타다; (마음 등에) 새겨지다
A burn is an injury that you get when something burns your skin.

on fire^{복습}

idiom (몸의 일부가) 화끈거리는; 열중하여, 흥분하여
If a part of your body is on fire, it is giving you a painful burning feeling.

blister
[blístər]

v. 물집이 잡히다; n. 물집
When your skin blisters or when something blisters it, painful swellings containing a clear liquid appear on it.

peel*
[pi:l]

v. 껍질이 벗겨지다; (과일·채소 등의) 껍질을 벗기다; n. 껍질
If you are peeling or if your skin is peeling, small pieces of skin are coming off, usually because you have been burned by the sun.

stiff**
[stif]

a. 결리는, 뻐근한; 뻣뻣한; 경직된; 심한; ad. 몹시, 극심하게 (stiffness n. 뻐근함)
If you are stiff, your muscles or joints hurt when you move, because of illness or because of too much exercise.

pilot^{복습}
[páilət]

n. 조종사, 비행사
A pilot is a person who is trained to fly an aircraft.

rage*
[reidʒ]

v. 맹위를 떨치다; 몹시 화를 내다; n. 격렬한 분노
You say that something powerful or unpleasant rages when it continues with great force or violence.

besides**
[bisáidz]

ad. 게다가, 뿐만 아니라; prep. ~외에
Besides is used to emphasize an additional point that you are making, especially one that you consider to be important.

swallow**
[swálou]

v. (음식 등을) 삼키다; 집어삼키다; n. (음식 등을) 삼키기; [동물] 제비
If you swallow something, you cause it to go from your mouth down into your stomach.

shore^{복습}
[ʃɔ:r]

n. 기슭, 해안, 호숫가
The shores or the shore of a sea, lake, or wide river is the land along the edge of it.

spring***
[spriŋ]

n. 샘; 봄; 생기, 활기; v. (갑자기) 뛰어오르다; 휙 움직이다; 튀다
A spring is a place where water comes up through the ground.

wreck*
[rek]

n. 충돌; 난파선; 사고 잔해; v. 망가뜨리다, 파괴하다
A wreck is an accident in which a moving vehicle hits something and is damaged or destroyed.

swell^{복습}
[swel]

v. 부풀다; (마음이) 벅차다; (소리가) 더 커지다; n. 증가, 팽창 (swollen a. 부어오른)
If a part of your body is swollen, it is larger and rounder than normal, usually as a result of injury or illness.

tear^{복습}
[teər]

① v. (tore-torn) 찢다, 뜯다; 뜯어 내다; n. 찢어진 곳, 구멍 ② n. 눈물
If a person or animal tears at something, they pull it violently and try to break it into pieces.

bank^{복습}
[bæŋk]

n. 둑; 은행; v. (비행기·차를) 좌우로 기울이다; 땔감을 쌓아 올리다
A bank is a sloping raised land, especially along the sides of a river.

murk
[mə:rk]

a. 흐림, 어두컴컴함 (murky a. 흐린)
Murky water or fog is so dark and dirty that you cannot see through it.

log*
[lɔ:g]

n. 통나무
A log is a piece of a thick branch or of the trunk of a tree that has been cut so that it can be used for fuel or for making things.

extend^{복습}
[iksténd]

v. (거리 · 기간을) 포괄하다; 관련시키다, 포함하다; (팔 · 다리를) 뻗다
If you say that something, usually something large, extends for a particular distance or extends from one place to another, you are indicating its size or position.

limb[*]
[lim]

n. (큰) 나뭇가지; (하나의) 팔, 다리
The limbs of a tree are its branches.

teeter
[tíːtər]

v. 불안정하게 움직이다; 망설이다; 시소를 타다; n. 시소
If someone or something teeters, they shake in an unsteady way, and seem to be about to lose their balance and fall over.

weed^{복습}
[wiːd]

n. 잡초; v. 잡초를 뽑다
A weed is a wild plant that grows in gardens or fields of crops and prevents the plants that you want from growing properly.

kneel[*]
[niːl]

v. 무릎을 꿇다
When you kneel, you bend your legs so that your knees are touching the ground.

sip[*]
[sip]

n. 한 모금; v. (음료를) 홀짝거리다, 조금씩 마시다
A sip is a small amount of drink that you take into your mouth.

cup^{***}
[kʌp]

v. 두 손을 동그랗게 모아 쥐다; n. 컵, 잔
If you cup your hands, you make them into a curved shape like a cup.

trickle
[trikl]

v. (액체가 가늘게) 흐르다; 천천히 가다; n. (물)방울; 소량
When a liquid trickles, or when you trickle it, it flows slowly in very small amounts.

tongue^{**}
[tʌŋ]

n. 혀; 말버릇
Your tongue is the soft movable part inside your mouth which you use for tasting, eating, and speaking.

stoop[*]
[stuːp]

v. 몸을 굽히다; n. 현관 입구의 계단; 구부정한 자세
If you stoop, you stand or walk with your shoulders bent forward.

gulp
[gʌlp]

n. 꿀꺽 마시기; v. 꿀꺽꿀꺽 삼키다; (숨을) 깊이 들이마시다
A gulp of air, food, or drink, is a large amount of it that you swallow at once.

stomach^{복습}
[stʌ́mək]

n. 복부, 배, 위(胃)
You can refer to the front part of your body below your waist as your stomach.

stagger[*]
[stǽgər]

v. 비틀거리다, 휘청거리다; 큰 충격을 주다
If you stagger, you walk very unsteadily, for example because you are ill or drunk.

trip^{***}
[trip]

v. 발을 헛디디다; ~를 넘어뜨리다; n. 여행; 발을 헛디딤
If you trip when you are walking, you knock your foot against something and fall or nearly fall.

immediate^{복습}
[imíːdiət]

a. 즉각적인; 당면한; 아주 가까이에 있는 (immediately ad. 즉시, 즉각)
If something happens immediately, it happens without any delay.

54

throw up ^{복습}

idiom ~을 토하다; ~을 두드러지게 하다
If you throw up, you bring food you have eaten back out of your mouth.

reduce ^{복습}
[ridjúːs]

v. (규모 · 크기 · 양 등을) 줄이다
If you reduce something, you make it smaller in size or amount, or less in degree.

out of place

idiom 맞지 않는, 부적절한
If someone or something seems out of place in a particular situation, they do not seem to belong there or to be suitable for that situation.

trigger[*]
[trígəːr]

v. 촉발시키다; n. (총의) 방아쇠; 폭파 장치
If something triggers an event or situation, it causes it to begin to happen or exist.

branch ^{복습}
[bræntʃ]

n. 나뭇가지; 지사, 분점; v. 갈라지다, 나뉘다
The branches of a tree are the parts that grow out from its trunk and have leaves, flowers, or fruit growing on them.

rough^{**}
[rʌf]

a. 매끈하지 않은, 거친; (행동이) 거친; 힘든, 골치 아픈; 개략적인
If a surface is rough, it is uneven and not smooth.

bark[*]
[baːrk]

n. 나무껍질; v. (명령 · 질문 등을) 빽 내지르다; (개가) 짖다
Bark is the tough material that covers the outside of a tree.

rear^{복습}
[riər]

n. 뒤쪽; 궁둥이; a. 뒤쪽의; v. 앞다리를 들어올리며 서다
The rear of something such as a building or vehicle is the back part of it.

shade^{**}
[ʃeid]

n. 그늘; 약간, 기미; v. 그늘지게 하다
Shade is an area of darkness under or next to an object such as a tree, where sunlight does not reach.

relative^{**}
[rélətiv]

a. 상대적인, 비교적인; 관계가 있는; n. 친척
You use relative to say that something is true to a certain degree, especially when compared with other things of the same kind.

comfort^{**}
[kʌ́mfərt]

n. 안락, 편안; 위로, 위안; v. 위로하다, 위안하다
If you are doing something in comfort, you are physically relaxed and contented, and are not feeling any pain or other unpleasant sensations.

sort out

idiom ~을 처리하다; ~을 정리하다
If you sort out something, you do what is necessary to deal with a problem, disagreement, or difficult situation successfully.

rush^{**}
[rʌʃ]

n. (감정이 갑자기) 치밀어 오름; 혼잡; v. 급히 움직이다; 서두르다
If you experience a rush of a feeling, you suddenly experience it very strongly.

confuse ^{복습}
[kənfjúːz]

v. (사람을) 혼란시키다; 혼동하다 (confused a. 혼란스러워하는)
If you are confused, you do not know exactly what is happening or what to do.

jumble ^{복습}
[dʒʌ́mbl]

n. 뒤죽박죽 뒤섞인 것; v. (마구) 뒤섞다
A jumble of things is a lot of different things that are all mixed together in a disorganized or confused way.

make sense 복습
idiom 이해가 되다; 타당하다; 이해하기 쉽다
If something makes sense, you can understand it.

heart attack 복습
[háːrt ətæk]
n. 심근 경색, 심장마비
If someone has a heart attack, their heart begins to beat very irregularly or stops completely.

sink 복습
[siŋk]
v. (sank–sunk) 가라앉다, 빠지다; 박다; (구멍을) 파다; n. (부엌의) 개수대
If a boat sinks or if someone or something sinks it, it disappears below the surface of a mass of water.

search **
[səːrtʃ]
v. 찾아보다, 수색하다; n. 찾기, 수색 (searcher n. 수색하는 사람)
Searchers are people who are looking for someone or something that is missing.

frantic *
[fræntik]
a. (두려움 · 걱정으로) 제정신이 아닌; 정신없이 서두는
If you are frantic, you are behaving in a wild and uncontrolled way because you are frightened or worried.

mount *
[maunt]
v. 시작하다; 끼우다, 고정시키다; n. 산
If you mount a campaign or event, you organize it and make it take place.

extensive *
[iksténsiv]
a. 대규모의; 광범위한, 폭넓은
Something that is extensive covers or includes a large physical area.

file *
[fail]
v. 발송하다; (문서 등을) 보관하다; n. 파일, 서류철; 정보
When someone files a report or a news story, they send or give it to their employer.

flight 복습
[flait]
n. 비행; 항공기; 계단, 층계; 탈출, 도피
A flight is a journey made by flying, usually in an airplane.

government **
[gʌ́vərnmənt]
n. 정부, 정권; 행정, 통치
The government of a country is the group of people who are responsible for governing it.

frown *
[fraun]
v. 얼굴을 찡그리다; 눈살을 찌푸리다; n. 찡그림, 찌푸림
When someone frowns, their eyebrows become drawn together, because they are annoyed or puzzled.

amphibious
[æmfíbiəs]
a. 수륙 양용의
An amphibious vehicle is able to move on both land and water.

float 복습
[flout]
n. 부표; v. (물 위나 공중에서) 떠가다; (물에) 뜨다
A float is a light object that is used to help someone or something float.

land 복습
[lænd]
v. (땅 · 표면에) 내려앉다, 착륙하다; 놓다, 두다; n. 육지, 땅; 지역
When someone or something lands, they come down to the ground after moving through the air or falling.

cheesy
[tʃíːzi]
a. 치즈 맛이 나는; 싸구려의, 저급한
Cheesy food is food that tastes or smells of cheese.

juicy *
[dʒúːsi]
a. 즙이 많은; 재미있는; 매력적인
If food is juicy, it has a lot of juice in it and is very enjoyable to eat.

hunger[*]
[hʌ́ŋgər]

n. 배고픔; 굶주림; 갈망
Hunger is the feeling of weakness or discomfort that you get when you need something to eat.

hold down

idiom ~을 억제하다; 유지하다
To hold something down means to keep it at a low level.

roar[복습]
[rɔːr]

v. 웅웅거리다; 고함치다; 굉음을 내며 질주하다; n. 함성; 울부짖는 듯한 소리
If something roars, it makes a very loud noise.

absolute[복습]
[ǽbsəlùːt]

a. 완전한, 완벽한 (absolutely ad. 극도로, 굉장히)
Absolute means total and complete.

strand[*]
[strænd]

v. 오도 가도 못 하게 하다; 발을 묶다; n. 가닥, 꼰 줄
If you are stranded, you are prevented from leaving a place, for example because of bad weather.

take care of

idiom ~을 처리하다; ~을 돌보다
To take care of someone or something means to do what is necessary to deal with a person or situation.

trap[*]
[træp]

n. 덫; 함정; v. (위험한 장소에) 가두다; 덫으로 잡다; 끌어모으다
A trap is a device which is placed somewhere or a hole which is dug somewhere in order to catch animals or birds.

slick
[slik]

a. 능란한; 교활한; (겉만) 번드르르한; v. 매끈하게 하다
A slick action is done quickly and smoothly, and without any obvious effort.

obvious[복습]
[ábviəs]

a. 분명한, 확실한; 너무 빤한; 명백한
If something is obvious, it is easy to see or understand.

as a matter of fact

idiom 사실은, 실제로
As a matter of fact is used when you are telling someone something interesting, new or important.

figure out[복습]

idiom ~을 이해하다, 알아내다; 계산하다, 산출하다
If you figure out someone or something, you come to understand them by thinking carefully.

stay on top of

idiom 무슨 일이 일어나는지 잘 알고 있다
If you stay on top of someone or something, you keep well-informed about them.

motivate[*]
[móutəvèit]

v. 동기를 부여하다; 이유가 되다
If someone motivates you to do something, they make you feel determined to do it.

knee[복습]
[niː]

n. 무릎; v. 무릎으로 치다
Your knee is the place where your leg bends.

pitiful
[pítifəl]

a. 한심한; 측은한, 가련한
If you describe something as pitiful, you mean that it is completely inadequate.

nail[복습]
[neil]

n. 손톱; 발톱; 못; v. (못 같은 것으로) 고정시키다 (fingernail n. 손톱)
Your fingernails are the thin hard areas at the end of each of your fingers.

clip^{복습}
[klip]

v. 깎다, 자르다; 핀으로 고정하다; n. 핀, 클립; 장전된 총알 한 세트
(clipper n. (무엇을) 깎는 도구)
Clippers are a tool used for cutting small amounts from something, especially from someone's hair or nails.

billfold
[bílfould]

n. 지갑
A billfold is a small flat folded case, usually made of leather or plastic, where you can keep banknotes and credit cards.

bill^{**}
[bil]

n. 지폐; 계산서; v. 청구서를 보내다
A bill is a piece of paper money.

in case^{복습}

idiom (~할) 경우에 대비해서
If you do something in case or just in case a particular thing happens, you do it because that thing might happen.

odd^{**}
[ad]

a. 잡다한; 이상한, 특이한
You use odd before a noun to indicate that you are not mentioning the type, size, or quality of something because it is not important.

hatchet^{복습}
[hǽtʃit]

n. 손도끼
A hatchet is a small ax that you can hold in one hand.

rust[*]
[rʌst]

n. 녹; v. 녹슬다, 부식하다
Rust is a brown substance that forms on iron or steel, for example when it comes into contact with water.

blade^{복습}
[bleid]

n. (칼·도구 등의) 날; 풀잎
The blade of a knife, ax, or saw is the edge, which is used for cutting.

thumb^{**}
[θʌm]

n. 엄지손가락; v. 엄지손가락으로 건드리다
Your thumb is the short thick part on the side of your hand next to your four fingers.

quit^{**}
[kwit]

v. 그만하다; 떠나다
If you quit an activity or quit doing something, you stop doing it.

mess around

idiom 꾸물대다, 어물어물하다
If you mess around, you behave in a silly and annoying way, especially instead of doing something useful.

underwear[*]
[ʌ́ndərwɛər]

n. 속옷
Underwear is clothing such as vests and pants which you wear next to your skin under your other clothes.

tatter
[tǽtər]

n. (pl.) 넝마, 누더기; v. 갈가리 찢다
Clothes that are in tatters are badly torn in several places, so that pieces can easily come off.

wrist[*]
[rist]

n. 손목
Your wrist is the part of your body between your hand and your arm which bends when you move your hand.

blank[*]
[blæŋk]

a. 빈; 멍한, 무표정한; n. 빈칸, 여백; v. (갑자기) 멍해지다
Something that is blank has nothing on it.

motion[*]
[móuʃən]

n. 동작, 몸짓; 운동, 움직임; v. (손·머리로) 몸짓을 해 보이다
A motion is an action, gesture, or movement.

58

drum into	idiom ~에게 ~을 주입시키다
	If you drum something into someone, you make them learn or understand it by repeating it many times.

valuable** [væljuəbl]	a. 소중한, 귀중한; 가치가 큰, 값비싼
	If you describe something or someone as valuable, you mean that they are very useful and helpful.

asset* [æset]	n. 자산(이 되는 사람·물건)
	Something or someone that is an asset is considered useful or helps a person or organization to be successful.

trade** [treid]	v. 주고받다, 교환하다; 거래하다; n. 거래, 교역, 무역
	If someone trades one thing for another or if two people trade things, they agree to exchange one thing for the other thing.

tone* [toun]	n. 어조, 말투; (글 등의) 분위기; 음색
	Someone's tone is a quality in their voice which shows what they are feeling or thinking.

yell복습 [jel]	v. 고함치다, 소리 지르다; n. 고함, 외침
	If you yell, you shout loudly, usually because you are excited, angry, or in pain.

click* [klik]	n. 찰칵 (하는 소리); v. 딸깍 하는 소리를 내다; 분명해지다
	A click is a short sound like the sound when you press a switch.

startle* [staːrtl]	v. 깜짝 놀라게 하다; 움찔하다; n. 깜짝 놀람
	If something sudden and unexpected startles you, it surprises and frightens you slightly.

realize** [ríːəlàiz]	v. 깨닫다, 알아차리다; 실현하다, 달성하다
	If you realize that something is true, you become aware of that fact or understand it.

last** [læst]	v. (특정한 시간 동안) 계속되다; 견디다, 버티다; 오래가다; ad. 맨 끝에, 마지막에
	If an event, situation, or problem lasts for a particular length of time, it continues to exist or happen for that length of time.

intense복습 [inténs]	a. 극심한, 강렬한; 치열한; 진지한
	Intense is used to describe something that is very great or extreme in strength or degree.

buzz복습 [bʌz]	v. 윙윙거리다; 부산스럽다, 활기가 넘치다; n. 윙윙거리는 소리
	If something buzzes or buzzes somewhere, it makes a long continuous sound, like the noise a bee makes when it is flying.

insect복습 [ínsekt]	n. 곤충
	An insect is a small animal that has six legs. Most insects have wings. Ants, flies, butterflies, and beetles are all insects.

chatter* [ʧǽtər]	v. 재잘거리다; 수다를 떨다; n. 수다, 재잘거림; 딱딱거리는 소리
	When birds or animals chatter, they make high-pitched noises.

caw [kɔː]	v. 까악까악 울다; n. 까악까악
	When a bird such as a crow or a rook caws, it makes a loud harsh sound.

coin** [kɔin]
n. 동전; v. (새로운 낱말·어구를) 만들다
A coin is a small piece of metal which is used as money.

weight** [weit]
n. 무게, 체중; 무거운 것
The weight of a person or thing is how heavy they are, measured in units such as kilograms, pounds, or tons.

mental^복습 [mentl]
a. 마음의, 정신의; 정신병의
Mental means relating to the process of thinking.

commercial** [kəmɔ́ːrʃəl]
n. (텔레비전·라디오의) 광고; a. 상업의; 상업적인
A commercial is an advertisement that is broadcast on television or radio.

thunder^복습 [θʌ́ndər]
v. 쏜살같이 보내다; 우르릉거리다; 천둥이 치다; n. 천둥; 천둥 같은 소리
If something or someone thunders somewhere, they move there quickly and with a lot of noise.

meat** [miːt]
n. 고기
Meat is flesh taken from a dead animal that people cook and eat.

bother^복습 [báðər]
v. 신경 쓰이게 하다; 귀찮게 하다; 귀찮게 말을 걸다; 신경 쓰다; n. 성가심
If something bothers you, or if you bother about it, it worries, annoys, or upsets you.

chew^복습 [ʧuː]
v. 심사숙고하다; 물어뜯다, 깨물다; (음식을) 씹다; n. 씹기, 깨물기
If you chew on or chew over something, you think about it carefully for a long time, before making a decision about it.

jerk^복습 [dʒɔːrk]
v. 홱 움직이다; n. 얼간이; 홱 움직임
If you jerk something or someone in a particular direction, or they jerk in a particular direction, they move a short distance very suddenly and quickly.

rudder^복습 [rʌ́dər]
n. (항공기의) 방향타; (배의) 키
An airplane's rudder is a vertical piece of metal at the back which is used to make the plane turn to the right or to the left.

pedal^복습 [pedl]
n. 페달, 발판; v. 페달을 밟다; (자전거를) 타고 가다
A pedal in a car or on a machine is a lever that you press with your foot in order to control the car or machine.

slew^복습 [sluː]
v. 홱 돌다, 미끄러지다; n. 많음, 다수, 대량
If a vehicle slews or is slewed across a road, it slides across it.

nudge [nʌdʒ]
v. (살짝) 쿡 찌르다; 조금씩 밀면서 가다; n. (팔꿈치로 살짝) 쿡 찌르기
If you nudge someone, you push them gently, usually with your elbow, in order to draw their attention to something.

assume** [əsúːm]
v. (특질·양상을) 띠다; (사실일 것으로) 추정하다
If something assumes a particular quality, it begins to have that quality.

swing** [swiŋ]
v. (swung-swung) 방향을 바꾸다; 휘두르다; 홱 움직이다; (전후·좌우로) 흔들다; n. 흔들기; 휘두르기
If a vehicle swings in a particular direction, or if the driver swings it in a particular direction, they turn suddenly in that direction.

beat ^{복습}
[biːt]

n. 고동, 맥박; 리듬; v. (게임 · 시합에서) 이기다; 때리다; (심장이) 고동치다
(heartbeat n. 심장 박동)
Your heartbeat is the regular movement of your heart as it pumps blood around your body.

explode ^{복습}
[iksplóud]

v. 폭발하다; 갑자기 ~하다; (강한 감정을) 터뜨리다
If something explodes, it increases suddenly and rapidly in number or intensity.

gradual[*]
[grǽdʒuəl]

a. 점진적인, 서서히 일어나는; 완만한 (gradually ad. 서서히)
If something changes or is done gradually, it changes or is done in small stages over a long period of time, rather than suddenly.

slosh
[slaʃ]

v. 철벅거리다; (물 · 진창 속을) 철벅거리며 걷다
If a liquid sloshes around or if you slosh it around, it moves around in different directions.

settle ^{복습}
[setl]

v. 진정되다; 자리를 잡다; (서서히) 가라앉다; 결정하다
If something is settled, it has all been decided and arranged.

finger^{***}
[fíŋgər]

v. 손으로 만지다, 더듬다; n. 손가락
If you finger something, you touch or feel it with your fingers.

weapon^{**}
[wépən]

n. 무기, 흉기
A weapon is an object such as a gun, a knife, or a missile, which is used to kill or hurt people in a fight or a war.

shelter ^{복습}
[ʃéltər]

n. 대피처, 피신처; 피신; v. 피하다; 막아 주다, 보호하다
A shelter is a small building or covered place which is made to protect people from bad weather or danger.

mosquito ^{복습}
[məskíːtou]

n. [곤충] 모기
Mosquitos are small flying insects which bite people and animals in order to suck their blood.

1분에 몇 단어를 읽는지 리딩 속도를 측정해보세요.

$$\frac{2,642 \text{ words}}{\text{reading time ( ) sec}} \times 60 = (\qquad) \text{ WPM}$$

Build Your Vocabulary

fool around
idiom 노닥거리다
If you fool around, you behave in a silly way for fun.

joke**
[dʒouk]
v. 농담하다; 농담 삼아 말하다; n. 농담; 웃음거리
If you joke, you tell someone something that is not true in order to amuse yourself.

make up***
idiom (이야기 등을) 만들어 내다; ~을 이루다
If you make up something, you invent something, such as an excuse or a story, often in order to deceive.

pretend***
[priténd]
v. ~라고 가장하다; ~인 척하다, ~인 것처럼 굴다
If children or adults pretend that they are doing something, they imagine that they are doing it, for example as part of a game.

figure***
[fígjər]
v. 생각하다; 중요하다; n. (멀리서 흐릿하게 보이는) 사람; 수치; (중요한) 인물
If you figure that something is the case, you think or guess that it is the case.

goody
[gúdi]
n. 매력적인 것; 맛있는 것
You can refer to pleasant, exciting, or attractive things as goodies.

gear*
[giər]
n. (특정 활동에 필요한) 장비; 기어
The gear involved in a particular activity is the equipment or special clothing that you use.

lean-to
[líːn-tu]
n. 기대어 지은 집
A lean-to is a building such as a shed or garage which is attached to one wall of a larger building, and which usually has a sloping roof.

set out
idiom (일·과제 등에) 착수하다; (여행을) 시작하다
If you set out, you start an activity with a particular aim.

brace***
[breis]
n. 버팀대; 치아 교정기; v. (스스로) 대비를 하다; (몸에) 단단히 힘을 주다
A brace is a piece of wood or metal used for supporting an object so that it does not fall down.

strike***
[straik]
v. (struck–struck/stricken) (생각 등이) 갑자기 떠오르다; (세게) 치다, 부딪치다; n. 공격; 치기, 때리기
If an idea or thought strikes you, it suddenly comes into your mind.

diminish*
[dimíniʃ]
v. 줄이다, 약화시키다; 폄하하다
When something diminishes, or when something diminishes it, it becomes reduced in size, importance, or intensity.

ridge ^{복습}
[ridʒ]

n. 산등성이, 산마루; v. (표면을) 이랑처럼 만들다
A ridge is a long, narrow piece of raised land.

check out

idiom (흥미로운 것을) 살펴보다; ~을 확인하다
If you check someone or something out, you look at them because they seem interesting or attractive.

scoop
[sku:p]

v. (큰 숟갈 같은 것으로) 뜨다; 재빨리 들어올리다; n. 한 숟갈(의 양)
If you scoop something from a container, you remove it with something such as a spoon.

glacier[*]
[gléiʃər]

n. 빙하
A glacier is an extremely large mass of ice which moves very slowly, often down a mountain valley.

bowl^{**}
[boul]

n. (우묵한) 그릇, 통; 한 그릇(의 양)
A bowl is a round container with a wide uncovered top. Some kinds of bowl are used, for example, for serving or eating food from, or in cooking, while other larger kinds are used for washing or cleaning.

ledge[*]
[ledʒ]

n. 절벽에서 튀어나온 바위; (벽에서 튀어나온) 선반
A ledge is a piece of rock on the side of a cliff or mountain, which is in the shape of a narrow shelf.

cave[*]
[keiv]

n. 동굴
A cave is a large hole in the side of a cliff or hill, or one that is under the ground.

smooth^{복습}
[smu:ð]

a. 매끈한; 부드러운; (소리가) 감미로운; v. 매끈하게 하다
A smooth surface has no roughness, lumps, or holes.

roof^{**}
[ru:f]

n. (터널·동굴 등의) 천장, 입천장; 지붕; v. 지붕을 씌우다
The roof of a building is the covering on top of it that protects the people and things inside from the weather.

slight^{복습}
[slait]

a. 약간의, 조금의; 작고 여윈 (slightly ad. 약간, 조금)
Slightly means to some degree but not to a very large degree.

tip^{복습}
[tip]

v. 기울어지다, 젖혀지다; 살짝 건드리다; n. (뾰족한) 끝
If you tip an object or part of your body or if it tips, it moves into a sloping position with one end or side higher than the other.

pulverize
[pʌ́lvəràiz]

v. 가루로 만들다, 분쇄하다; 쳐부수다
If you pulverize something, you make it into a powder by crushing it.

edge^{복습}
[edʒ]

n. 끝, 가장자리; 우위; v. 조금씩 움직이다; 테두리를 두르다
The edge of something is the place or line where it stops, or the part of it that is furthest from the middle.

overhang[*]
[òuvərhǽŋ]

n. 돌출부; v. 돌출하다, 쑥 나오다
An overhang is the part of something that sticks out over and above something else.

opening[*]
[óupəniŋ]

n. (사람 등이 지나가거나 할 수 있는) 틈; 첫 부분; (사람을 쓸 수 있는) 빈자리;
a. 첫, 시작 부분의
An opening is a hole or empty space through which things or people can pass.

doorway*
[dɔ́:rwèi]

n. 출입구
A doorway is a space in a wall where a door opens and closes.

watertight
[wɔ́:tərtait]

a. 물이 새지 않는; 빈틈없는
Something that is watertight does not allow water to pass through it, for example because it is tightly sealed.

crawl^{복습}
[krɔ:l]

v. 기어가다; 우글거리다; n. 기어가기
When you crawl, you move forward on your hands and knees.

shade^{복습}
[ʃeid]

n. 그늘; 약간, 기미; v. 그늘지게 하다
Shade is an area of darkness under or next to an object such as a tree, where sunlight does not reach.

blister^{복습}
[blístər]

v. 물집이 잡히다; n. 물집
When your skin blisters or when something blisters it, painful swellings containing a clear liquid appear on it.

rubbery
[rʌ́bə:ri]

a. 힘이 없는, 후들거리는; 고무 같은
If your legs or knees are rubbery, they feel weak or unsteady.

swallow^{복습}
[swálou]

n. (음식 등을) 삼키기; [동물] 제비; v. (음식 등을) 삼키다; 집어삼키다
A swallow is a movement in your throat that makes food or drink go down into your stomach.

thirst^{복습}
[θə:rst]

n. 갈증; 물의 부족; 갈망 (thirsty a. 목이 마른, 갈증이 나는)
If you are thirsty, you feel a need to drink something.

take the edge off

idiom (강도를) 약화시키다
To take the edge off means to make something unpleasant have less of an effect on someone.

hunger^{복습}
[hʌ́ngər]

n. 배고픔; 굶주림; 갈망
Hunger is the feeling of weakness or discomfort that you get when you need something to eat.

sharpen^{복습}
[ʃá:rpən]

v. 더 강렬해지다; (날카롭게) 갈다; (기량 등을) 갈고 닦다
If disagreements or differences between people sharpen, or if they are sharpened, they become bigger or more important.

drag*
[dræg]

v. 끌다, 끌고 가다; 힘들게 움직이다; n. 끌기, 당기기; 장애물
If you drag something, you pull it along the ground, often with difficulty.

crash^{복습}
[kræʃ]

n. (자동차 · 항공기) 사고; 요란한 소리; v. 충돌하다; 부딪치다; 굉음을 내다
A crash is an accident in which a moving vehicle hits something and is damaged or destroyed.

injure^{**}
[índʒər]

v. 부상을 입히다; (평판 · 자존심 등을) 해치다 (injury n. 부상)
An injury is damage done to a person's or an animal's body.

lean^{복습}
[li:n]

v. ~에 기대다; 기울이다, (몸을) 숙이다; a. 군살이 없는, 호리호리한
If you lean on or against someone or something, you rest against them so that they partly support your weight.

64

icebox
[áisbàks]

n. 냉장고
An icebox is the same as a refrigerator which is a large container kept cool inside, usually by electricity, so that the food and drink in it stays fresh.

divorce^{복습}
[divɔ́:rs]

n. 이혼; v. 이혼하다
A divorce is the formal ending of a marriage by law.

move out

idiom (살던 집에서) 이사를 나가다
If you move out from a place, you vacate your residence or place of business.

break up^{복습}

idiom 헤어지다; (휴대전화의 통화가) 끊기다
If a relationship breaks up, it ends.

work out

idiom ~을 해결하다; ~을 계획해 내다
If you work things out, you solve problems by considering the facts.

yard**
[ja:rd]

n. 마당, 뜰; (학교의) 운동장; 정원 (back yard n. 뒷마당)
A yard is a piece of land next to someone's house, with grass and plants growing in it.

barbecue
[bá:rbikjù:]

n. 바비큐용 그릴; v. 바비큐하다
A barbecue is a piece of equipment which you use for cooking on in the open air.

charcoal
[ʧá:rkòul]

n. 숯; 목탄
Charcoal is a black substance obtained by burning wood without much air. It can be burned as a fuel, and small sticks of it are used for drawing with.

lid*
[lid]

n. 뚜껑
A lid is the top of a box or other container which can be removed or raised when you want to open the container.

chip**
[ʧip]

n. 조각, 토막; 감자칩; v. 깨지다, 이가 빠지다; 잘게 썰다
A chip is a small piece of something or a small piece which has been broken off something.

unbelievable^{복습}
[ʌnbilí:vəbl]

a. 믿기 어려울 정도인; 믿기 힘든
If you say that something is unbelievable, you are emphasizing that it is very good, impressive, intense, or extreme.

meat^{복습}
[mi:t]

n. 고기
Meat is flesh taken from a dead animal that people cook and eat.

saliva
[səláivə]

n. 침, 타액
Saliva is the watery liquid that forms in your mouth and helps you to chew and digest food.

twist^{복습}
[twist]

v. 휘다, 구부리다; (고개·몸 등을) 돌리다; n. 돌리기; (고개·몸 등을) 돌리기
If you twist something, especially a part of your body, or if it twists, it moves into an unusual, uncomfortable, or bent position, for example because of being hit or pushed, or because you are upset.

growl*
[graul]

v. 으르렁거리다; 으르렁거리듯 말하다; n. 으르렁거리는 소리
If something growls, it makes a low or harsh rumbling sound.

wilderness [복습]
[wildərnis]

n. 황야, 황무지; 버려진 땅
A wilderness is a desert or other area of natural land which is not used by people.

force[***]
[fɔːrs]

n. 군대; 작용력; 힘; 영향력; v. 억지로 ~하다; ~를 강요하다 (air force n. 공군)
An air force is the part of a country's armed forces that is concerned with fighting in the air.

survive[복습]
[sərváiv]

v. 살아남다, 생존하다 (survival n. 생존)
If you refer to the survival of something or someone, you mean that they manage to continue or exist in spite of difficult circumstances.

desert[**]
[dézərt]

① n. 사막 ② v. (어떤 장소를) 떠나다; 버리다
A desert is a large area of land, usually in a hot region, where there is almost no water, rain, trees, or plants.

sheet[**]
[ʃiːt]

n. (종이 등의) 한 장; (물 · 불 등이) 가득 퍼짐; 침대에 깔거나 위로 덮는 얇은 천
A sheet of glass, metal, or wood is a large, flat, thin piece of it.

dew[*]
[djuː]

n. 이슬
Dew is small drops of water that form on the ground and other surfaces outdoors during the night.

gather[**]
[gǽðər]

v. (여기저기 있는 것을) 모으다; (사람들이) 모이다
If you gather things, you collect them together so that you can use them.

device[복습]
[diváis]

n. 장치, 기구; 폭발물; 방법
A device is an object that has been invented for a particular purpose, for example for recording or measuring something.

lizard
[lízərd]

n. [동물] 도마뱀
A lizard is a reptile with short legs and a long tail.

crystal[*]
[kristl]

n. (시계의) 뚜껑; 결정체; 수정
A crystal is the piece of glass or plastic that protects the face of a clock or watch.

magnify[*]
[mǽgnəfài]

v. 확대하다; 과장하다
To magnify an object means to make it appear larger than it really is, by means of a special lens or mirror.

raw[**]
[rɔː]

a. 익히지 않은; 가공되지 않은; 다듬어지지 않은
Raw food is food that is eaten uncooked, that has not yet been cooked, or that has not been cooked enough.

bean[**]
[biːn]

n. 콩
Beans such as green beans, French beans, or broad beans are the seeds of a climbing plant or the long thin cases which contain those seeds.

bush[**]
[buʃ]

n. 관목, 덤불; 우거진 것
A bush is a large plant which is smaller than a tree and has a lot of branches.

stew[*]
[stjuː]

n. 스튜; v. (음식을) 뭉근히 끓이다
A stew is a meal which you make by cooking meat and vegetables in liquid at a low temperature.

66

tin[*]
[tin]

n. (= tin can) 깡통; 주석
A tin is a metal container with a lid in which things such as biscuits, cakes, or tobacco can be kept.

exercise[**]
[éksərsàiz]

n. (신체적 · 정신적 건강을 위한) 운동; 연습, 훈련; v. 운동하다
Exercises are a series of movements or actions which you do in order to get fit, remain healthy, or practise for a particular physical activity.

jet[*]
[dʒet]

n. 분출; 제트기; v. 급속히 움직이다; 분출하다
A jet of liquid or gas is a strong, fast, thin stream of it.

sight[**]
[sait]

n. 광경, 모습; 보기, 봄; 시야; v. 갑자기 보다
(lose sight of idiom ~이 더는 안 보이게 되다)
If you lose sight of someone or something, you are no longer able to see them.

distance[**]
[dístəns]

n. 거리; 먼 곳; v. (~에) 관여하지 않다
The distance between two points or places is the amount of space between them.

limb[복습]
[lim]

n. (큰) 나뭇가지; (하나의) 팔, 다리
The limbs of a tree are its branches.

breeze[*]
[bri:z]

n. 산들바람, 미풍; 식은 죽 먹기; v. 경쾌하게 움직이다
A breeze is a gentle wind.

sigh[*]
[sai]

v. 한숨을 쉬다, 한숨짓다; 탄식하듯 말하다; n. 한숨
When you sigh, you let out a deep breath, as a way of expressing feelings such as disappointment, tiredness, or pleasure.

belt[**]
[belt]

n. (특정) 지대; 벨트, 허리띠; v. 세게 치다, 강타하다
A belt of land or sea is a long, narrow area of it that has some special feature.

lusty
[lʌ́sti]

a. 건장한, 튼튼한, 활기찬 (lustily ad. 건장하게)
If you say that something is lusty, you mean that it is healthy and full of strength and energy.

joint[**]
[dʒɔint]

n. 관절; 연결 부위; a. 공동의, 합동의
A joint is a part of your body such as your elbow or knee where two bones meet and are able to move together.

sparrow[*]
[spǽrou]

n. [동물] 참새
A sparrow is a small brown bird that is very common in Britain.

flock[복습]
[flak]

n. (동물의) 떼; (사람들) 무리; v. (많은 수가) 모이다; 떼 지어 가다
A flock of birds, sheep, or goats is a group of them.

reddish
[rédiʃ]

a. 발그레한, 불그스름한
Reddish means slightly red in color.

beak[*]
[bi:k]

n. (새의) 부리
A bird's beak is the hard curved or pointed part of its mouth.

slash[복습]
[slæʃ]

n. (칼 등으로) 긋기; v. 긋다, 베다; 대폭 줄이다
A slash is a long deep cut.

solid ^{복습}
[sálid]

a. 완전한; 확실한; 단단한; 견고한, 속이 꽉 찬; n. 고체, 고형물
A solid metal or color is pure and does not have anything else mixed together with it.

undergrowth
[Ándərgrouθ]

n. 덤불, 관목
Undergrowth consists of bushes and plants growing together under the trees in a forest.

slender *
[sléndər]

a. 가느다란; 날씬한, 호리호리한
If you describe something as slender, you mean that it is not very wide.

droop *
[dru:p]

v. 아래로 처지다; 풀이 죽다, (기가) 꺾이다
If something droops, it hangs or leans downward with no strength or firmness.

cluster *
[klÁstər]

n. 무리, 집단; v. 무리를 이루다, (소규모로) 모이다
A cluster of people or things is a small group of them close together.

bunch *
[bÁntʃ]

n. 다발, 송이, 묶음; (양 · 수가) 많음
A bunch of bananas or grapes is a group of them growing on the same stem.

glisten
[glisn]

v. 반짝이다, 번들거리다
If something glistens, it shines, usually because it is wet or oily.

pace *
[peis]

n. 속도; 걸음; v. 서성거리다; (일의) 속도를 유지하다
Your pace is the speed at which you walk.

quicken *
[kwíkən]

v. 더 빠르게 하다; 더 활발해지다
If something quickens or if you quicken it, it becomes faster or moves at a greater speed.

scatter ^{복습}
[skætər]

v. 황급히 흩어지다; 흩뿌리다; n. 흩뿌리기; 소수, 소량
If a group of people scatter or if you scatter them, they suddenly separate and move in different directions.

grab ^{복습}
[græb]

v. (와락 · 단단히) 붙잡다; 급히 ~하다; n. 와락 잡아채려고 함
If you grab something, you take it or pick it up suddenly and roughly.

strip *
[strip]

v. (물건을) 다 뜯어내다; 옷을 벗다; n. 가느다란 조각
To strip something means to remove everything that covers it.

bitter **
[bítər]

a. 맛이 쓴; 쓰라린
A bitter taste is sharp, not sweet, and often slightly unpleasant.

lack **
[læk]

v. ~이 없다, 부족하다; n. 부족, 결핍
If you say that someone or something lacks a particular quality or that a particular quality is lacking in them, you mean that they do not have any or enough of it.

tart
[ta:rt]

a. (맛이) 시큼털털한; 쏘아붙이는
If something such as fruit is tart, it has a sharp taste.

flavor *
[fléivər]

n. (음식 · 술의) 맛; 운치, 정취; 특징; v. 맛을 내다
The flavor of a food or drink is its taste.

68

pit[*]
[pit]

n. (과일의) 씨; (크고 깊은) 구덩이; v. 자국을 남기다, 구멍을 남기다
A pit is the stone of a fruit or vegetable.

handful[*]
[hǽndfùl]

n. 줌, 움큼; 몇 안 되는 수
A handful of something is the amount of it that you can hold in your hand.

jam[복습]
[dʒæm]

v. 밀어 넣다; 움직이지 못하게 되다; n. 교통 체증; 혼잡; 잼
If you jam something somewhere, you push or put it there roughly.

shrink[*]
[ʃriŋk]

v. (shrank–shrunk) 줄어들다; (놀람·충격으로) 움츠러들다
If something shrinks or something else shrinks it, it becomes smaller.

drive[복습]
[draiv]

n. 충동, 욕구; 드라이브, 자동차 여행; v. 운전하다; 만들다; 박아넣다; 몰아가다
A drive is a very strong need or desire in human beings that makes them act in particular ways.

pouch
[pautʃ]

n. 주머니; (캥거루 같은 동물의) 새끼 주머니
A pouch is a flexible container like a small bag.

judge[복습]
[dʒʌdʒ]

v. 판단하다; 심판을 보다; 짐작하다; n. 판사; 심판, 심사위원
If you judge something or someone, you form an opinion about them after you have examined the evidence or thought carefully about them.

camp[**]
[kæmp]

n. 야영지; 수용소; 진영; v. 야영하다
A camp is a collection of tents or caravans where people are living or staying, usually temporarily while they are traveling.

glance[복습]
[glæns]

v. 흘깃 보다; 대충 훑어보다; 비스듬히 맞다; n. 흘깃 봄
If you glance at something or someone, you look at them very quickly and then look away again immediately.

rueful
[rú:fəl]

a. 후회하는, 유감스러워하는 (ruefully ad. 유감스러운 듯이)
If someone is rueful, they feel or express regret or sorrow in a quiet and gentle way.

lakeside
[léiksàid]

n. 호반, 호숫가
The lakeside is the area of land around the edge of a lake.

driftwood
[dríftwud]

n. 유목(流木)
Driftwood is wood which has been carried onto the shore by the motion of the sea or a river, or which is still floating on the water.

firewood
[fáiərwud]

n. 장작
Firewood is wood that has been cut into pieces so that it can be burned on a fire.

tuck[*]
[tʌk]

v. 집어 넣다; 끼워 넣다; 밀어넣다; n. 주름, 단
If you tuck something somewhere, you put it there so that it is safe, comfortable, or neat.

disgust[*]
[disgʌ́st]

n. 혐오감, 역겨움; v. 혐오감을 유발하다, 역겹게 하다
Disgust is a feeling of very strong dislike or disapproval.

livable
[lívəbl]

a. 살기에 적합한; 살 만한
If you describe a place as livable, you mean that the place is pleasant enough to live in.

interlace
[intə́ːrleis]

a. 꼬다, 엮다

To interlace means to join different parts together to make a whole, especially by crossing one thing over another or fitting one part into another.

weave 복습
[wiːv]

v. (wove—woven) (옷감 등을) 짜다; 이리저리 빠져 나가다;
n. 엮어서 만든 것; (직물을) 짜는 법

If you weave something such as a basket, you make it by crossing long plant stems or fibers over and under each other.

twinge
[twindʒ]

n. 찌릿한 통증; (불쾌하게) 찌르르한 느낌

A twinge is a sudden sharp pain.

tighten 복습
[taitn]

v. (더 단단히) 조이다; (더) 팽팽해지다; 더 엄격하게 하다

If a part of your body tightens, the muscles in it become tense and stiff, for example because you are angry or afraid.

slope**
[sloup]

v. 경사지다, 기울어지다; n. 경사지; (산)비탈

If a surface slopes, it is at an angle, so that one end is higher than the other.

nod 복습
[nad]

v. (고개를) 끄덕이다, 까딱하다; n. (고개를) 끄덕임

If you nod, you move your head downward and upward to show that you are answering 'yes' to a question, or to show agreement, understanding, or approval.

initial 복습
[iníʃəl]

a. 처음의, 초기의; n. 이름의 첫 글자

You use initial to describe something that happens at the beginning of a process.

cloud***
[klaud]

v. 구름으로 덮다, 어둡게 하다; 흐리다, 흐려지다; n. 구름

If something clouds, it becomes difficult to see through.

dump*
[dʌmp]

v. (아무렇게나) 내려놓다; 버리다; n. (쓰레기) 폐기장

If you dump something somewhere, you put it or unload it there quickly and carelessly.

sleeve*
[sliːv]

n. (옷의) 소매, 소맷자락

The sleeves of a coat, shirt, or other item of clothing are the parts that cover your arms.

wrap**
[ræp]

v. 둘러싸다; (무엇의 둘레를) 두르다; 포장하다; n. 포장지; 랩

When you wrap something, you fold paper or cloth tightly round it to cover it completely, for example in order to protect it or so that you can give it to someone as a present.

huddle*
[hʌdl]

v. 몸을 움츠리다; 모이다; n. 모여 서 있는 것; 혼잡

If you huddle somewhere, you sit, stand, or lie there holding your arms and legs close to your body, usually because you are cold or frightened.

70

1. How did Brian feel when he saw his reflection in the lake?
   A. He did not care at all about his appearance.
   B. He was not surprised at all at his appearance.
   C. He felt more confident in his looks.
   D. He felt sorry for himself.

2. What did he learn after getting sick from the gut cherries?
   A. He should wash them well before eating them.
   B. He should only eat the light red ones that were not yet ripe.
   C. He should not eat too many, but just enough to make him less hungry.
   D. He should not store so many in the shelter, as they would rot.

3. What did he realize about the bear?
   A. The bear was not interested in hurting him.
   B. The bear was not as big as he originally thought.
   C. The bear might have followed him back to the shelter.
   D. The bear might have been traveling with other bears.

4. What did he think about in the shelter after encountering the bear?
   A. He wondered if the bear was lonely.
   B. He wondered if the bear felt threatened by him.
   C. He wondered if the bear was stunned to see him.
   D. He wondered if the bear could break into the shelter.

5. How did he know he was attacked by a porcupine?
   A. He knew the slithering sound that porcupines made.
   B. He was familiar with the distinct scent that porcupines had.
   C. He caught a glimpse of the porcupine's quills in the moonlight.
   D. He recognized the texture of the quills stuck in his leg.

6. What was the most important rule of survival that he learned?
   A. Self-pity was a natural part of life.
   B. Self-pity did not help solve problems.
   C. Crying could always make a person feel better.
   D. Crying required too much effort, and so it was not worth it.

7. What did he realize about the hatchet?
   A. The hatchet was unbreakable, so he could use it anytime.
   B. The hatchet could protect him from animals.
   C. The hatchet could be used to make fire.
   D. The hatchet was a symbol of the people he loved.

1분에 몇 단어를 읽는지 리딩 속도를 측정해보세요.

$$\frac{993 \text{ words}}{\text{reading time } (\quad) \text{ sec}} \times 60 = (\qquad) \text{ WPM}$$

Build Your Vocabulary

awaken[*]
[əwéikən]

v. (잠에서) 깨다; (감정을) 불러일으키다
When you awaken, or when something or someone awakens you, you wake up.

abdomen[*]
[ǽbdəmən]

n. 배, 복부
Your abdomen is the part of your body below your chest where your stomach and intestines are.

jolt[복습]
[dʒoult]

n. 충격; 덜컥 하고 움직임; v. 갑자기 거칠게 움직이다; (~하도록) 충격을 주다
A jolt is an unpleasant shock or surprise.

double[**]
[dʌbl]

v. (통증으로) 몸을 구부리다; 두 배로 만들다; a. 두 배의; 이중의; n. 두 배, 갑절
If you double over, or if something doubles you over, you suddenly bend forward and down, usually because of pain or laughter.

moan[*]
[moun]

v. 신음하다; 투덜거리다; n. 신음; 투덜거림
If you moan, you make a low sound, usually because you are unhappy or in pain.

pit[복습]
[pit]

n. (과일의) 씨; (크고 깊은) 구덩이; v. 자국을 남기다, 구멍을 남기다
A pit is the stone of a fruit or vegetable.

rip[복습]
[rip]

v. (재빨리·거칠게) 떼어 내다, 뜯어 내다; (갑자기) 찢다; n. (길게) 찢어진 곳
When something rips or when you rip it, you tear it forcefully with your hands or with a tool such as a knife.

doorway[복습]
[dɔ́:rwèi]

n. 출입구
A doorway is a space in a wall where a door opens and closes.

vomit[복습]
[vámit]

v. 토하다, 게우다; n. 토함, 게움
If you vomit, food and drink comes back up from your stomach and out through your mouth.

diarrhea
[dàiərí:ə]

n. 설사
If someone has diarrhea, a lot of liquid faeces comes out of their body because they are ill.

drain[복습]
[drein]

v. (힘·돈 등을) 빼내 가다; (액체를) 따라 내다; n. 배수관
If something drains you, it leaves you feeling physically and emotionally exhausted.

blond[복습]
[bland]

a. 금발의
If you describe someone's hair as blond, you mean that it is pale yellow or golden.

friendly ∗∗
[fréndli]

a. 상냥한, 다정한; 우호적인; (행동이) 친절한
If someone is friendly, they behave in a pleasant, kind way, and like to be with other people.

peck ∗
[pek]

n. 가벼운 입맞춤; 쪼기; v. (새가) 쪼다, 쪼아 먹다
If you give someoen a peck, you give them a quick light kiss.

angle 복습
[æŋgl]

n. 기울기; 각도, 각; 관점; v. 비스듬히 움직이다
An angle is the difference in direction between two lines or surfaces. Angles are measured in degrees.

cheek ∗∗
[ʧi:k]

n. 뺨, 볼; 엉덩이
Your cheeks are the sides of your face below your eyes.

forehead 복습
[fɔ́:rhèd]

n. 이마
Your forehead is the area at the front of your head between your eyebrows and your hair.

shame ∗∗
[ʃeim]

n. 수치심, 창피; 애석한 일; v. 창피스럽게 하다; 망신시키다
Shame is an uncomfortable feeling that you get when you have done something wrong or embarrassing, or when someone close to you has.

fade ∗
[feid]

v. 서서히 사라지다; (색깔이) 바래다, 희미해지다
If memories, feelings, or possibilities fade, they slowly become less intense or less strong.

stream 복습
[stri:m]

v. (액체·기체가) 줄줄 흐르다; 줄을 지어 이어지다; n. 개울, 시내; (액체·기체의) 줄기
When light streams into or out of a place, it shines strongly into or out of it.

whine 복습
[hwain]

n. 윙 하는 소리; 불평; v. 윙 소리를 내다; 우는 소리를 하다; 낑낑거리다
A whine is a high sound made by a machine or insect.

brush 복습
[brʌʃ]

v. (솔이나 손으로) 털다; 솔질을 하다; ~을 스치다; n. 덤불, 잡목 숲; 붓; 솔
If you brush something somewhere, you remove it with quick light movements of your hands.

welt
[welt]

v. (피부가) 부풀어오르다; n. (맞거나 쓸려서 피부가) 부은 자국
If a part of your skin is welted, you have a red raised area on the skin caused by injury or illness.

bite 복습
[bait]

n. (짐승·곤충에게) 물린 상처; 한 입; 물기; v. (곤충·뱀 등이) 물다; 베어 물다
A bite is an injury or a mark on your body where an animal, snake, or small insect has bitten you.

lump ∗
[lʌmp]

n. 혹; 덩어리, 응어리; v. 함께 묶다 (lumpy a. 혹투성이의)
A lump on or in someone's body is a small, hard swelling that has been caused by an injury or an illness.

deal ∗∗
[di:l]

n. 많은; 거래, 합의; 대우, 처리; v. 처리하다
If you say that you need or have a great deal of or a good deal of a particular thing, you are emphasizing that you need or have a lot of it.

awful 복습
[ɔ́:fəl]

a. 끔찍한, 지독한; (정도가) 대단한, 아주 심한
If you say that something is awful, you mean that it is extremely unpleasant, shocking, or bad.

pile[pail]

n. 무더기; 쌓아 놓은 것, 더미; v. (차곡차곡) 쌓다; 우르르 가다

A pile of things is a mass of them that is high in the middle and has sloping sides.

gut[gʌt]

n. 소화관; 배; 직감; v. 내부를 파괴하다

The gut is the tube inside the body of a person or animal through which food passes while it is being digested.

mess[mes]

v. 엉망으로 만들다; n. (지저분하고) 엉망인 상태; (많은 문제로) 엉망인 상황

If you mess up something, you make it dirty or untidy.

dawn[dɔːn]

n. 새벽, 여명; v. 분명해지다, 이해되기 시작하다; 밝다

Dawn is the time of day when light first appears in the sky, just before the sun rises.

reflect[riflékt]

v. (상을) 비추다; 반사하다; 깊이 생각하다 (reflection n. (거울 등에 비친) 상)

A reflection is an image that you can see in a mirror or in glass or water.

frighten[fraitn]

v. 겁먹게 하다, 놀라게 하다

If something or someone frightens you, they cause you to suddenly feel afraid, anxious, or nervous.

bleed[bliːd]

v. 피를 흘리다, 출혈하다

When you bleed, you lose blood from your body as a result of injury or illness.

matted[mǽtid]

a. 엉겨 붙은

If you describe someone's hair as matted, you mean that it has become a thick untidy mass, often because it is wet or dirty.

heal[hiːl]

v. 치유되다, 낫다; 치료하다, 고치다

When a broken bone or other injury heals or when something heals it, it becomes healthy and normal again.

scab[skæb]

n. (상처의) 딱지

A scab is a hard, dry covering that forms over the surface of a wound.

slit[slít]

n. (좁고 기다란) 구멍; v. (좁고) 길게 자르다

A slit is a long narrow cut.

slap[slæp]

v. (손바닥으로) 철썩 때리다; 털썩 놓다; n. 철썩 때리기, 치기

If you slap someone, you hit them with the palm of your hand.

overcome[ouvərkʌ́m]

v. (overcame–overcome) 꼼짝 못하게 되다; 압도당하다; 극복하다

If you are overcome by a feeling or event, it is so strong or has such a strong effect that you cannot think clearly.

pity[píti]

n. 연민, 동정; v. 애석해 하다; 불쌍하다, 동정하다 (self-pity n. 자기 연민)

Self-pity is a feeling of unhappiness that you have about yourself and your problems, especially when this is unnecessary or greatly exaggerated.

starve[staːrv]

v. 굶주리다, 굶어죽다

If people starve, they suffer greatly from lack of food which sometimes leads to their death.

miserable*
[mízərəbl]

a. 비참한; 우울하게 하는; 보잘것없는
If you are miserable, you are very unhappy.

bank ^{복습}
[bæŋk]

n. 둑; 은행; v. (비행기 · 차를) 좌우로 기울이다; 땔감을 쌓아 올리다
A bank is a sloping raised land, especially along the sides of a river.

waste**
[weist]

v. 낭비하다; 헛되이 쓰다; n. 낭비, 허비; (pl.) 쓰레기, 폐기물
If you waste something such as time, money, or energy, you use too much of it doing something that is not important or necessary, or is unlikely to succeed.

cramp ^{복습}
[kræmp]

n. (근육의) 경련; 꺾쇠; v. 경련을 일으키다; (비좁은 곳에) 처박아 넣다
Cramp is a sudden strong pain caused by a muscle suddenly contracting.

recede**
[risíːd]

v. (느낌 · 특질이) 약해지다, 희미해지다; (서서히) 물러나다
When something such as a quality, problem, or illness recedes, it becomes weaker, smaller, or less intense.

dump ^{복습}
[dʌmp]

v. (아무렇게나) 내려놓다; 버리다; n. (쓰레기) 폐기장
If you dump something somewhere, you put it or unload it there quickly and carelessly.

stave off

idiom (안 좋은 일을) 피하다
To stave off means to stop something from happening.

ripe*
[raip]

a. 익은, 여문 (ripeness n. 성숙)
Ripe fruit or grain is fully grown and ready to eat.

handful ^{복습}
[hǽndfùl]

n. 줌, 움큼; 몇 안 되는 수
A handful of something is the amount of it that you can hold in your hand.

splash ^{복습}
[splæʃ]

v. 첨벙거리다; (물 등을) 끼얹다; n. 첨벙 하는 소리; (어디에 떨어지는) 방울
If you splash about or splash around in water, you hit or disturb the water in a noisy way, causing some of it to fly up into the air.

hook**
[huk]

n. (낚시) 바늘; (갈)고리; v. (낚싯바늘로) 낚다; 갈고리로 잠그다
A hook is a bent piece of metal or plastic that is used for catching or holding things, or for hanging things up.

spit ^{복습}
[spit]

v. (침 · 음식 등을) 뱉다; n. 침; (침 등을) 뱉기
If you spit liquid or food somewhere, you force a small amount of it out of your mouth.

tart ^{복습}
[taːrt]

a. (맛이) 시큼털털한; 쏘아붙이는
If something such as fruit is tart, it has a sharp taste.

numb*
[nʌm]

a. (신체 부위가) 감각이 없는; 멍한; v. 감각이 없게 하다; 멍하게 만들다
If a part of your body is numb, you cannot feel anything there.

go through ^{복습}

idiom ~을 살펴보다; 거치다; ~을 겪다
If you go through something, you look at, check, or examine it closely and carefully, especially in order to find something.

breeze ^{복습}
[briːz]

n. 산들바람, 미풍; 식은 죽 먹기; v. 경쾌하게 움직이다
A breeze is a gentle wind.

sight^{복습}
[sait]

n. 시야; 광경, 모습; 보기, 봄; v. 갑자기 보다
If something is in sight or within sight, you can see it.

crude*
[kru:d]

a. 대충 만든; 대충의, 대강의
If you describe an object that someone has made as crude, you mean that it has been made in a very simple way or from very simple parts.

weather tight
[wéðər tàit]

a. 비바람을 막는
Something that is weather tight does not allow rain or wind to pass through it, for example because it is tightly sealed.

cut off

idiom ~을 차단하다; (말을) 중단시키다; 단절시키다
To cut off something means to block or get in the way of it.

set off

idiom 출발하다; (폭탄 등을) 터뜨리다
If you set off, you begin a journey.

bush^{복습}
[buʃ]

n. 관목, 덤불; 우거진 것
A bush is a large plant which is smaller than a tree and has a lot of branches.

pause**
[pɔ:z]

v. (말·일을 하다가) 잠시 멈추다; 정지시키다; n. (말·행동 등의) 멈춤
If you pause while you are doing something, you stop for a short period and then continue.

merely**
[míərli]

ad. 한낱, 그저, 단지
You use merely to emphasize that something is only what you say and not better, more important, or more exciting.

go on

idiom (어떤 상황이) 계속되다; 말을 계속하다; 자자, 어서
To go on something means to continue an activity without stopping.

tricky
[tríki]

a. 까다로운, 곤란한
If you describe a task or problem as tricky, you mean that it is difficult to do or deal with.

fierce*
[fiərs]

a. 극심한, 맹렬한; 사나운, 험악한
Fierce conditions are very intense, great, or strong.

snap^{복습}
[snæp]

v. 딱 부러지다; 급히 움직이다; 딱 소리 내다; (동물이) 물려고 하다; n. 탁 하는 소리
If something snaps or if you snap it, it breaks suddenly, usually with a sharp cracking noise.

halfway^{복습}
[hǽfwèi]

ad. (거리·시간상으로) 가운데쯤에; 부분적으로, 불완전하게
Halfway means in the middle of a place or between two points, at an equal distance from each of them.

rot*
[rat]

v. 썩다, 부패하다; n. 썩음, 부식, 부패
When food, wood, or another substance rots, or when something rots it, it becomes softer and is gradually destroyed.

snag
[snæg]

n. 날카로운 것; 문제; v. 잡아채다, 낚아채다; (날카롭거나 튀어나온 것에) 걸리다
A snag is something rough or sharp that can cause damage.

poke*
[pouk]

v. 쑥 내밀다; (손가락 등으로) 쿡 찌르다; n. (손가락 등으로) 찌르기
If something pokes out of or through another thing, you can see part of it appearing from behind or underneath the other thing.

clearing [klíəriŋ]

n. (숲 속의) 빈터
A clearing is a small area in a forest where there are no trees or bushes.

thorn [θɔːrn]

n. (식물의) 가시 (thorny a. 가시가 있는)
A thorny plant or tree is covered with thorns.

cluster [klʌ́stər]

n. 무리, 집단; v. 무리를 이루다, (소규모로) 모이다
A cluster of people or things is a small group of them close together.

tiny [táini]

a. 아주 작은
Something or someone that is tiny is extremely small.

tang [tæŋ]

n. 톡 쏘는 듯한 맛
A tang is a strong, sharp smell or taste.

gorge [gɔːrdʒ]

v. 잔뜩 먹다; n. 협곡
If you gorge on something or gorge yourself on it, you eat lots of it in a very greedy way.

cram [kræm]

v. (억지로) 밀어 넣다
If you cram things or people into a container or place, you put them into it, although there is hardly enough room for them.

tongue [tʌŋ]

n. 혀; 말버릇
Your tongue is the soft movable part inside your mouth which you use for tasting, eating, and speaking.

stain [stein]

v. 더러워지다, 얼룩지게 하다; n. 얼룩, 오점
If a liquid stains something, the thing becomes colored or marked by the liquid.

roof [ruːf]

n. 입천장; (터널 · 동굴 등의) 천장, 지붕; v. 지붕을 씌우다
The roof of your mouth is the highest part of the inside of your mouth.

stare [stɛər]

v. 빤히 쳐다보다, 응시하다; n. 빤히 쳐다보기, 응시
If you stare at someone or something, you look at them for a long time.

fur [fəːr]

n. (동물의) 털; 모피
Fur is the thick and usually soft hair that grows on the bodies of many mammals.

silky [sílki]

a. 비단 같은; 보드라운, 광택 있는
If something has a silky texture, it is smooth, soft, and shiny, like silk.

hind [haind]

a. 뒤쪽의, 후방의
An animal's hind legs are at the back of its body.

wuffle [wʌfl]

v. 킁킁거리다
If an animal wuffles, it snort or sniff gently.

delicate [délikət]

a. 섬세한, 우아한; 연약한, 여린 (delicately ad. 우아하게)
A delicate task, movement, action, or product needs or shows great skill and attention to detail.

stem[**] [stem]

n. 줄기, 대
The stem of a plant is the thin, upright part on which the flowers and leaves grow.

disbelief [dìsbilíːf]

n. 믿기지 않음, 불신감
Disbelief is not believing that something is true or real.

opposite[**] [ápəzit]

a. (정)반대의; 건너편의; 맞은편의; prep. 맞은편에
Opposite is used to describe things of the same kind which are completely different in a particular way.

panic[복습] [pǽnik]

n. 극심한 공포, 공황; 허둥지둥함; v. 어쩔 줄 모르다, 공황 상태에 빠지다
Panic is a very strong feeling of anxiety or fear, which makes you act without thinking carefully.

take over

idiom 장악하다, 탈취하다; (~을) 인계받다
If you take over something, you take control of it.

run away

idiom (~에서) 달아나다
If you run away, you move quickly away from someone or a place.

threaten[**] [θretn]

v. 위협하다; 협박하다; (나쁜 일이 있을) 조짐을 보이다
If something or someone threatens a person or thing, they are likely to harm that person or thing.

harm[**] [haːrm]

n. 해, 피해, 손해; v. 해치다; 해를 끼치다, 손상시키다
Harm is physical injury to a person or an animal which is usually caused on purpose.

stand[복습] [stænd]

n. 수목, 관목; 가판대, 좌판; v. 서다; (어떤 위치에) 세우다
A stand is a group of growing plants of a specified kind, especially trees.

move on

idiom (새로운 일 · 주제로) 옮기다
To move on to means to stop discussing or doing something and begin discussing or doing something different.

indicate[복습] [índikèit]

v. 보여 주다; (계기가) 가리키다; (손가락이나 고갯짓으로) 가리키다
If you indicate an opinion, an intention, or a fact, you mention it in an indirect way.

convince[*] [kənvíns]

v. 납득시키다, 확신시키다; 설득하다
If someone or something convinces you of something, they make you believe that it is true or that it exists.

patch[*] [pætʃ]

n. 작은 땅; 부분; 조각; v. 덧대다, 때우다
A patch of land is a small area of land where a particular plant or crop grows.

caution[**] [kɔ́ːʃən]

n. 조심; 경고, 주의; v. 주의를 주다; ~에게 경고하다
Caution is great care which you take in order to avoid possible danger.

squirrel[*] [skwə́ːrəl]

n. [동물] 다람쥐
A squirrel is a small animal with a long furry tail.

rustle *
[rʌsl]

v. 바스락거리다; n. 바스락거리는 소리
When something thin and dry rustles or when you rustle it, it makes soft sounds as it moves.

pine 복습
[pain]

n. 소나무
A pine tree or a pine is a tall tree which has very thin, sharp leaves and a fresh smell. Pine trees have leaves all year round.

needle 복습
[niːdl]

n. (pl.) 솔잎; 바늘, 침; (계기의) 바늘, 지침
The needles of a fir or pine tree are its thin, hard, pointed leaves.

jump out of one's skin

idiom (기쁨 · 놀람 등으로) 펄쩍 뛰다
If you jump out of your skin, you are extremely surprised by something.

thicken *
[θíkən]

v. 짙어지다; 걸쭉해지다
If something thickens, it becomes more closely grouped together or more solid than it was before.

trot *
[trat]

v. 빨리 걷다; 총총걸음을 걷다; n. 속보, 빠른 걸음
If you trot somewhere, you move fairly fast at a speed between walking and running, taking small quick steps.

pouch 복습
[pautʃ]

n. 주머니; (캥거루 같은 동물의) 새끼 주머니
A pouch is a flexible container like a small bag.

make it

idiom 가다; 해내다; (힘든 경험 등을) 버텨 내다
If you make it to a place, you succeed in reaching that place.

sheet 복습
[ʃiːt]

n. (물 · 불 등이) 가득 퍼짐; (종이 등의) 한 장; 침대에 깔거나 위로 덮는 얇은 천
A sheet of something is a thin wide layer of it over the surface of something else.

drench
[drentʃ]

v. 흠뻑 적시다
To drench something or someone means to make them completely wet.

rivulet
[rívjulit]

n. 시내, 개울
A rivulet is a small stream.

snug *
[snʌg]

a. 포근한, 아늑한; 꼭 맞는
If you feel snug or are in a snug place, you are very warm and comfortable, especially because you are protected from cold weather.

notice 복습
[nóutis]

v. 알아채다, 인지하다; 주의하다; n. 신경 씀, 주목, 알아챔
If you notice something or someone, you become aware of them.

seep 복습
[siːp]

v. 스미다, 배다
If something such as liquid or gas seeps somewhere, it flows slowly and in small amounts into a place where it should not go.

apparent 복습
[əpǽrənt]

a. 분명한; ~인 것처럼 보이는 (apparently ad. 보아하니)
You use apparently to refer to something that seems to be true, although you are not sure whether it is or not.

crush 복습
[krʌʃ]

v. 으스러뜨리다; 밀어 넣다; n. 홀딱 반함
To crush something means to press it very hard so that its shape is destroyed or so that it breaks into pieces.

weight ^{복습}
[weit]

n. 무게, 체중; 무거운 것
The weight of a person or thing is how heavy they are, measured in units such as kilograms, pounds, or tons.

liquid**
[líkwid]

n. 액체; a. 액체의
A liquid is a substance which is not solid but which flows and can be poured, for example water.

tangy
[tǽŋi]

a. (맛이) 찌릿한, (냄새가) 톡 쏘는
A tangy flavor or smell is one that is sharp, especially a flavor like that of lemon juice or a smell like that of sea air.

pop ^{복습}
[pap]

n. 탄산수; 펑 (하는 소리); v. 불쑥 나타나다; 펑 하는 소리가 나다; 눈이 휘둥그레지다
You can refer to fizzy drinks such as lemonade as pop.

fizz
[fiz]

n. (음료 속의) 거품; 쉬익 하는 소리; v. 쉬익 하는 소리를 내다
Fizz is bubbles of gas in a liquid.

grin**
[grin]

v. 활짝 웃다; n. 활짝 웃음
When you grin, you smile broadly.

seepage
[síːpidʒ]

n. (물기 등의) 침투, 누수
Seepage is the slow flow of a liquid through something.

drip*
[drip]

v. (액체가) 뚝뚝 흐르다; 가득 담고 있다; n. (액체가) 뚝뚝 떨어짐
When liquid drips somewhere, or you drip it somewhere, it falls in individual small drops.

pour ^{복습}
[pɔːr]

v. 마구 쏟아지다; 붓다, 따르다; 쏟아져 들어오다
When it rains very heavily, you can say that it is pouring.

syrup
[sírəp]

n. 시럽
Syrup is a sweet liquid made by cooking sugar with water, and sometimes with fruit juice as well.

stiff ^{복습}
[stif]

a. 결리는, 뻐근한; 뻣뻣한; 경직된; 심한; ad. 몹시, 극심하게 (stiffness n. 뻐근함)
If you are stiff, your muscles or joints hurt when you move, because of illness or because of too much exercise.

belly*
[béli]

n. 배, 복부
The belly of a person or animal is their stomach or abdomen.

sticky ^{복습}
[stíki]

a. 끈적거리는, 끈적끈적한; 힘든, 불쾌한
A sticky substance is soft, or thick and liquid, and can stick to other things.

catch up

idiom 결국 ~의 발목을 잡다; 따라잡다, 따라가다; (소식 등을) 듣다
If something catches up with you, it begins to have an effect on you.

1분에 몇 단어를 읽는지 리딩 속도를 측정해보세요.

$$\frac{1{,}930 \text{ words}}{\text{reading time ( ) sec}} \times 60 = (\quad) \text{ WPM}$$

Build Your Vocabulary

growl^{복습}
[graul]

n. 으르렁거리는 소리; v. 으르렁거리다; 으르렁거리듯 말하다
A growl is a frightening or unfriendly low noise.

shelter^{복습}
[ʃéltər]

n. 대피처, 피신처; 피신; v. 피하다; 막아 주다, 보호하다
A shelter is a small building or covered place which is made to protect people from bad weather or danger.

terrify[*]
[térəfài]

v. (몹시) 무섭게 하다
If something terrifies you, it makes you feel extremely frightened.

rot^{복습}
[rat]

n. 썩음, 부식, 부패; v. 썩다, 부패하다
If there is rot in something, especially something that is made of wood, parts of it have decayed and fallen apart.

musty
[mʌ́sti]

a. 퀴퀴한 냄새가 나는
Something that is musty smells old and damp.

grave^{**}
[greiv]

n. 무덤, 묘; a. 심각한
A grave is a place where a dead person is buried.

cobweb
[kábwèb]

n. 거미줄
A cobweb is the net which a spider makes for catching insects.

nostril^{복습}
[nástrəl]

n. 콧구멍
Your nostrils are the two openings at the end of your nose.

widen[*]
[waidn]

v. 넓어지다; (정도 · 범위 등이) 커지다
If you widen something or if it widens, it becomes greater in measurement from one side or edge to the other.

monster[*]
[mánstər]

n. 괴물; a. 기이하게 큰, 거대한
A monster is a large imaginary creature that looks very ugly and frightening.

fright[*]
[frait]

n. 놀람, 두려움
Fright is a sudden feeling of fear, especially the fear that you feel when something unpleasant surprises you.

hammer^{복습}
[hǽmər]

v. 쿵쿵 치다; 망치로 치다; n. 망치, 해머
If your heart hammers, you feel it beating strongly and quickly.

slither
[slíðər]

v. (매끄럽게) 스르르 나아가다; 미끄러지듯 나아가다
If an animal such as a snake slithers, it moves along in a curving way.

hatchet ^{복습}
[hǽtʃit]

n. 손도끼
A hatchet is a small ax that you can hold in one hand.

sail^{**}
[seil]

v. 미끄러지듯 나아가다; 항해하다; n. 돛
If a person or thing sails somewhere, they move there smoothly and fairly quickly.

shower[*]
[ʃáuər]

n. 소나기(처럼 쏟아지는 것들); 샤워; v. 샤워를 하다; 소나기처럼 쏟아져 내리다
You can refer to a lot of things that are falling as a shower of them.

spark[*]
[spɑːrk]

n. 불꽃, 불똥; (전류의) 스파크; v. 촉발시키다; 불꽃을 일으키다
A spark is a tiny bright piece of burning material that flies up from something that is burning.

instant ^{복습}
[ínstənt]

a. 즉각적인; n. 순간, 아주 짧은 동안 (instantly ad. 즉각, 즉시)
You use instant to describe something that happens immediately.

tear ^{복습}
[tɛər]

① v. (tore–torn) 찢다, 뜯다; 뜯어 내다; n. 찢어진 곳, 구멍 ② n. 눈물
If you are torn between two or more things, you cannot decide which to choose, and so you feel anxious or troubled.

drive ^{복습}
[draiv]

v. 박아 넣다; 운전하다; 만들다; 몰아가다; n. 드라이브, 자동차 여행; 충동, 욕구
If you drive something such as a nail into something else, you push it in or hammer it in using a lot of effort.

skitter
[skítər]

v. 잽싸게 나아가다
If something skitters, it moves about very lightly and quickly.

strain^{**}
[strein]

v. 안간힘을 쓰다; 한계에 이르게 하다; n. 부담, 압박
If you strain to do something, you make a great effort to do it when it is difficult to do.

terror ^{복습}
[térər]

n. 두려움, 공포; 공포의 대상
Terror is very great fear.

bulk[*]
[bʌlk]

n. 육중한 것; 큰 규모
You can refer to something's bulk when you want to emphasize that it is very large.

scrape[*]
[skreip]

v. (무엇을) 긁어내다; (상처가 나도록) 긁다; n. 긁기; 긁힌 상처
If something scrapes against something else or if someone or something scrapes something else, it rubs against it, making a noise or causing slight damage.

opening ^{복습}
[óupəniŋ]

n. (사람 등이 지나가거나 할 수 있는) 틈; 첫 부분; (사람을 쓸 수 있는) 빈자리; a. 첫, 시작 부분의
An opening is a hole or empty space through which things or people can pass.

rasp
[ræsp]

v. 거친 소리를 내다; 쉰 목소리로 말하다; n. 거친 소리
If someone rasps, their voice or breathing is harsh and unpleasant to listen to.

calf
[kæf]

n. 종아리; 송아지
Your calf is the thick part at the back of your leg, between your ankle and your knee.

spread ^{복습}
[spred]

v. 퍼지다, 확산되다; (넓은 범위에 걸쳐) 펼쳐지다; 펴다; n. 확산, 전파
If something spreads or is spread, it becomes larger or moves so that it affects more people or a larger area.

gingerly
[dʒíndʒərli]

ad. 조심조심
If you do something gingerly, you do it in a careful manner, usually because you expect it to be dangerous, unpleasant, or painful.

flesh ^{복습}
[fleʃ]

n. (사람 · 동물의) 살; (사람의) 피부 (fleshy a. 살집이 있는)
Fleshy parts of the body or fleshy plants are thick and soft.

stumble[*]
[stʌmbl]

v. 비틀거리다; 발을 헛디디다; (말 · 글 읽기를 하다가) 더듬거리다
(stumble into idiom ~를 우연히 만나다)
If you stumble into something, you become involved in it by chance.

tail[*]
[teil]

n. (동물의) 꼬리; 끝부분; v. 미행하다
The tail of an animal, bird, or fish is the part extending beyond the end of its body.

quill
[kwil]

n. (고슴도치의) 가시; (새 날개 · 꼬리의 커다란) 깃
The quills of a porcupine are the long sharp points on its body.

dozen ^{복습}
[dʌzn]

n. (pl.) 다수, 여러 개; 십여 개; 12개
If you refer to dozens of things or people, you are emphasizing that there are very many of them.

slam ^{복습}
[slæm]

v. 세게 치다, 놓다; 쾅 닫다; n. 쾅 하고 놓기; 탕 하는 소리
If you slam something down, you put it there quickly and with great force.

pin^{**}
[pin]

v. (핀으로) 고정시키다; 꼼짝 못하게 하다; n. 핀
If you pin something on or to something, you attach it with a pin.

skin ^{복습}
[skin]

n. 피부; (동물의) 껍질; 거죽, 외피; v. (동물의) 가죽을 벗기다; (피부가) 까지다
Your skin is the natural covering of your body.

intense[*]
[inténs]

a. 극심한, 강렬한; 치열한; 진지한
Intense is used to describe something that is very great or extreme in strength or degree.

satisfaction^{**}
[sætisfækʃən]

n. 만족(감), 흡족; 보상
Satisfaction is the pleasure that you feel when you do something or get something that you wanted or needed to do or get.

grasp[*]
[græsp]

v. 꽉 잡다; 완전히 이해하다, 파악하다; n. 움켜잡기; 통제; 이해
If you grasp something, you take it in your hand and hold it very firmly.

hold one's breath

idiom (흥분 · 공포 등으로) 숨을 죽이다
If you say that someone is holding their breath, you mean that they are waiting anxiously or excitedly for something to happen.

jerk ^{복습}
[dʒəːrk]

v. 홱 움직이다; n. 얼간이; 홱 움직임
If you jerk something or someone in a particular direction, or they jerk in a particular direction, they move a short distance very suddenly and quickly.

signal ^{복습}
[sígnəl]

n. 신호; 징조; v. 암시하다; (동작 · 소리로) 신호를 보내다
A signal is a gesture, sound, or action which is intended to give a particular message to the person who sees or hears it.

wave ^{복습}
[weiv]

n. (감정 · 움직임의) 파도; (열 · 소리 · 빛 등의) −파; 물결; (팔 · 손 · 몸을) 흔들기; v. (손 · 팔을) 흔들다; 손짓하다
If you refer to a wave of a particular feeling, you mean that it increases quickly and becomes very intense, and then often decreases again.

pointed[*]
[pɔ́intid]

a. (끝이) 뾰족한; (말 등이) 날카로운
Something that is pointed has a point at one end.

injure ^{복습}
[índʒər]

v. 부상을 입히다; (평판 · 자존심 등을) 해치다 (injury n. 부상)
An injury is damage done to a person's or an animal's body.

smear ^{복습}
[smiə:r]

n. 얼룩, 자국; v. 마구 바르다; 더럽히다
A smear is a dirty or oily mark.

catch one's breath

idiom 한숨 돌리다, 잠시 숨을 가다듬다
When you catch your breath while you are doing something energetic, you stop for a short time so that you can start breathing normally again.

pause ^{복습}
[pɔ:z]

v. (말 · 일을 하다가) 잠시 멈추다; 정지시키다; n. (말 · 행동 등의) 멈춤
If you pause while you are doing something, you stop for a short period and then continue.

pity ^{복습}
[píti]

n. 연민, 동정; v. 애석해 하다; 불쌍해하다, 동정하다 (self−pity n. 자기 연민)
Self-pity is a feeling of unhappiness that you have about yourself and your problems, especially when this is unnecessary or greatly exaggerated.

ache ^{복습}
[eik]

v. (계속) 아프다; n. (계속적인) 아픔
If you ache or a part of your body aches, you feel a steady, fairly strong pain.

mosquito ^{복습}
[məskí:tou]

n. [곤충] 모기
Mosquitos are small flying insects which bite people and animals in order to suck their blood.

upright[*]
[Ápràit]

a. (자세가) 똑바른, 꼿꼿한; 수직으로 세워 둔
If you are sitting or standing upright, you are sitting or standing with your back straight, rather than bending or lying down.

cave ^{복습}
[keiv]

n. 동굴
A cave is a large hole in the side of a cliff or hill, or one that is under the ground.

knee ^{복습}
[ni:]

n. 무릎; v. 무릎으로 치다
Your knee is the place where your leg bends.

look back

idiom (과거를) 되돌아보다
If you look back on something, you think about a time or event in the past.

accomplish[*]
[əkámpliʃ]

v. 완수하다, 성취하다, 해내다
If you accomplish something, you succeed in doing it.

86

doze
[douz]

n. 잠깐 잠, 낮잠; v. 깜빡 잠이 들다, 졸다
When you doze, you sleep lightly or for a short period, especially during the daytime.

awaken ^{복습}
[əwéikən]

v. (잠에서) 깨다; (감정을) 불러일으키다
When you awaken, or when something or someone awakens you, you wake up.

period ^{복습}
[pí:əriəd]

n. 기간, 시기; 시대; 끝; int. 끝, 이상이다
A period is a length of time.

daylight *
[déilait]

n. 낮; (낮의) 햇빛, 일광
Daylight is the time of day when it begins to get light.

segment *
[ségmənt]

n. 부분, 조각; v. 나누다, 분할하다
A segment of something is one part of it, considered separately from the rest.

whisper ^{복습}
[hwíspər]

n. 속삭임, 소곤거리는 소리; v. 속삭이다, 소곤거리다
A whisper is a very quiet way of saying something so that other people cannot hear you.

gesture **
[dʒéstʃər]

n. 몸짓; (감정·의도의) 표시; v. (손·머리 등으로) 가리키다; 몸짓을 하다
A gesture is a movement that you make with a part of your body, especially your hands, to express emotion or information.

scratch ^{복습}
[skrætʃ]

v. 긁다; 긁힌 자국을 내다; n. 긁힌 자국; 긁는 소리
If a sharp object scratches someone or something, it makes small shallow cuts on their skin or surface.

cross ***
[krɔːs]

a. 짜증난, 약간 화가 난; v. 서로 겹치게 놓다; (가로질러) 건너다; n. 십자 기호
Someone who is cross is rather angry or irritated.

fade ^{복습}
[feid]

v. 서서히 사라지다; (색깔이) 바래다, 희미해지다
When something that you are looking at fades, it slowly becomes less bright or clear until it disappears.

fog **
[fɔːg]

n. 안개; 혼미, 혼란; v. 수증기가 서리다; 헷갈리게 하다
When there is fog, there are tiny drops of water in the air which form a thick cloud and make it difficult to see things.

bench ^{복습}
[bentʃ]

n. 벤치; 판사석
A bench is a long seat of wood or metal that two or more people can sit on.

barbecue ^{복습}
[báːrbikjùː]

n. 바비큐용 그릴; v. 바비큐하다
A barbecue is a piece of equipment which you use for cooking on in the open air.

pit ^{복습}
[pit]

n. (크고 깊은) 구덩이; (과일의) 씨; v. 자국을 남기다, 구멍을 남기다
A pit is a large hole that is dug in the ground.

charcoal ^{복습}
[tʃáːrkòul]

n. 숯; 목탄
Charcoal is a black substance obtained by burning wood without much air. It can be burned as a fuel, and small sticks of it are used for drawing with.

fluid *
[flu:id]

n. 유체(流體), 유동체; a. 부드러운, 우아한; 가변적인
A fluid is a liquid.

flick
[flik]

n. 재빨리 움직임; v. 튀기다, 털다; 잽싸게 움직이다
A flick is a sudden quick movement.

burn 복습
[bəːrn]

v. 불에 타다; 화끈거리다; 데다, (햇볕 등에) 타다; (마음 등에) 새겨지다; n. 화상
If something is burning, it is on fire.

grocery
[gróusəri]

n. 식료 잡화점; (pl.) 식료 잡화류
A grocery or a grocery store is a grocer's shop.

sack 복습
[sæk]

n. (종이) 봉지, 부대
A sack is a paper or plastic bag, which is used to carry things bought in a food shop.

contain **
[kəntéin]

v. ~이 들어 있다; (감정을) 억누르다
If something such as a box, bag, room, or place contains things, those things are inside it.

chip 복습
[ʧip]

n. 감자칩; 조각, 토막; v. 깨지다, 이가 빠지다; 잘게 썰다
Chips or potato chips are very thin slices of fried potato that are eaten cold as a snack.

mustard *
[mʌ́stərd]

n. 겨자, 머스터드 (소스)
Mustard is a yellow or brown paste usually eaten with meat. It tastes hot and spicy.

flame **
[fleim]

n. 불길, 불꽃; 격정; v. 활활 타오르다; 시뻘게지다
A flame is a hot bright stream of burning gas that comes from something that is burning.

frustrate 복습
[frʌ́streit]

v. 좌절감을 주다, 불만스럽게 하다; 방해하다 (frustration n. 불만, 좌절감)
If something frustrates you, it upsets or angers you because you are unable to do anything about the problems it creates.

dim *
[dim]

a. (빛이) 어둑한; (형체가) 흐릿한; v. (빛의 밝기가) 낮아지다, 어둑해지다
Dim light is not bright.

wipe 복습
[waip]

v. (먼지 · 물기 등을) 닦다; 지우다; n. 닦기
If you wipe something, you rub its surface to remove dirt or liquid from it.

stiffen *
[stífən]

v. 뻣뻣해지다; (화 · 공포로 몸이) 경직되다; (태도 · 생각을) 강화시키다
If your muscles or joints stiffen, or if something stiffens them, they become difficult to bend or move.

spoil **
[spɔil]

v. 상하다; 망치다, 버려 놓다; (아이를) 버릇없게 키우다
If food spoils or if it is spoilt, it is no longer fit to be eaten.

mushy
[mʌ́ʃi]

a. 죽 같은, 걸쭉한
Vegetables and fruit that are mushy are soft and have lost most of their shape.

crush 복습
[krʌʃ]

v. 으스러뜨리다; 밀어 넣다; n. 홀딱 반함
To crush something means to press it very hard so that its shape is destroyed or so that it breaks into pieces.

flash ^{복습}
[flæʃ]

n. (잠깐) 반짝임; 갑자기 떠오름; v. (잠깐) 비치다; 휙 내보이다; 휙 움직이다
A flash is a sudden burst of light or of something shiny or bright.

catch one's eye

idiom 눈에 띄다; 눈길을 끌다
If something catches your eye, you suddenly notice it.

scootch ^{복습}
[skuːʃ]

v. 약간 옮기다, 살짝 움직이다
To scootch means to hunch or draw yourself up and move.

wince ^{복습}
[wins]

v. (통증 · 당혹감으로) 움찔하고 놀라다
If you wince, the muscles of your face tighten suddenly because you have felt a pain or because you have just seen, heard, or remembered something unpleasant.

bend ^{**}
[bend]

v. (bent-bent) (몸 · 머리를) 굽히다, 숙이다; 구부리다; n. (도로 · 강의) 굽이, 굽은 곳
When you bend a part of your body such as your arm or leg, or when it bends, you change its position so that it is no longer straight.

nick
[nik]

n. (칼로) 새긴 자국; v. (칼로) 베다
A nick is a small cut made in the surface of something, usually in someone's skin.

tool ^{**}
[tuːl]

n. 도구, 연장; 수단
A tool is any instrument or simple piece of equipment that you hold in your hands and use to do a particular kind of work.

staff ^{**}
[stæf]

n. 지팡이
A staff is a strong stick or pole.

lance
[læns]

n. 긴 창
A lance is a long spear used in former times by soldiers on horseback.

pin down

idiom ~을 정확히 이해하다
If you pin down something, you identify or understand it exactly.

scramble [*]
[skræmbl]

v. 재빨리 움직이다; 허둥지둥 해내다; n. (힘들게) 기어가기; 서로 밀치기
If you scramble to a different place or position, you move there in a hurried, awkward way.

stretch ^{복습}
[streʧ]

v. 기지개를 켜다; (팔 · 다리를) 뻗다; 펼쳐지다; n. (길게) 뻗은 구간; 기간
When you stretch, you put your arms or legs out straight and tighten your muscles.

muscle ^{복습}
[mʌsl]

n. 근육
A muscle is a piece of tissue inside your body which connects two bones and which you use when you make a movement.

sore ^{**}
[sɔːr]

a. 아픈, 화끈거리는; 화가 난, 감정이 상한
If part of your body is sore, it causes you pain and discomfort.

ray [*]
[rei]

n. 광선; 약간, 소량
Rays of light are narrow beams of light.

faint ^{복습}
[feint]

a. 희미한, 약한; v. 실신하다, 기절하다; n. 실신, 기절
A faint sound, color, mark, feeling, or quality has very little strength or intensity.

brilliant*
[briljənt]

a. 눈부신; 훌륭한, 멋진; (재능이) 뛰어난, 우수한
A brilliant color is extremely bright.

imbed
[imbéd]

v. (단단히) 박다
If an object imbeds itself in a substance or thing, it becomes fixed there firmly and deeply.

rear복습
[riər]

n. 뒤쪽; 궁둥이; a. 뒤쪽의; v. 앞다리를 들어올리며 서다
The rear of something such as a building or vehicle is the back part of it.

glance복습
[glæns]

v. 비스듬히 맞다; 흘깃 보다; 대충 훑어보다; n. 흘깃 봄 (glancing a. 비스듬히 치는)
A glancing blow is one that hits something at an angle rather than from directly in front.

blow복습
[blou]

n. 세게 때림, 강타; 충격; v. (입으로) 불다; (바람·입김에) 날리다; 폭파하다
If someone receives a blow, they are hit with a fist or weapon.

skip복습
[skip]

v. 표면을 스치며 날다; (일을) 거르다; 생략하다; n. 깡충깡충 뛰기
To skip means to move quickly over the surface of something, or to make something do this.

immediate복습
[imí:diət]

a. 즉각적인; 당면한; 아주 가까이에 있는 (immediately ad. 즉시, 즉각)
If something happens immediately, it happens without any delay.

swing복습
[swiŋ]

v. (swung–swung) 휘두르다; 방향을 바꾸다; 휙 움직이다; (전후·좌우로) 흔들다; n. 흔들기; 휘두르기
If you swing at a person or thing, you try to hit them with your arm or with something that you are holding.

slide복습
[slaid]

v. 미끄러지듯이 움직이다; 슬며시 넣다; n. 떨어짐; 미끄러짐
When something slides somewhere or when you slide it there, it moves there smoothly over or against something.

explode복습
[iksplóud]

v. 폭발하다; 갑자기 ~하다; (강한 감정을) 터뜨리다
If an object such as a bomb explodes or if someone or something explodes it, it bursts loudly and with great force, often causing damage or injury.

90

1. What did Brian do with the birchbark in order to make fire?
   A. He chopped it into large blocks.
   B. He cut it into very thin pieces.
   C. He placed it on top of some grass and twigs.
   D. He put it against the black rock and hit it with the hatchet.

2. What was the final step he took to get the fire started?
   A. He made the nest wider and removed some of the bark hairs.
   B. He hit the bark gently and then fanned the hairs.
   C. He blew gently on the sparks that hit the bark.
   D. He struck the rock until it turned into flames.

3. What did he consider the fire to be?
   A. A curse
   B. A mystery
   C. An enemy
   D. A guard

4. What was one of the benefits of having a fire?
   A. It kept the mosquitoes away.
   B. It did not require much fuel.
   C. It reduced Brian's pain and tiredness.
   D. Its smoke would prevent Brian from getting lost.

5. Why did he inspect the pile of sand?
   A. He was hoping there would be eggs buried in it.
   B. He assumed an animal was hiding in it.
   C. He wanted to find out why an animal had gone up to it.
   D. He thought there might be wood in it that he could add to his fire.

6. What did he do with the eggs?
   A. He cooked some of them over the fire and stored the rest.
   B. He ate some of them raw and decided to save the rest.
   C. He only managed to eat a few because they made him feel sick.
   D. He ate all six of them, including the shells.

7. What did he think about the possibility of being rescued?
   A. His chances of being found were getting smaller and smaller.
   B. The searchers had probably already stopped looking for him.
   C. He would run out of food before the searchers could find him.
   D. He needed to remain optimistic about the searchers finding him.

1분에 몇 단어를 읽는지 리딩 속도를 측정해보세요.

$$\frac{1,469 \text{ words}}{\text{reading time ( ) sec}} \times 60 = (\quad) \text{ WPM}$$

Build Your Vocabulary

spark^{복습}
[spa:rk]

n. 불꽃, 불똥; (전류의) 스파크; v. 촉발시키다; 불꽃을 일으키다
A spark is a tiny bright piece of burning material that flies up from something that is burning.

ignite
[ignáit]

v. 불을 붙이다, 점화하다
When you ignite something or when it ignites, it starts burning or explodes.

tinder
[tíndər]

n. 부싯깃, 불쏘시개
Tinder consists of small pieces of something dry, especially wood or grass, that burns easily and can be used for lighting a fire.

kindling
[kíndliŋ]

n. 불쏘시개
Kindling is small pieces of dry wood and other materials that you use to start a fire.

tap[*]
[tæp]

v. (가볍게) 톡톡 두드리다; n. (가볍게) 두드리기
If you tap something, you hit it with a quick light blow or a series of quick light blows.

twig[*]
[twig]

n. (나무의) 잔가지
A twig is a very small thin branch that grows out from a main branch of a tree or bush.

combination^{**}
[kàmbənéiʃən]

n. 조합, 결합; 연합
A combination of things is a mixture of them.

sputter
[spʌ́tər]

v. (엔진·불길 등이) 펑펑 하는 소리를 내다; 식식거리며 말하다
If something such as an engine or a flame sputters, it works or burns in an uneven way and makes a series of soft popping sounds.

settle^{복습}
[setl]

v. 자리를 잡다; 진정되다; (서서히) 가라앉다; 결정하다
If you settle yourself somewhere or settle somewhere, you sit down or make yourself comfortable.

haunch
[hɔ:nʧ]

n. (pl.) 궁둥이, 둔부
If you get down on your haunches, you lower yourself toward the ground so that your legs are bent under you and you are balancing on your feet.

exasperate
[igzǽspərèit]

v. 몹시 화나게 하다, 짜증나게 하다 (exasperation n. 격분, 분노)
If someone or something exasperates you, they annoy you and make you feel frustrated or upset.

pitiful ^{복습}
[pítifəl]

a. 한심한; 측은한, 가련한
If you describe something as pitiful, you mean that it is completely inadequate.

clump
[klʌmp]

n. 무리, 무더기; 수풀; v. 무리를 짓다, 함께 모이다
A clump of things such as wires or hair is a group of them collected together in one place.

fine^{***}
[fain]

a. 아주 가는; 질 높은, 좋은; 괜찮은; n. 벌금
Something that is fine is very delicate, narrow, or small.

fluff
[flʌf]

n. (동물이나 새의) 솜털; 보풀; v. 망치다; 부풀리다 (fluffy a. 푹신해 보이는, 솜털 같은)
If you describe something such as a towel or a toy animal as fluffy, you mean that it is very soft.

shred[*]
[ʃred]

v. (갈가리) 자르다, 찢다; n. (가늘고 작은) 조각; 아주 조금
If you shred something such as food or paper, you cut it or tear it into very small, narrow pieces.

limp[*]
[limp]

v. 다리를 절다, 절뚝거리다; n. 절뚝거림; a. 기운이 없는, 축 처진
If a person or animal limps, they walk with difficulty or in an uneven way because one of their legs or feet is hurt.

sore ^{복습}
[sɔːr]

a. 아픈, 화끈거리는; 화가 난, 감정이 상한
If part of your body is sore, it causes you pain and discomfort.

dig^{**}
[dig]

v. (dug-dug) (무엇을 찾기 위해) 뒤지다; (구멍 등을) 파다; 찌르다; n. 쿡 찌르기
If you dig into something such as a deep container, you put your hand in it to search for something.

bill ^{복습}
[bil]

n. 지폐; 계산서; v. 청구서를 보내다
A bill is a piece of paper money.

worthless[*]
[wə́ːrθlis]

a. 가치 없는, 쓸모없는
Something that is worthless is of no real value or use.

pile ^{복습}
[pail]

n. 무더기; 쌓아 놓은 것, 더미; v. (차곡차곡) 쌓다; 우르르 가다
A pile of things is a mass of them that is high in the middle and has sloping sides.

lean ^{복습}
[liːn]

v. 기울이다, (몸을) 숙이다; ~에 기대다; a. 군살이 없는, 호리호리한
When you lean in a particular direction, you bend your body in that direction.

register[*]
[rédʒistər]

v. 알아채다, 기억하다; (이름을) 등록하다; n. 기록부, 명부
If a piece of information does not register or if you do not register it, you do not really pay attention to it, and so you do not remember it or react to it.

bark ^{복습}
[baːrk]

n. 나무껍질; v. (명령 · 질문 등을) 빽 내지르다; (개가) 짖다
Bark is the tough material that covers the outside of a tree.

slight ^{복습}
[slait]

a. 약간의, 조금의; 작고 여윈 (slightly ad. 약간, 조금)
Slightly means to some degree but not to a very large degree.

speckle
[spekl]

n. 작은 반점 (speckled a. 작은 반점들이 있는, 얼룩덜룩한)
A speckled surface is covered with small marks, spots, or shapes.

peel ^{복습}
[pi:l]

v. 껍질이 벗겨지다; (과일·채소 등의) 껍질을 벗기다; n. 껍질
If you peel off something that has been sticking to a surface or if it peels off, it comes away from the surface.

trunk *
[trʌŋk]

n. 나무의 몸통; 트렁크 (가방); (코끼리의) 코
The trunk of a tree is the large main stem from which the branches grow.

tendril
[téndril]

n. 덩굴 모양의 것; [식물] 덩굴손
A tendril is something light and thin, for example a piece of hair which hangs loose and is away from the main part.

pluck *
[plʌk]

v. (잡아 당겨) 빼내다; (기타 등의 현을) 뜯다
If you pluck something from somewhere, you take it between your fingers and pull it sharply from where it is.

flammable
[flǽməbl]

a. 가연성의, 불에 잘 타는
Flammable chemicals, gases, cloth, or other things catch fire and burn easily.

powder **
[páudər]

n. 가루, 분말; v. 파우더를 바르다 (powdery a. 가루 같은)
Something that is powdery looks or feels like powder.

twist ^{복습}
[twist]

v. 휘다, 구부리다; (고개·몸 등을) 돌리다; n. 돌리기; (고개·몸 등을) 돌리기
If you twist something, you turn it to make a spiral shape, for example by turning the two ends of it in opposite directions.

pack ^{복습}
[pæk]

v. (짐을) 싸다; (사람·물건으로) 가득 채우다; n. 꾸러미; 무리
When you pack a bag, you put clothes and other things into it, because you are leaving a place or going on holiday.

gather ^{복습}
[gǽðər]

v. (여기저기 있는 것을) 모으다; (사람들이) 모이다
If you gather things, you collect them together so that you can use them.

wad
[wad]

n. (종이·돈 등의) 뭉치; 덩이; v. 뭉치다
A wad of something such as paper or cloth is a tight bundle or ball of it.

afterthought
[ǽftərθɔːt]

n. 나중에 생각한 것
If you do or say something as an afterthought, you do or say it after something else as an addition, perhaps without careful thought.

strike ^{복습}
[straik]

v. (struck−struck/stricken) (세게) 치다, 부딪치다; (생각 등이) 갑자기 떠오르다; n. 공격; 치기, 때리기
If you strike someone or something, you deliberately hit them.

stream ^{복습}
[striːm]

n. (액체·기체의) 줄기; 개울, 시내; v. (액체·기체가) 줄줄 흐르다; 줄을 지어 이어지다
A stream of smoke, air, or liquid is a narrow moving mass of it.

hair ***
[hɛər]

n. (식물의 나뭇잎·줄기에 난) 털 모양의 것; 머리(털); 털
Hairs are short, very fine threads that grow on some insects and plants.

thread **
[θred]

n. (가느다란) 줄기; 실; v. (실 등을) 꿰다
Thread or a thread is a long very thin piece of a material such as cotton, nylon, or silk, especially one that is used in sewing.

glow[*]
[glou]

v. 빛나다, 타다; (얼굴이) 상기되다; n. (은은한) 불빛; 홍조
If something glows, it produces a dull, steady light.

material[**]
[mətíəriəl]

n. 재료; 직물, 천; 소재; a. 물질적인; 중요한
Materials are the things that you need for a particular activity.

incredible[복습]
[inkrédəbl]

a. 믿을 수 없는, 믿기 힘든 (incredibly ad. 믿을 수 없을 정도로, 엄청나게)
If you describe something or someone as incredible, you like them
very much or are impressed by them, because they are extremely or
unusually good.

nest[*]
[nest]

n. 둥지; 보금자리; v. 둥지를 틀다
A nest is a home that a group of insects or other creatures make in
order to live in and give birth to their young in.

nail[복습]
[neil]

n. 손톱; 못; v. ~을 완벽하게 하다; 못으로 박다 (fingernail n. 손톱)
Your fingernails are the thin hard areas at the end of each of your
fingers.

edge[복습]
[edʒ]

n. 끝, 가장자리; 우위; v. 조금씩 움직이다; 테두리를 두르다
The edge of something is the place or line where it stops, or the part
of it that is furthest from the middle.

sliver
[slívər]

n. (깨지거나 잘라 낸) 조각
A sliver of something is a small thin piece or amount of it.

painstaking
[péinsteikiŋ]

a. 공들인
A painstaking search, examination, or investigation is done extremely
carefully and thoroughly.

grapefruit[*]
[gréipfru:t]

n. 자몽
A grapefruit is a large, round, yellow fruit, similar to an orange, that
has a sharp, slightly bitter taste.

thumb[복습]
[θʌm]

n. 엄지손가락; v. 엄지손가락으로 건드리다
Your thumb is the short thick part on the side of your hand next to
your four fingers.

depress[복습]
[diprés]

v. (기계의 어느 부분을) 누르다; 우울하게 하다 (depression n. 오목한 곳)
A depression in a surface is an area which is lower than the parts
surrounding it.

fuel[복습]
[fjú:əl]

n. 연료; v. (감정 등을) 부채질하다; 연료를 공급하다
Fuel is a substance such as coal, oil, or petrol that is burned to
provide heat or power.

smolder
[smóuldər]

v. (서서히) 타다; (불만 등이) 들끓다; n. 연기
If something smolders, it burns slowly, producing smoke but not
flames.

go out

idiom (불·전깃불이) 꺼지다; 외출하다
If the fire or the light goes out, it stops burning or shining.

dent
[dent]

n. 움푹 들어간 곳; v. 찌그러뜨리다; (자신감·명성 등을) 훼손하다
A dent is a hollow in the surface of something which has been caused
by hitting or pressing it.

chapter nine

cave ^{복습}
[keiv]

n. 동굴
A cave is a large hole in the side of a cliff or hill, or one that is under the ground.

dwell *
[dwel]

v. ~에 살다 (dweller n. 거주자)
A city dweller or slum dweller, for example, is a person who lives in the kind of place or house indicated.

pour ^{복습}
[pɔːr]

v. 마구 쏟아지다; 붓다, 따르다; 쏟아져 들어오다
When a liquid or other substance pours somewhere, for example through a hole, it flows quickly and in large quantities.

waterfall *
[wɔ́ːtərfɔ̀ːl]

n. 폭포
A waterfall is a place where water flows over the edge of a steep, high cliff in hills or mountains, and falls into a pool below.

brief *
[briːf]

a. (시간이) 짧은; 간단한; v. ~에게 보고하다 (briefly ad. 잠시)
Something that is brief lasts for only a short time.

starve ^{복습}
[staːrv]

v. 굶주리다, 굶어죽다 (starved a. 부족한)
If a person or thing is starved of something that they need, they are suffering because they are not getting enough of it.

quantity **
[kwántəti]

n. 양, 분량
You can use quantity to refer to the amount of something that there is, especially when you want to contrast it with its quality.

book ***
[buk]

n. (책처럼 엮은) 묶음; 책; (회계) 장부; v. 예약하다
A book of something such as stamps, matches, or tickets is a small number of them fastened together between thin cardboard covers.

oxygen **
[áksidʒen]

n. [화학] 산소
Oxygen is a colorless gas that exists in large quantities in the air. All plants and animals need oxygen in order to live.

fan *
[fæn]

v. (바람을 일으켜 불길을) 거세게 하다; 부채질을 하다; n. 선풍기
If you fan a fire, you wave something flat next to it in order to make it burn more strongly.

tense **
[tens]

v. 긴장하다; a. 긴장한, 신경이 날카로운
If your muscles tense, if you tense, or if you tense your muscles, your muscles become tight and stiff, often because you are anxious or frightened.

aim ^{복습}
[eim]

v. 겨누다; 목표하다; n. 겨냥, 조준; 목적
If you aim a weapon or object at something or someone, you point it toward them before firing or throwing it.

spot **
[spat]

n. (특정한) 곳; (작은) 점; v. 발견하다, 찾다, 알아채다
You can refer to a particular place as a spot.

mass ^{복습}
[mæs]

n. (많은 사람·사물의) 무리; (pl.) (수·양이) 많은; a. 대량의, 대규모의
A mass of things is a large number of them grouped together.

worm **
[wəːrm]

n. 벌레; v. 꿈틀거리며 나아가다
A worm is a small animal with a long thin body, no bones and no legs.

crawl [복습]
[krɔ:l]

v. 기어가다; 우글거리다; n. 기어가기
When an insect crawls somewhere, it moves there quite slowly.

coal *
[koul]

n. 석탄
Coal is a hard black substance that is extracted from the ground and burned as fuel.

run out of [복습]

idiom ~을 다 써버리다; ~이 없어지다
If you run out of something like money or time, you use up all of them.

inhale [복습]
[inhéil]

v. 숨을 들이마시다, 들이쉬다
When you inhale, you breathe in.

burst [복습]
[bə:rst]

v. (burst–burst) 갑자기 ~하다; 불쑥 움직이다; 터지다;
n. (갑자기) ~을 함; 파열, 폭발
To burst into flames means to suddenly start burning with large flames.

flame [복습]
[fleim]

n. 불길, 불꽃; 격정; v. 활활 타오르다; 시뻘게지다
A flame is a hot bright stream of burning gas that comes from something that is burning.

yell [복습]
[jel]

v. 고함치다, 소리 지르다; n. 고함, 외침
If you yell, you shout loudly, usually because you are excited, angry, or in pain.

consume [복습]
[kənsú:m]

v. 소모하다; (강렬한 감정이) 사로잡다; 먹다
To consume an amount of fuel, energy, or time means to use it up.

gasoline **
[gǽsəlì:n]

n. 휘발유, 가솔린
Gasoline is a liquid which is used as a fuel for motor vehicles.

feed **
[fi:d]

v. 공급하다; 먹이를 주다; 먹여 살리다; n. (동물의) 먹이
To feed something to a place, means to supply it to that place in a steady flow.

gratify *
[grǽtəfài]

v. 기쁘게 하다, 만족시키다 (gratified a. 만족한, 기뻐하는)
If you are gratified by something, it gives you pleasure or satisfaction.

limb [복습]
[lim]

n. (큰) 나뭇가지; (하나의) 팔, 다리
The limbs of a tree are its branches.

squat *
[skwat]

v. 웅크리다, 쪼그리고 앉다; a. 땅딸막한; 쪼그리고 앉은
If you squat, you lower yourself toward the ground, balancing on your feet with your legs bent.

brace [복습]
[breis]

n. 버팀대; 치아 교정기; v. (스스로) 대비를 하다; (몸에) 단단히 힘을 주다
A brace is a piece of wood or metal used for supporting an object so that it does not fall down.

curve **
[kə:rv]

n. 커브, 곡선; v. 곡선으로 나아가다, 곡선을 이루다
A curve is a smooth, gradually bending line, for example part of the edge of a circle.

flue
[flu:]

n. (굴뚝의) 연통, 연관
A flue is a pipe or long tube that acts as a chimney, taking smoke away from a device such as a heater, fire, or cooker.

crack ^{복습}
[kræk]

n. (좁은)·틈; 날카로운 소리; 금; v. 갈라지다; 깨지다. 부서지다
A crack is a very narrow gap between two things, or between two parts of a thing.

curl **
[kə:rl]

v. 돌돌 감기다; (몸을) 웅크리다; 곱슬곱슬하다; n. 곱슬곱슬한 머리카락
If something curls somewhere, or if you curl it there, it moves there in a spiral or curve.

1분에 몇 단어를 읽는지 리딩 속도를 측정해보세요.

$$\frac{2{,}018 \text{ words}}{\text{reading time } (\quad) \text{ sec}} \times 60 = (\quad) \text{ WPM}$$

Build Your Vocabulary

precious*
[préʃəs]

a. 소중한; 귀중한, 값비싼; ad. 정말 거의 없는
If something is precious to you, you regard it as important and do not want to lose it.

brighten*
[braitn]

v. 밝아지다, 반짝이다; (얼굴 등이) 환해지다
When a light brightens a place or when a place brightens, it becomes brighter or lighter.

interior**
[intíəriər]

n. 내부; a. 내부의
The interior of something is the inside part of it.

crackle
[krækl]

n. 탁탁 하는 소리; v. 탁탁 소리를 내다
A crackle is a short, dry, sharp sound.

chop*
[ʧap]

v. (장작 같은 것을) 패다; 내려치다; n. 내리치기, 찍기
(chop off idiom ~을 (~에서) 잘라 내다)
If you chop something off, you remove it by cutting it with a sharp heavy tool.

feed복습
[fiːd]

v. (fed-fed) 공급하다; 먹이를 주다; 먹여 살리다; n. (동물의) 먹이
To feed something to a place, means to supply it to that place in a steady flow.

go out복습
[gou]

idiom (불 · 전깃불이) 꺼지다; 외출하다
If the fire or the light goes out, it stops burning or shining.

stock*
[stak]

n. 비축물, 저장품; 재고; (총의) 개머리판; v. 채우다, 갖추다
If you have a stock of things, you have a supply of them stored in a place ready to be used.

thirst복습
[θəːrst]

n. 갈증; 물의 부족; 갈망 (thirsty a. 목이 마른, 갈증이 나는)
If you are thirsty, you feel a need to drink something.

stack*
[stæk]

v. (깔끔하게 정돈하여) 쌓다; n. 무더기, 더미
If you stack a number of things, you arrange them in neat piles.

bank복습
[bæŋk]

v. 땔감을 쌓아 올리다; (비행기 · 차를) 좌우로 기울이다; n. 둑; 은행
To bank a fire means to cover a fire with wood or coal to keep it going for a long time.

search복습
[səːrʧ]

v. 찾아보다, 수색하다; n. 찾기, 수색
If you search for something or someone, you look carefully for them.

fuel^{복습}
[fjúːəl]

n. 연료; v. (감정 등을) 부채질하다; 연료를 공급하다
Fuel is a substance such as coal, oil, or petrol that is burned to provide heat or power.

supply^{복습}
[səplái]

n. 공급; (pl.) 용품, 비품; 비축(량); v. 공급하다, 제공하다
A supply of something is an amount of it which someone has or which is available for them to use.

camp^{복습}
[kæmp]

n. 야영지; 수용소; 진영; v. 야영하다 (campsite n. 야영지)
A campsite is a place where people who are on holiday can stay in tents.

site[*]
[sait]

n. 위치, 장소; (사건 등의) 현장; 대지, 용지
A site is a piece of ground that is used for a particular purpose or where a particular thing happens.

windstorm
[wíndstɔːrm]

n. (비ㆍ눈은 거의 동반하지 않는) 폭풍
A windstorm is a storm with very strong wind but little or no rain or snow.

land^{복습}
[lænd]

v. (땅ㆍ표면에) 내려앉다, 착륙하다; 놓다, 두다; n. 육지, 땅; 지역
When someone or something lands, they come down to the ground after moving through the air or falling.

pine^{복습}
[pain]

n. 소나무
A pine tree or a pine is a tall tree which has very thin, sharp leaves and a fresh smell. Pine trees have leaves all year round.

weathered
[wéðərd]

a. 비바람을 맞은
If something is weathered, it is changed in color or form over a period of time because of the effects of sun, wind, rain, or other conditions in the air.

overhang^{복습}
[òuvərhǽŋ]

n. 돌출부; v. 돌출하다, 쑥 나오다
An overhang is the part of something that sticks out over and above something else.

enormous[*]
[inɔ́ːrməs]

a. 막대한, 거대한
Something that is enormous is extremely large in size or amount.

notice^{복습}
[nóutis]

v. 알아채다, 인지하다; 주의하다; n. 신경 씀, 주목, 알아챔
If you notice something or someone, you become aware of them.

advantage^{**}
[ædvǽntidʒ]

n. 이점; 장점; v. (~에게) 유리하게 하다
An advantage is a way in which one thing is better than another.

shade^{복습}
[ʃeid]

n. 그늘; 약간, 기미; v. 그늘지게 하다
Shade is an area of darkness under or next to an object such as a tree, where sunlight does not reach.

swarm^{복습}
[swɔːrm]

v. 무리를 지어 다니다; 많이 모여들다; n. (곤충의) 떼, 무리; 군중
When bees or other insects swarm, they move or fly in a large group.

eddy
[édi]

v. 회오리를 일으키다, 소용돌이치다; n. (공기ㆍ먼지ㆍ물의) 회오리
If a current of water or air eddies, it moves against the main current in a circular pattern.

102

swirl
[swəːrl]

v. 빙빙 돌다, 소용돌이치다; n. 소용돌이
If you swirl something liquid or flowing, or if it swirls, it moves round and round quickly.

insect^{복습}
[ínsekt]

n. 곤충
An insect is a small animal that has six legs. Most insects have wings. Ants, flies, butterflies, and beetles are all insects.

discovery**
[diskÁvəri]

n. 발견
If someone makes a discovery, they become aware of something that they did not know about before.

drive ^{복습}
[draiv]

v. (drove—driven) 만들다; 운전하다; 박아 넣다; 몰아가다; n. 드라이브; 충동, 욕구
To drive someone into a particular state or situation means to force them into that state or situation.

be rid of

idiom (귀찮은 것에서) 벗어나다, 해방되다
If you are rid of someone or something that you did not want or that caused problems for you, they are no longer with you or causing problems for you.

spirit**
[spírit]

n. (pl.) 기분, 마음; 영혼; 태도
Your spirits are your feelings at a particular time, especially feelings of happiness or unhappiness.

curl^{복습}
[kəːrl]

v. 돌돌 감기다; (몸을) 웅크리다; 곱슬곱슬하다; n. 곱슬곱슬한 머리카락
If something curls somewhere, or if you curl it there, it moves there in a spiral or curve.

realize^{복습}
[ríːəlàiz]

v. 깨닫다, 알아차리다; 실현하다, 달성하다
If you realize that something is true, you become aware of that fact or understand it.

dusk*
[dʌsk]

n. 땅거미, 황혼, 어스름
Dusk is the time just before night when the daylight has almost gone but when it is not completely dark.

loosen^{복습}
[luːsn]

v. 느슨하게 하다; 풀다; (통제 · 구속 등을) 완화하다
If you loosen something that is stretched across something else, you make it less stretched or tight.

ache^{복습}
[eik]

v. (계속) 아프다; n. (계속적인) 아픔
If you ache or a part of your body aches, you feel a steady, fairly strong pain.

rub^{복습}
[rʌb]

v. (손 · 손수건 등을 대고) 문지르다; (두 손 등을) 맞비비다; n. 문지르기, 비비기
If you rub a part of your body, you move your hand or fingers backward and forward over it while pressing firmly.

crash^{복습}
[kræʃ]

n. (자동차 · 항공기) 사고; 요란한 소리; v. 충돌하다; 부딪치다; 꽝음을 내다
A crash is an accident in which a moving vehicle hits something and is damaged or destroyed.

get a handle on

idiom ～을 이해하다
If you get a handle on a subject or problem, you have a way of approaching it that helps you to understand it or deal with it.

stare^{복습}
[stɛər]

v. 빤히 쳐다보다, 응시하다; n. 빤히 쳐다보기, 응시
If you stare at someone or something, you look at them for a long time.

stir[*]
[stə:r]

v. 약간 움직이다; 자극하다; 젓다; n. 동요, 충격; 젓기
If you stir, you move slightly, for example because you are uncomfortable or beginning to wake up.

bed^{***}
[bed]

n. ~을 깐 바닥; 침대; v. (단단히) 놓다
A bed of something is a flat base or foundation on which something rests or is supported.

coal^{복습}
[koul]

n. 석탄
Coal is a hard black substance that is extracted from the ground and burned as fuel.

glow^{복습}
[glou]

v. 빛나다, 타다; (얼굴이) 상기되다; n. (은은한) 불빛; 홍조
If something glows, it produces a dull, steady light.

blaze[*]
[bleiz]

n. 불길; 휘황찬란한 빛; v. 눈부시게 빛나다; 활활 타다
A blaze is a large fire which is difficult to control and which destroys a lot of things.

interval^{복습}
[íntərvəl]

n. (두 사건 사이의) 간격; 잠깐
An interval between two events or dates is the period of time between them.

regulate[*]
[régjulèit]

v. 규제하다; 조절하다
To regulate an activity or process means to control it, especially by means of rules.

slither^{복습}
[slíðər]

v. (매끄럽게) 스르르 나아가다; 미끄러지듯 나아가다
If an animal such as a snake slithers, it moves along in a curving way.

drag^{복습}
[dræg]

v. 끌다, 끌고 가다; 힘들게 움직이다; n. 끌기, 당기기; 장애물
If you drag something, you pull it along the ground, often with difficulty.

slosh^{복습}
[slaʃ]

v. 철벅거리다; (물 · 진창 속을) 철벅거리며 걷다
If a liquid sloshes around or if you slosh it around, it moves around in different directions.

shoreline
[[ʃɔ́:rlàin]

n. 해안선
A shoreline is the edge of a sea, lake, or wide river.

doze^{복습}
[douz]

v. 깜빡 잠이 들다, 졸다; n. 잠깐 잠, 낮잠
When you doze, you sleep lightly or for a short period, especially during the daytime.

dawn^{복습}
[dɔ:n]

n. 새벽, 여명; v. 분명해지다, 이해되기 시작하다; 밝다
Dawn is the time of day when light first appears in the sky, just before the sun rises.

knot^{복습}
[nat]

n. (긴장 · 화 등으로) 뻣뻣한 느낌; 매듭; v. 매듭을 묶다
If you feel a knot in your stomach, you get an uncomfortable tight feeling in your stomach, usually because you are afraid or excited.

104

hunger 복습
[hʌ́ŋɡər]

n. 배고픔; 굶주림; 갈망
Hunger is the feeling of weakness or discomfort that you get when you need something to eat.

stomach 복습
[stʌ́mək]

n. 위(胃), 복부, 배
Your stomach is the organ inside your body where food is digested before it moves into the intestines.

track **
[træk]

n. 자국; 경주로, 트랙; 길; v. 추적하다; 뒤쫓다
Tracks are marks left in the ground by the feet of animals or people.

claw 복습
[klɔː]

n. (동물·새의) 발톱; v. 헤치며 나아가다; (손톱·발톱으로) 할퀴다
The claws of a bird or animal are the thin, hard, curved nails at the end of its feet.

squat 복습
[skwat]

v. 웅크리다, 쪼그리고 앉다; a. 땅딸막한; 쪼그리고 앉은
If you squat, you lower yourself toward the ground, balancing on your feet with your legs bent.

make sense 복습

idiom 이해가 되다; 타당하다; 이해하기 쉽다
If something makes sense, you can understand it.

apparent 복습
[əpǽrənt]

a. 분명한; ~인 것처럼 보이는 (apparently ad. 보아하니)
You use apparently to refer to something that seems to be true, although you are not sure whether it is or not.

waste 복습
[weist]

v. 낭비하다; 헛되이 쓰다; n. 낭비, 허비; (pl.) 쓰레기, 폐기물
If you waste something such as time, money, or energy, you use too much of it doing something that is not important or necessary, or is unlikely to succeed.

make it 복습

idiom 해내다; 가다; (힘든 경험 등을) 버텨 내다
If you make it, you succeed in a particular activity.

brush 복습
[brʌʃ]

v. (솔이나 손으로) 털다; 솔질을 하다; ~을 스치다; n. 덤불, 잡목 숲; 붓; 솔
If you brush something somewhere, you remove it with quick light movements of your hands.

damp *
[dæmp]

a. 축축한; n. 축축한 곳
Something that is damp is slightly wet.

scrape 복습
[skreip]

v. (무엇을) 긁어내다; (상처가 나도록) 긁다; n. 긁기; 긁힌 상처
If you scrape something from a surface, you remove it, especially by pulling a sharp object over the surface.

dig 복습
[dig]

v. (구멍 등을) 파다; (무엇을 찾기 위해) 뒤지다; 찌르다; n. 쿡 찌르기
If people or animals dig, they make a hole in the ground or in a pile of earth, stones, or rubbish.

chamber *
[ʧéimbər]

n. (지하의) 공간; (기계의) ~실(室); 회의실
A chamber is a room designed and equipped for a particular purpose.

turtle *
[tə́ːrtl]

n. [동물] (바다) 거북
A turtle is a large reptile which has a thick shell covering its body and which lives in the sea most of the time.

snap ^{복습}
[snæp]

v. (동물이) 물려고 하다; 급히 움직이다; 딱 소리 내다; 딱 부러지다; n. 탁 하는 소리
If an animal such as a dog snaps at you, it opens and shuts its jaws quickly near you, as if it were going to bite you.

tighten ^{복습}
[taitn]

v. (더 단단히) 조이다; (더) 팽팽해지다; 더 엄격하게 하다
If a part of your body tightens, the muscles in it become tense and stiff, for example because you are angry or afraid.

belong***
[bilɔ́ːŋ]

v. ~에 속하다; 제자리에 있다; 소속감을 느끼다
You say that something belongs to a particular person when you are guessing, discovering, or explaining that it was produced by or is part of that person.

control ^{복습}
[kəntróul]

v. 조정하다; 지배하다; n. (기계 · 차량의) 제어 장치; 통제, 제어
If you control yourself, or if you control your feelings, voice, or expression, you make yourself behave calmly even though you are feeling angry, excited, or upset.

dormant
[dɔ́ːrmənt]

a. 휴면기의, 활동을 중단한
Something that is dormant is not active, growing, or being used at the present time but is capable of becoming active later on.

crave
[kreiv]

v. 열망하다, 갈망하다; 간절히 원하다
If you crave something, you want to have it very much.

intense ^{복습}
[inténs]

a. 극심한, 강렬한; 치열한; 진지한 (intensity n. 강렬함)
Intense is used to describe something that is very great or extreme in strength or degree.

quicken ^{복습}
[kwíkən]

v. 더 빠르게 하다; 더 활발해지다
If something quickens or if you quicken it, it becomes faster or moves at a greater speed.

nest ^{복습}
[nest]

n. 둥지; 보금자리; v. 둥지를 틀다
A nest is a home that a group of insects or other creatures make in order to live in and give birth to their young in.

leathery
[léðəri]

a. 가죽 같은, 딱딱하고 질긴
If the texture of something, for example someone's skin, is leathery, it is tough and hard, like leather.

shell**
[ʃel]

n. 껍데기; 포탄; 뼈대, 외부 구조; v. 껍질을 까다
The shell of a nut or egg is the hard covering which surrounds it.

squeeze*
[skwiːz]

v. (꼭) 쥐다; (좁은 곳에) 비집고 들어가다; n. (손으로 꼭) 쥐기
If you squeeze something, you press it firmly, usually with your hands.

heap*
[hiːp]

v. (아무렇게나) 쌓다; n. (쌓아 놓은) 더미; 많음
If you heap things somewhere, you arrange them in a large pile.

pyramid*
[pírəmìd]

n. 피라미드형으로 쌓은 것; (고대 이집트의) 피라미드
A pyramid is a shape, object, or pile of things with a flat base and sloping triangular sides that meet at a point.

container*
[kəntéinər]

n. 용기, 그릇; (화물 수송용) 컨테이너
A container is something such as a box or bottle that is used to hold or store things in.

106

raw ^{복습}
[rɔː]

a. 익히지 않은; 가공되지 않은; 다듬어지지 않은
Raw food is food that is eaten uncooked, that has not yet been cooked, or that has not been cooked enough.

runny
[rʌ́ni]

a. 물기가 많은, 묽은; 콧물이 흐르는
Something that is runny is more liquid than usual or than was intended.

gulp ^{복습}
[gʌlp]

n. 꿀꺽 마시기; v. 꿀꺽꿀꺽 삼키다; (숨을) 깊이 들이마시다
A gulp of air, food, or drink, is a large amount of it that you swallow at once.

backbone
[bǽkbòun]

n. 척추, 등뼈
Your backbone is the column of small linked bones down the middle of your back.

fussy
[fʌ́si]

a. 까다로운, 야단스런; 신경질적인
Someone who is fussy is very concerned with unimportant details and is difficult to please.

native^{**}
[néitiv]

n. 원주민, 토착민; a. 출생의, 출생지의; 토착의, 본국의
A native of a particular country or region is someone who was born in that country or region.

grasshopper
[grǽshàpər]

n. 메뚜기
A grasshopper is an insect with long back legs that jumps high into the air and makes a high, vibrating sound.

sharpen ^{복습}
[ʃáːrpən]

v. (날카롭게) 갈다; (기량 등을) 갈고 닦다; 더 강렬해지다
If you sharpen an object, you make its edge very thin or you make its end pointed.

poke ^{복습}
[pouk]

v. (손가락 등으로) 쿡 찌르다; 쑥 내밀다; n. (손가락 등으로) 찌르기
If you poke someone or something, you quickly push them with your finger or with a sharp object.

widen ^{복습}
[waidn]

v. 넓어지다; (정도·범위 등이) 커지다
If you widen something or if it widens, it becomes greater in measurement from one side or edge to the other.

yolk
[jouk]

n. (달걀 등의) 노른자
The yolk of an egg is the yellow part in the middle.

suck ^{복습}
[sʌk]

v. 빨아 먹다; (특정한 방향으로) 빨아들이다; n. 빨기, 빨아 먹기
If you suck something, you hold it in your mouth and pull at it with the muscles in your cheeks and tongue, for example in order to get liquid out of it.

swallow ^{복습}
[swálou]

v. (음식 등을) 삼키다; 집어삼키다; n. (음식 등을) 삼키기; [동물] 제비
If you swallow something, you cause it to go from your mouth down into your stomach.

grease[*]
[griːs]

n. 기름, 지방; v. 기름을 바르다 (greasy a. 기름투성이의, 기름이 많이 묻은)
Something that is greasy has grease on it or in it.

throw up ^{복습}

idiom ~을 토하다; ~을 두드러지게 하다
If you throw up, you bring food you have eaten back out of your mouth.

convulse
[kənvʌ́ls]

v. 경련하다, 몸부림치게 하다
If someone convulses or if they are convulsed by or with something, their body moves suddenly in an uncontrolled way.

hold back

idiom ~을 저지하다; (감정을) 누르다
If you hold back, you decide not to do something, often because of fear or because you do not want to make a bad situation worse.

roar^{복습}
[rɔːr]

v. 웅웅거리다; 고함치다; 굉음을 내며 질주하다; n. 함성; 울부짖는 듯한 소리
(roaringly ad. 으르렁대며)
If something roars, it makes a very loud noise.

rip^{복습}
[rip]

v. (재빨리·거칠게) 떼어 내다, 뜯어 내다; (갑자기) 찢다; n. (길게) 찢어진 곳
When something rips or when you rip it, you tear it forcefully with your hands or with a tool such as a knife.

lick[*]
[lik]

v. 핥다; 핥아먹다; n. 한 번 핥기, 핥아먹기
When people or animals lick something, they move their tongue across its surface.

chew^{복습}
[ʧuː]

v. (음식을) 씹다, 물어뜯다, 깨물다; 심사숙고하다; n. 씹기, 깨물기
When you chew food, you use your teeth to break it up in your mouth so that it becomes easier to swallow.

literally[*]
[lítərəli]

ad. 정말로, 완전히; 그야말로; 말 그대로
You use literally to emphasize that what you are saying is true, even though it seems exaggerated or surprising.

1. In what way did Brian change?
   A. He gained a little bit of weight.
   B. He built a lot of muscle in his arms and legs.
   C. He became much more observant.
   D. He learned to ignore the sounds around him.

2. Why did he put wood on the bluff over his shelter?
   A. To avoid making the inside of the shelter too crowded with wood
   B. To scare away any animals that came near his shelter
   C. So that he could start a signal fire quickly if needed
   D. So that he would have enough wood to last several days

3. What made him think of catching fish for food?
   A. He saw a bird snatch a fish out of the water.
   B. He happened to find many fish swimming in the lake.
   C. He came across a small fish jumping in and out of the water.
   D. He remembered a fishing trip he once took with his family.

4. Why couldn't he catch fish with the spear?
   A. The fish were too big for the spear.
   B. The fish swam away too quickly.
   C. The spear was not sharp enough.
   D. The spear was not long enough.

5. Why did he decide to make a bow and arrow?
   A. It would be more practical than the spear.
   B. It would be easier to carry than the spear.
   C. He knew it would be the easiest tool to make.
   D. He would be able to catch multiple fish at a time with it.

6. Why did it take him a while to realize a plane was flying toward the area?
   A. The strong wind made the plane hard to hear.
   B. He assumed the sound of the plane was just the trees moving.
   C. He thought the sound of the plane was just his imagination.
   D. He was too focused on making a bow out of wood.

7. What happened when he could no longer hear the plane?
   A. He figured the plane was not real.
   B. He lost all hope in being rescued.
   C. He was sure the pilot had seen him and would return.
   D. He believed another plane would come searching for him soon.

1분에 몇 단어를 읽는지 리딩 속도를 측정해보세요.

$$\frac{1,538 \text{ words}}{\text{reading time ( ) sec}} \times 60 = (\qquad) \text{ WPM}$$

Build Your Vocabulary

transfer[*]
[trænsfɔ́ːr]

v. 이동하다, (장소를) 옮기다; (병을) 옮기다; n. 이동
If you transfer something or someone from one place to another, or they transfer from one place to another, they go from the first place to the second.

shelter[복습]
[ʃéltər]

n. 대피처, 피신처; 피신; v. 피하다; 막아 주다, 보호하다
A shelter is a small building or covered place which is made to protect people from bad weather or danger.

bury[**]
[béri]

v. (땅에) 묻다; 뒤덮다; 감추다 (rebury v. 다시 묻다)
To bury something means to put it into a hole in the ground and cover it up with earth.

will[***]
[wil]

n. 의지; (바라는) 뜻; v. 의지력을 발휘하다; 유언으로 남기다
Will is the determination to do something.

sight[복습]
[sait]

n. 시야; 광경, 모습; 보기, 봄; v. 갑자기 보다
If something is out of sight, you cannot see it.

soak[*]
[souk]

v. 흠뻑 적시다; (지식 등을) 흡수하다; n. (액체 속에) 담그기
If a liquid soaks through something, it passes through it.

smooth[복습]
[smuːð]

v. 매끈하게 하다; a. 매끈한; 부드러운; (소리가) 감미로운
If you smooth something, you move your hands over its surface to make it smooth and flat.

mental[복습]
[mentl]

a. 마음의, 정신의; 정신병의
Mental means relating to the process of thinking.

depress[복습]
[diprés]

v. 우울하게 하다; (기계의 어느 부분을) 누르다 (depression n. 우울함)
If someone or something depresses you, they make you feel sad and disappointed.

square away

idiom ~을 정리하다
If you square away something, you do the things necessary to complete it.

on hand

idiom 구할 수 있는
If someone or something is on hand, they are near and able to be used if they are needed.

stagger[복습]
[stǽgər]

v. 큰 충격을 주다; 비틀거리다, 휘청거리다 (staggering a. 충격적인, 믿기 어려운)
Something that is staggering is very surprising.

chop ^{복습}
[ʧap]

v. (장작 같은 것을) 패다; 내려치다; n. 내려치기, 찍기
If you chop something, you cut it into pieces with strong downward movements of a knife or an ax.

neat^{**}
[niːt]

a. 정돈된, 단정한; 깔끔한; 뛰어난 (neatly ad. 깔끔하게)
A neat place, thing, or person is tidy and smart, and has everything in the correct place.

reflect ^{복습}
[riflékt]

v. (상을) 비추다; 반사하다; 깊이 생각하다 (reflection n. (거울 등에 비친) 상)
A reflection is an image that you can see in a mirror or in glass or water.

swell ^{복습}
[swel]

v. 부풀다; (마음이) 벅차다; (소리가) 더 커지다; n. 증가, 팽창
(swelling n. (몸의) 부어오른 곳)
A swelling is a raised, curved shape on the surface of your body which appears as a result of an injury or an illness.

assume ^{복습}
[əsúːm]

v. (사실일 것으로) 추정하다; (특질·양상을) 띠다
If you assume that something is true, you imagine that it is true, sometimes wrongly.

take care of ^{복습}

idiom ~을 처리하다; ~을 돌보다
To take care of someone or something means to do what is necessary to deal with a person or situation.

rough ^{복습}
[rʌf]

a. 개략적인; 매끈하지 않은, 거친; (행동이) 거친; 힘든, 골치 아픈
If you give someone a rough idea, description, or drawing of something, you indicate only the most important features, without much detail.

quill ^{복습}
[kwil]

n. (고슴도치의) 가시; (새 날개·꼬리의 커다란) 깃
The quills of a porcupine are the long sharp points on its body.

nail ^{복습}
[neil]

v. (못 같은 것으로) 고정시키다; n. 손톱; 발톱; 못
If you nail something somewhere, you fix it there using a device with pointed end.

shore ^{복습}
[ʃɔːr]

n. 기슭, 해안, 호숫가
The shores or the shore of a sea, lake, or wide river is the land along the edge of it.

take stock

idiom 꼼꼼히 살펴보다; 재고 조사를 하다
If you take stock, you pause to think about all the aspects of a situation or event before deciding what to do next.

weight ^{복습}
[weit]

n. 무게, 체중; 무거운 것
The weight of a person or thing is how heavy they are, measured in units such as kilograms, pounds, or tons.

cave in

idiom 무너지다, 함몰되다
If a ceiling, roof, or other structure caves in, it breaks and falls into the space below.

burn ^{복습}
[bəːrn]

v. 데다; (햇볕 등에) 타다; 불에 타다; 화끈거리다; (마음 등에) 새겨지다; n. 화상
If you burn part of your body, burn yourself, or are burnt, you are injured by fire or by something very hot.

tan[*]
[tæn]

v. (피부가 갈색으로) 햇볕에 타다, 그을리다; n. 선탠
If a part of your body tans or if you tan it, your skin becomes darker than usual because you spend a lot of time in the sun.

swing[복습]
[swiŋ]

v. 휙 움직이다; 휘두르다; 방향을 바꾸다; (전후 · 좌우로) 흔들다; n. 흔들기; 휘두르기
If someone swings around, they turn around quickly, usually because they are surprised.

twig[복습]
[twig]

n. (나무의) 잔가지
A twig is a very small thin branch that grows out from a main branch of a tree or bush.

wave[복습]
[weiv]

n. (열 · 소리 · 빛 등의) −파; 물결; (감정 · 움직임의) 파도; (팔 · 손 · 몸을) 흔들기; v. (손 · 팔을) 흔들다; 손짓하다
Waves are the form in which things such as sound, light, and radio signals travel.

bush[복습]
[buʃ]

n. 관목, 덤불; 우거진 것
A bush is a large plant which is smaller than a tree and has a lot of branches.

ripple[복습]
[ripl]

n. 잔물결, 파문 (모양의 것); v. 잔물결을 이루다; (감정 등이) 파문처럼 번지다
Ripples are little waves on the surface of water caused by the wind or by something moving in or on the water.

feather[*]
[féðər]

n. (새의) 털, 깃털; v. 깃털로 덮다
A bird's feathers are the soft covering on its body. Each feather consists of a lot of smooth hairs on each side of a thin stiff center.

blow[복습]
[blou]

v. (바람 · 입김에) 날리다; (입으로) 불다; 폭파하다; n. 세게 때림, 강타; 충격
If the wind blows something somewhere or if it blows there, the wind moves it there.

come together

idiom (하나로) 합치다
If two or more people or things come together, they form one group or one piece.

deal[복습]
[di:l]

v. 처리하다; n. 많음; 거래, 합의; 대우, 처리
If you deal with something, you accept and control a difficult emotional situation so that you can start to live a normal life again despite it.

signal[복습]
[sígnəl]

n. 신호; 징조; v. 암시하다; (동작 · 소리로) 신호를 보내다
A signal is a gesture, sound, or action which is intended to give a particular message to the person who sees or hears it.

ridge[복습]
[ridʒ]

n. 산등성이, 산마루; v. (표면을) 이랑처럼 만들다
A ridge is a long, narrow piece of raised land.

comprise[*]
[kəmpráiz]

v. 구성되다, 이뤄지다
If you say that something comprises or is comprised of a number of things or people, you mean it has them as its parts or members.

bluff
[blʌf]

n. (바다나 강가의) 절벽; 허세, 엄포; v. 허세를 부리다, 엄포를 놓다
A bluff is a cliff or very steep bank by the sea or river.

114

pleased[*]
[pliːzd]

a. 기쁜, 기뻐하는, 만족해하는
If you are pleased, you are happy about something or satisfied with something.

moan[복습]
[moun]

v. 신음하다; 투덜거리다; n. 신음; 투덜거림
If you moan, you make a low sound, usually because you are unhappy or in pain.

inward[*]
[ínwərd]

a. 마음속의, 내심의; 안쪽으로 향한; ad. 안쪽으로 (inwardly ad. 마음속으로)
Your inward thoughts or feelings are the ones that you do not express or show to other people.

bonfire
[bánfàiər]

n. 모닥불
A bonfire is a fire that is made outdoors, usually to burn rubbish. Bonfires are also sometimes lit as part of a celebration.

initial[복습]
[iníʃəl]

a. 처음의, 초기의; n. 이름의 첫 글자 (initially ad. 처음에)
Initially means soon after the beginning of a process or situation, rather than in the middle or at the end of it.

supply[복습]
[səplái]

n. 공급; (pl.) 용품, 비품; 비축(량); v. 공급하다, 제공하다
A supply of something is an amount of it which someone has or which is available for them to use.

set off[복습]

idiom (폭탄 등을) 터뜨리다; 출발하다
If you set off something, you make it explode.

overlook[복습]
[ouvərlúk]

v. 바라보다, 내려다보다; 눈감아주다; n. 전망이 좋은 곳, 높은 곳
If a building or window overlooks a place, you can see the place clearly from the building or window.

terror[복습]
[térər]

n. 두려움, 공포; 공포의 대상
Terror is very great fear.

be caught up in

idiom (사건ㆍ흥분 등에) 휘말려 들다
If you are caught up in something, you are completely absorbed in an activity or your own feelings.

scenery[복습]
[síːnəri]

n. 풍경; 배경, 무대 장치
The scenery in a country area is the land, water, or plants that you can see around you.

constant[복습]
[kánstənt]

a. 끊임없는; 거듭되는; 변함없는
You use constant to describe something that happens all the time or is always there.

hum[복습]
[hʌm]

n. 윙윙거리는 소리; v. 윙윙거리다; 왁자지껄하다; (노래를) 흥얼거리다
A hum is a low continuous noise made by a machine or a lot of people talking.

snaggle
[snægl]

n. 뒤죽박죽 모아 놓은 것; v. 뒤엉키다, 뒤죽박죽이 되다 (snaggly a. 뒤엉킨)
if you describe something as snaggly, it is covered in snaggles and knotty.

bend[복습]
[bend]

v. (bent–bent) 구부리다; (몸ㆍ머리를) 굽히다, 숙이다; n. (도로ㆍ강의) 굽이, 굽은 곳
If you bend something that is flat or straight, you use force to make it curved or to put an angle in it.

gnarl
[naːrl]

v. 비틀다; 마디지게 하다; n. (나무) 마디, 옹이 (gnarled a. 울퉁불퉁하고 비틀린)
A gnarled tree is twisted and strangely shaped because it is old.

crest*
[krest]

n. (조류 머리 위의) 볏, 관모; 꼭대기; v. 꼭대기에 이르다
A bird's crest is a group of upright feathers on the top of its head.

beak^{복습}
[biːk]

n. (새의) 부리
A bird's beak is the hard curved or pointed part of its mouth.

branch^{복습}
[brænʧ]

n. 나뭇가지; 지사, 분점; v. 갈라지다, 나뉘다
The branches of a tree are the parts that grow out from its trunk and have leaves, flowers, or fruit growing on them.

dive^{복습}
[daiv]

v. (물 속으로) 뛰어들다; 급강하하다; 급히 움직이다; n. (물 속으로) 뛰어들기
If you dive into some water, you jump in head-first with your arms held straight above your head.

emerge*
[imə́ːrdʒ]

v. 나오다, 모습을 드러내다; (어려움 등을) 헤쳐 나오다
To emerge means to come out from an enclosed or dark space such as a room or a vehicle, or from a position where you could not be seen.

split second
[split sékənd]

n. 아주 짧은 순간; 눈 깜짝할 사이
A split second is an extremely short period of time.

wiggle^{복습}
[wigl]

v. 꿈틀꿈틀 움직이다; n. 꿈틀꿈틀 움직이기
If you wiggle something or if it wiggles, it moves up and down or from side to side in small quick movements.

juggle
[dʒʌgl]

v. (공·접시 등으로) 곡예를 하다; (일을 동시에) 곡예하듯 하다
If you juggle, you entertain people by throwing things into the air, catching each one and throwing it up again so that there are several of them in the air at the same time.

scramble^{복습}
[skræmbl]

v. 재빨리 움직이다; 허둥지둥 해내다; n. (힘들게) 기어가기; 서로 밀치기
If you scramble to a different place or position, you move there in a hurried, awkward way.

trot^{복습}
[trat]

v. 빨리 걷다; 총총걸음을 걷다; n. 속보, 빠른 걸음
If you trot somewhere, you move fairly fast at a speed between walking and running, taking small quick steps.

surface^{복습}
[sə́ːrfis]

n. 표면, 지면, 수면; 외관; v. 수면으로 올라오다; (갑자기) 나타나다
The surface of something is the flat top part of it or the outside of it.

flash^{복습}
[flæʃ]

v. (잠깐) 비치다; 휙 내보이다; 휙 움직이다; n. 갑자기 떠오름; (잠깐) 반짝임
If a light flashes or if you flash a light, it shines with a sudden bright light, especially as quick, regular flashes of light.

wade
[weid]

v. (물·진흙 속을 힘겹게) 헤치며 걷다
If you wade through something that makes it difficult to walk, usually water or mud, you walk through it.

literally^{복습}
[lítərəli]

ad. 정말로, 완전히; 그야말로; 말 그대로
You use literally to emphasize that what you are saying is true, even though it seems exaggerated or surprising.

pack ^{복습}
[pæk]

v. (사람 · 물건으로) 가득 채우다; (짐을) 싸다; n. 꾸러미; 무리
If people or things pack into a place or if they pack a place, there are so many of them that the place is full.

patch ^{복습}
[pætʃ]

n. 부분; 작은 땅; 조각; v. 덧대다, 때우다
A patch on a surface is a part of it which is different in appearance from the area around it.

mud ^{복습}
[mʌd]

n. 진흙, 진창
Mud is a sticky mixture of earth and water.

shell ^{복습}
[ʃel]

n. 껍데기; 포탄; 뼈대, 외부 구조; v. 껍질을 까다
The shell of a nut or egg is the hard covering which surrounds it.

tiny ^{복습}
[táini]

a. 아주 작은
Something or someone that is tiny is extremely small.

roundish
[ráundiʃ]

a. 둥그스름한, 약간 둥근
Something that is roundish is somewhat round.

tense ^{복습}
[tens]

v. 긴장하다; a. 긴장한, 신경이 날카로운
If your muscles tense, if you tense, or if you tense your muscles, your muscles become tight and stiff, often because you are anxious or frightened.

stab [*]
[stæb]

n. 찌르기; 찌르는 듯한 통증; v. 찌르다
A stab is a thrusting movement with a finger or other pointed object.

grab ^{복습}
[græb]

v. (와락 · 단단히) 붙잡다; 급히 ~하다; n. 와락 잡아채려고 함
If you grab something, you take it or pick it up suddenly and roughly.

explode ^{복습}
[iksplóud]

v. 갑자기 ~하다; 폭발하다; (강한 감정을) 터뜨리다
To explode means to move very quickly.

flick ^{복습}
[flik]

n. 재빨리 움직임; v. 튀기다, 털다; 잽싸게 움직이다
A flick is a sudden quick movement.

curious ^{**}
[kjúəriəs]

a. 궁금한, 호기심이 많은; 별난, 특이한 (curiosity n. 호기심)
If you are curious about something, you are interested in it and want to know more about it.

hook ^{복습}
[huk]

n. (낚시) 바늘; (갈)고리; v. (낚싯바늘로) 낚다; 갈고리로 잠그다
A hook is a bent piece of metal or plastic that is used for catching or holding things, or for hanging things up.

string ^{**}
[striŋ]

n. 줄; (악기의) 현; 일련; v. 묶다, 매달다; (실 등에) 꿰다
String is thin rope made of twisted threads, used for tying things together or tying up parcels.

lure [*]
[luər]

v. 꾀다, 유혹하다; n. 유혹, 매력; 미끼
To lure someone means to trick them into a particular place or to trick them into doing something that they should not do.

shallow ^{복습}
[ʃǽlou]

n. (pl.) (강 · 바다의) 얕은 곳; a. 얕은; 피상적인
The shallows are the shallow part of an area of water.

spear
[spiər]

n. 창; v. (창 등으로) 찌르다; (물고기를) 작살로 잡다
A spear is a weapon consisting of a long pole with a sharp metal point attached to the end.

slim
[slim]

a. (보통 것보다) 얇은; 날씬한, 호리호리한
A slim book, wallet, or other object is thinner than usual.

hatchet^{복습}
[hǽtʃit]

n. 손도끼
A hatchet is a small ax that you can hold in one hand.

reward
[riwɔ́ːrd]

v. 보상하다, 사례하다; n. 보상; 현상금, 보상금
If you do something and are rewarded with a particular benefit, you receive that benefit as a result of doing that thing.

dessert
[dizɔ́ːrt]

n. 디저트, 후식
Dessert is something sweet, such as fruit or a pudding, that you eat at the end of a meal.

fancy
[fǽnsi]

a. 고급의; 복잡한; 장식이 많은; v. 생각하다, 상상하다
If you describe something as fancy, you mean that it is very expensive or of very high quality, and you often dislike it because of this.

118

1분에 몇 단어를 읽는지 리딩 속도를 측정해보세요.

$$\frac{1{,}968 \text{ words}}{\text{reading time ( ) sec}} \times 60 = (\qquad) \text{ WPM}$$

Build Your Vocabulary

spear 복습
[spiər]

n. 창; v. (창 등으로) 찌르다; (물고기를) 작살로 잡다
A spear is a weapon consisting of a long pole with a sharp metal point attached to the end.

lunge
[lʌndʒ]

v. 달려들다, 돌진하다; n. 돌진
If you lunge in a particular direction, you move in that direction suddenly and clumsily.

jab
[dʒæb]

v. (쿡) 찌르다; n. 비난; (쿡) 찌르기; (권투에서) 잽
If you jab one thing into another, you push it there with a quick, sudden movement and with a lot of force.

flail
[fleil]

v. 마구 움직이다; (팔다리를) 마구 흔들다
If your arms or legs flail or if you flail them about, they wave about in an energetic but uncontrolled way.

absolute 복습
[ǽbsəlùːt]

a. 완전한, 완벽한 (absolutely ad. 극도로, 굉장히)
Absolute means total and complete.

peel 복습
[piːl]

v. 껍질이 벗겨지다; (과일 · 채소 등의) 껍질을 벗기다; n. 껍질
If you peel off something that has been sticking to a surface or if it peels off, it comes away from the surface.

bark 복습
[baːrk]

n. 나무껍질; v. (명령 · 질문 등을) 빽 내지르다; (개가) 짖다
Bark is the tough material that covers the outside of a tree.

staff 복습
[stæf]

n. 지팡이
A staff is a strong stick or pole.

prop
[prap]

v. 떠받치다; n. (연극 · 영화에 쓰이는) 소품; 지주, 버팀목
If you prop an object on or against something, you support it by putting something underneath it or by resting it somewhere.

crack 복습
[kræk]

n. (좁은) 틈; 날카로운 소리; 금; v. 갈라지다; 깨지다, 부서지다
A crack is a very narrow gap between two things, or between two parts of a thing.

carve *
[kaːrv]

v. 조각하다, 깎아서 만들다; 새기다
If you carve an object, you make it by cutting it out of a substance such as wood or stone.

taper
[téipər]

v. (폭이) 점점 가늘어지다; n. 점점 가늘어짐
If something tapers, or if you taper it, it becomes gradually thinner at one end.

needle ^{복습}
[níːdl]

n. 바늘, 침; (계기의) 바늘, 지침; (pl.) 솔잎
A needle is a small, very thin piece of polished metal which is used for sewing.

satisfied*
[sǽtisfàid]

a. 만족하는, 흡족해하는; 납득하는
If you are satisfied with something, you are happy because you have got what you wanted or needed.

split ^{복습}
[split]

v. 나뉘다; 찢어지다, 쪼개지다; 분열되다; n. 분열; (길게 찢어진) 틈
If something splits or if you split it, it is divided into two or more parts.

jam ^{복습}
[dʒæm]

v. 밀어 넣다; 움직이지 못하게 되다; n. 교통 체증; 혼잡; 잼
If you jam something somewhere, you push or put it there roughly.

prong
[prɔːŋ]

n. (뾰족하게 나뉘어져 있는) 갈래
The prongs of something such as a fork are the long, thin pointed parts.

crude ^{복습}
[kruːd]

a. 대충 만든; 대충의, 대강의
If you describe an object that someone has made as crude, you mean that it has been made in a very simple way or from very simple parts.

effective**
[iféktiv]

a. 효과적인; 시행되는
Something that is effective works well and produces the results that were intended.

heft
[heft]

v. 들어올리다; 들어서 무게를 대중하다; n. 무게, 중량
If you heft something, you lift and hold something, especially a weapon.

tool ^{복습}
[tuːl]

n. 도구, 연장; 수단
A tool is any instrument or simple piece of equipment that you hold in your hands and use to do a particular kind of work.

frighten ^{복습}
[fraitn]

v. 겁먹게 하다, 놀라게 하다
If something or someone frightens you, they cause you to suddenly feel afraid, anxious, or nervous.

thrust*
[θrʌst]

v. 찌르다; (거칠게) 밀다; n. 추진력; 찌르기
If you thrust something or someone somewhere, you push or move them there quickly with a lot of force.

telegraph*
[téligræf]

v. (무심코) 의향을 드러내다; 전보를 보내다; n. 전신, 전보
If someone telegraphs something that they are planning or intending to do, they make it obvious, either deliberately or accidentally, that they are going to do it.

motion ^{복습}
[móuʃən]

n. 동작, 몸짓; 운동, 움직임; v. (손·머리로) 몸짓을 해 보이다
A motion is an action, gesture, or movement.

spring ^{복습}
[spriŋ]

v. 휙 움직이다; 튀다; (갑자기) 뛰어오르다; n. 샘; 봄; 생기, 활기
If something springs in a particular direction, it moves suddenly and quickly.

motive*
[móutiv]

a. 움직이게 하는, 원동력이 되는; n. 동기, 이유
Motive means producing or causing movement.

120

force ^{복습}
[fɔːrs]

n. 작용력; 군대; 힘; 영향력; v. 억지로 ~하다; ~를 강요하다
In physics, a force is the pulling or pushing effect that something has on something else.

string ^{복습}
[striŋ]

n. 줄; (악기의) 현; 일련; v. 묶다, 매달다; (실 등에) 꿰다
String is thin rope made of twisted threads, used for tying things together or tying up parcels.

bow [*]
[bou]

① n. 활 ② n. 절, (고개 숙여 하는) 인사; v. (허리를 굽혀) 절하다
A bow is a weapon for shooting arrows which consists of a long piece of curved wood with a string attached to both its ends.

arrow [*]
[ǽrou]

n. 화살; 화살표
An arrow is a long thin weapon which is sharp and pointed at one end and which often has feathers at the other end. An arrow is shot from a bow.

release ^{복습}
[rilíːs]

v. 놓아 주다; 풀다; (감정을) 발산하다; n. 풀어 줌; 발표, 공개
If you release someone or something, you stop holding them.

invent ^{복습}
[invént]

v. 발명하다; (사실이 아닌 것을) 지어내다
If you invent something such as a machine or process, you are the first person to think of it or make it.

primitive [*]
[prímətiv]

a. 원시의; 원시 사회의; 초기의
Primitive means belonging to a very early period in the development of an animal or plant.

discovery ^{복습}
[diskʌ́vəri]

n. 발견
If someone makes a discovery, they become aware of something that they did not know about before.

bury ^{복습}
[béri]

v. (땅에) 묻다; 뒤덮다; 감추다 (rebury v. 다시 묻다)
To bury something means to put it into a hole in the ground and cover it up with earth.

settle ^{복습}
[setl]

v. 자리를 잡다; 진정되다; (서서히) 가라앉다; 결정하다
If something settles or if you settle it, it sinks slowly down and becomes still.

set off ^{복습}

idiom 출발하다; (폭탄 등을) 터뜨리다
If you set off, you begin a journey.

bother ^{복습}
[báðər]

v. 신경 쓰이게 하다; 귀찮게 하다, 귀찮게 말을 걸다; 신경 쓰다; n. 성가심
If something bothers you, or if you bother about it, it worries, annoys, or upsets you.

patch ^{복습}
[pætʃ]

n. 작은 땅; 부분; 조각; v. 덧대다, 때우다
A patch of land is a small area of land where a particular plant or crop grows.

ripe ^{복습}
[raip]

a. 익은, 여문 (overripe a. 지나치게 익은)
Ripe fruit or grain is fully grown and ready to eat.

limb ^{복습}
[lim]

n. (큰) 나뭇가지; (하나의) 팔, 다리
The limbs of a tree are its branches.

cheek ^{복습}
[ʧiːk]

n. 뺨, 볼; 엉덩이
Your cheeks are the sides of your face below your eyes.

turtle ^{복습}
[təːrtl]

n. [동물] (바다) 거북
A turtle is a large reptile which has a thick shell covering its body and which lives in the sea most of the time.

handful ^{복습}
[hǽndfùl]

n. 줌, 움큼; 몇 안 되는 수
A handful of something is the amount of it that you can hold in your hand.

cave in ^{복습}

idiom 무너지다, 함몰되다
If a ceiling, roof, or other structure caves in, it breaks and falls into the space below.

bulge
[bʌldʒ]

v. 툭 불거져 나오다; 가득 차다; n. 툭 튀어 나온 것, 불룩한 것
If something such as a person's stomach bulges, it sticks out.

freeze ^{복습}
[friːz]

v. 얼다; (두려움 등으로 몸이) 얼어붙다; n. 얼어붙음; 동결; 한파 (freezy a. 차가운)
If something is freezy, it is chilled almost to freezing.

shrink ^{복습}
[ʃriŋk]

v. (shrank–shrunk) 줄어들다; (놀람 · 충격으로) 움츠러들다
If something shrinks or something else shrinks it, it becomes smaller.

tear ^{복습}
[tɛər]

① v. 찢다, 뜯다; 뜯어 내다; n. 찢어진 곳, 구멍 ② n. 눈물
If a person or animal tears at something, they pull it violently and try to break it into pieces.

automatic[*]
[ɔ̀ːtəmǽtik]

a. 무의식적인, 반사적인; 자동의 (automatically ad. 무의식적으로)
An automatic action is one that you do without thinking about it.

edge ^{복습}
[edʒ]

n. 끝, 가장자리; 우위; v. 조금씩 움직이다; 테두리를 두르다
The edge of something is the place or line where it stops, or the part of it that is furthest from the middle.

springy
[spríŋi]

a. (용수철같이) 탄력 있는; 생기 넘치는
If something is springy, it returns quickly to its original shape after you press it.

lack ^{복습}
[læk]

v. ~이 없다, 부족하다; n. 부족, 결핍
If you say that someone or something lacks a particular quality or that a particular quality is lacking in them, you mean that they do not have any or enough of it.

whip[*]
[hwip]

v. 격렬하게 움직이다; 휙 빼내다; n. 채찍
If something, for example the wind, whips something, it strikes it sharply.

halfway ^{복습}
[hǽfwèi]

ad. (거리 · 시간상으로) 가운데쯤에; 부분적으로, 불완전하게
Halfway means in the middle of a place or between two points, at an equal distance from each of them.

log ^{복습}
[lɔːg]

n. 통나무
A log is a piece of a thick branch or of the trunk of a tree that has been cut so that it can be used for fuel or for making things.

terrify ^{복습}
[térəfài]

v. (몹시) 무섭게 하다 (terrified a. (몹시) 무서워하는, 겁이 난)
If something terrifies you, it makes you feel extremely frightened.

122

feather [복습]
[féðər]
v. 깃털로 덮다; n. (새의) 털, 깃털 (feathered a. 깃털이 있는)
If you describe something as feathered, you mean that it has feathers on it.

bomb [**]
[bam]
n. 폭탄; v. 폭탄으로 공격하다, 폭격하다
A bomb is a device which explodes and damages or destroys a large area.

flurry
[flə́:ri]
n. 질풍, 한 줄기의 바람; (잠시 한바탕 벌어지는) 소동
A flurry is a small swirling mass of something, especially snow or leaves, moved by sudden gusts of wind.

thunder [복습]
[θʌ́ndər]
n. 천둥 같은 소리; 천둥; v. 우르릉거리다; 천둥이 치다; 쏜살같이 보내다
The thunder of something that is moving or making a sound is the loud deep noise it makes.

fantail
[fǽntèil]
n. 부채 모양의 꼬리
A fantail is a tail shaped like an outspread fan.

stub
[stʌb]
n. (쓰다 남은 물건의) 토막; v. ~에 발가락이 차이다 (stubby a. 뭉툭한, 짤막한)
An object that is stubby is shorter and thicker than usual.

slam [복습]
[slæm]
v. 세게 치다, 놓다; 쾅 닫다; n. 쾅 하고 놓기; 탕 하는 소리
If you slam something down, you put it there quickly and with great force.

speckle [복습]
[spekl]
n. 작은 반점 (speckled a. 작은 반점들이 있는, 얼룩덜룩한)
A speckled surface is covered with small marks, spots, or shapes.

bake [**]
[beik]
v. (음식을) 굽다; (열로) 굽다
If you bake, you spend some time preparing and mixing together ingredients to make bread, cakes, pies, or other food which is cooked in the oven.

crackle [복습]
[krækl]
v. 탁탁 소리를 내다; n. 탁탁 하는 소리
If something crackles, it makes a rapid series of short, harsh noises.

drive out
idiom ~을 몰아내다, 사라지게 하다
To drive someone or something out means to force them to leave or stop doing something.

vicious [복습]
[víʃəs]
a. 지독한, 극심한; 사나운, 공격적인; 잔인한, 악랄한
Something that is vicious is very bad or severe.

chip [복습]
[ʧip]
n. 조각, 토막; 감자칩; v. 깨지다, 이가 빠지다; 잘게 썰다
A chip is a small piece of something or a small piece which has been broken off something.

concentrate [**]
[kάnsəntrèit]
v. (정신을) 집중하다; (한 곳에) 모으다; n. 농축물
If you concentrate on something, or concentrate your mind on it, you give all your attention to it.

persistent [*]
[pərsístənt]
a. 끊임없이 지속되는; 끈질긴, 집요한
Something that is persistent continues to exist or happen for a long time; used especially about bad or undesirable states or situations.

whine [복습]
[hwain]
n. 윙 하는 소리; 불평; v. 윙 소리를 내다; 우는 소리를 하다; 낑낑거리다
A whine is a high sound made by a machine or insect.

steady ^{복습}
[stédi]

a. 꾸준한; 흔들림 없는, 안정된; v. 진정되다; 가라앉히다
A steady situation continues or develops gradually without any interruptions and is not likely to change quickly.

motor **
[móutər]

n. 모터, 전동기; v. 자동차로 가다
The motor in a machine, vehicle, or boat is the part that uses electricity or fuel to produce movement, so that the machine, vehicle, or boat can work.

bluff ^{복습}
[blʌf]

n. (바다나 강가의) 절벽; 허세, 엄포; v. 허세를 부리다, 엄포를 놓다
A bluff is a cliff or very steep bank by the sea or river.

swivel
[swívəl]

v. (몸 · 눈 · 고개를) 홱 돌리다; 돌리다, 회전시키다; n. 회전 고리
If you swivel in a particular direction, you turn suddenly in that direction.

lung ^{복습}
[lʌŋ]

n. 폐, 허파
Your lungs are the two organs inside your chest which fill with air when you breathe in.

waggle
[wǽgl]

v. (상하 · 좌우로) 흔들다, 움직거리다
If you waggle something, or if something waggles, it moves up and down or from side to side with short quick movements.

float ^{복습}
[flout]

n. 부표; v. (물 위나 공중에서) 떠가다; (물에) 뜨다
A float is a light object that is used to help someone or something float.

pilot ^{복습}
[páilət]

n. 조종사, 비행사
A pilot is a person who is trained to fly an aircraft.

amaze *
[əméiz]

v. (대단히) 놀라게 하다; 경악하게 하다 (amazed a. 놀란)
If something amazes you, it surprises you very much.

liquid ^{복습}
[líkwid]

n. 액체; a. 액체의
A liquid is a substance which is not solid but which flows and can be poured, for example water.

flame ^{복습}
[fleim]

n. 불길, 불꽃; 격정; v. 활활 타오르다; 시뻘게지다
A flame is a hot bright stream of burning gas that comes from something that is burning.

abrupt *
[əbrʌ́pt]

a. 돌연한, 갑작스런; 퉁명스러운
An abrupt change or action is very sudden, often in a way which is unpleasant.

shield *
[ʃiːld]

v. 보호하다, 가리다; n. 방패; 보호 장치
If you shield your eyes, you put your hand above your eyes to protect them from direct sunlight.

faint ^{복습}
[feint]

a. 희미한, 약한; v. 실신하다, 기절하다; n. 실신, 기절
A faint sound, color, mark, feeling, or quality has very little strength or intensity.

kneel ^{복습}
[niːl]

v. 무릎을 꿇다
When you kneel, you bend your legs so that your knees are touching the ground.

124

bonfire ^{복습}
[bánfàiər]

n. 모닥불
A bonfire is a fire that is made outdoors, usually to burn rubbish. Bonfires are also sometimes lit as part of a celebration.

whisper ^{복습}
[hwíspər]

v. 속삭이다, 소곤거리다; n. 속삭임, 소곤거리는 소리
When you whisper, you say something very quietly, using your breath rather than your throat, so that only one person can hear you.

fade ^{복습}
[feid]

v. 서서히 사라지다; (색깔이) 바래다, 희미해지다
When something that you are looking at fades, it slowly becomes less bright or clear until it disappears.

imagination ^{복습}
[imædʒənéiʃən]

n. 상상력, 상상; 착각; 창의력
Your imagination is the part of your mind which allows you to form pictures or ideas of things that do not necessarily exist in real life.

soul^{**}
[soul]

n. 마음; 영혼
Your soul is the part of you that consists of your mind, character, thoughts, and feelings.

ash[*]
[æʃ]

n. 재
Ash is the grey or black powdery substance that is left after something is burnt.

flight ^{복습}
[flait]

n. 비행; 항공기; 계단; 층계; 탈출, 도피
A flight is a journey made by flying, usually in an airplane.

knee ^{복습}
[niː]

n. 무릎; v. 무릎으로 치다
Your knee is the place where your leg bends.

silly^{**}
[síli]

a. 어리석은, 바보 같은; 우스꽝스러운; n. 바보
If you say that someone or something is silly, you mean that they are foolish, childish, or ridiculous.

1. How did Brian overcome his fear of the wolf?
   A. He understood that the wolf was a part of nature.
   B. He sensed that the wolf was actually afraid of him.
   C. He noticed that the wolf was too far away to attack him.
   D. He realized that he could use his fishing tools as a weapon against the wolf.

2. Why had he cut himself?
   A. His hand accidentally slipped when he was cutting an egg.
   B. He was trying to chop wood but missed the tree.
   C. He needed to remove poison in his body.
   D. He wanted to escape his suffering and die.

3. How was he finally able to catch a fish?
   A. He aimed his arrow under the fish instead of directly at it.
   B. He shot a few arrows at a time instead of just one.
   C. He placed his arrow farther away from the fish so that he would not scare it.
   D. He only targeted bigger, slower fish that swam near him.

4. How did he feel after his first day of catching fish?
   A. He felt a new sense of optimism about being rescued soon.
   B. He felt more confident in his ability to survive on his own.
   C. He felt depressed that he had no one to share his feast with.
   D. He felt motivated to hunt for more delicious food in the woods.

5. What did he think about little mistakes in the wilderness?

    A. Little mistakes were worse than big mistakes.

    B. Little mistakes were not a big deal.

    C. Little mistakes could lead to huge problems.

    D. Little mistakes could always be prevented.

6. What lesson did he learn after encountering the skunk?

    A. He should bury food even deeper in the shelter.

    B. He should make a bigger fire at night to keep animals away.

    C. It was important not to store food for a long time.

    D. It was important to keep food safe from other animals.

7. Why did he make an enclosure in the lake to trap fish?

    A. He wanted to raise some fish as pets.

    B. He could not store dead fish in his food shelf.

    C. He was bored with using a bow and arrow to catch fish.

    D. He was tired of looking for fish every time he was hungry.

1분에 몇 단어를 읽는지 리딩 속도를 측정해보세요.

$$\frac{2{,}006 \text{ words}}{\text{reading time ( ) sec}} \times 60 = (\qquad) \text{ WPM}$$

Build Your Vocabulary

jerk^{복습}
[dʒəːrk]

v. 홱 움직이다; n. 얼간이; 홱 움직임
If you jerk something or someone in a particular direction, or they jerk in a particular direction, they move a short distance very suddenly and quickly.

sideways^{복습}
[sáidwèiz]

ad. 옆으로; 옆에서
Sideways means in a direction to the left or right, not forward or backward.

ripple^{복습}
[ripl]

n. 잔물결, 파문 (모양의 것); v. 잔물결을 이루다; (감정 등이) 파문처럼 번지다
Ripples are little waves on the surface of water caused by the wind or by something moving in or on the water.

bow^{복습}
[bou]

① n. 활 ② n. 절, (고개 숙여 하는) 인사; v. (허리를 굽혀) 절하다
A bow is a weapon for shooting arrows which consists of a long piece of curved wood with a string attached to both its ends.

pouch^{복습}
[pauʧ]

n. 주머니; (캥거루 같은 동물의) 새끼 주머니
A pouch is a flexible container like a small bag.

arrow^{복습}
[ǽrou]

n. 화살; 화살표
An arrow is a long thin weapon which is sharp and pointed at one end and which often has feathers at the other end. An arrow is shot from a bow.

meat^{복습}
[miːt]

n. 고기
Meat is flesh taken from a dead animal that people cook and eat.

foolish^{***}
[fúːliʃ]

a. 어리석은; 바보 같은 (기분이 들게 하는)
If someone's behavior or action is foolish, it is not sensible and shows a lack of good judgment.

fool[*]
[fuːl]

n. 바보; a. 바보 같은; v. 속이다, 기만하다
If you call someone a fool, you are indicating that you think they are not at all sensible and show a lack of good judgment.

flock^{복습}
[flɑk]

n. (동물의) 떼; (사람들) 무리; v. (많은 수가) 모이다; 떼 지어 가다
A flock of birds, sheep, or goats is a group of them.

female^{**}
[fíːmeil]

a. 암컷의; 여성인; n. 암컷; 여성
You can refer to any creature that can lay eggs or produce babies from its body as a female.

cub[*]
[kʌb]

n. (곰 · 사자 · 여우 등의) 새끼
A cub is a young wild animal such as a lion, wolf, or bear.

128

threaten^{복습}
[θretn]

v. 위협하다; 협박하다; (나쁜 일이 있을) 조짐을 보이다
If a person threatens to do something unpleasant to you, or if they threaten you, they say or imply that they will do something unpleasant to you, especially if you do not do what they want.

patient^{**}
[péiʃənt]

a. 참을성 있는, 인내심 있는; n. 환자 (patiently ad. 참을성 있게)
If you are patient, you stay calm and do not get annoyed, for example when something takes a long time, or when someone is not doing what you want them to do.

opening^{복습}
[óupəniŋ]

n. (사람 등이 지나가거나 할 수 있는) 틈; 첫 부분; (사람을 쓸 수 있는) 빈자리;
a. 첫, 시작 부분의
An opening is a hole or empty space through which things or people can pass.

throw^{***}
[θrou]

v. (threw–thrown) 충격을 주다, 놀라게 하다; 던지다; n. 던지기, 투구
If something such as a remark or an experience throws you, it surprises you or confuses you because it is unexpected.

claim^{***}
[kleim]

v. 차지하다; 주장하다; 요구하다; n. 주장
If you claim something, you try to get it because you think you have a right to it.

tense^{복습}
[tens]

v. 긴장하다; a. 긴장한, 신경이 날카로운 (tension n. 팽팽함; 장력)
The tension in something such as a rope or wire is the extent to which it is stretched tight.

nod^{복습}
[nad]

v. (고개를) 끄덕이다, 까딱하다; n. (고개를) 끄덕임
If you nod, you bend your head once, as a way of saying hello or goodbye.

effortless
[éfərtlis]

a. 힘이 들지 않는; 수월해 보이는 (effortlessly ad. 쉽게)
Something that is effortless is done easily and well.

brush^{복습}
[brʌʃ]

n. 덤불, 잡목 숲; 붓; 솔; v. (솔이나 손으로) 털다; 솔질을 하다; ~을 스치다
Brush is an area of rough open land covered with small bushes and trees. You also use brush to refer to the bushes and trees on this land.

measure^{복습}
[méʒər]

v. 측정하다; 판단하다; n. 조치, 정책; 척도
If you measure a quantity that can be expressed in numbers, such as the length of something, you discover it using a particular instrument or device, for example a ruler.

crash^{복습}
[kræʃ]

n. (자동차·항공기) 사고; 요란한 소리; v. 충돌하다; 부딪치다; 굉음을 내다
A crash is an accident in which a moving vehicle hits something and is damaged or destroyed.

gut^{복습}
[gʌt]

v. 내부를 파괴하다; n. 소화관; 배; 직감
To gut a building means to destroy the inside of it so that only its outside walls remain.

go out^{복습}

idiom (불·전깃불이) 꺼지다; 외출하다
If the fire or the light goes out, it stops burning or shining.

funk
[fʌŋk]

n. 두려움, 걱정; 펑크(강한 비트의 음악)
If you are in a funk, you are very unhappy and without hope.

madness[*]
[mǽdnis]

n. 어리석은 행동; 광기
Madness refers to ideas or actions that show a lack of good judgment and careful thought.

hiss^{복습}
[his]

v. 쉿 하는 소리를 내다; (화난 어조로) 낮게 말하다; n. 쉭쉭거리는 소리
To hiss means to make a sound like a long 's.'

awful^{복습}
[ɔ́:fəl]

a. 끔찍한, 지독한; (정도가) 대단한, 아주 심한
If you say that something is awful, you mean that it is extremely unpleasant, shocking, or bad.

disappoint^{**}
[dìsəpɔ́int]

v. 실망시키다, 실망을 안겨 주다; 좌절시키다 (disappointment n. 실망, 낙심)
Disappointment is the feeling of sadness or displeasure caused by the non-fulfilment of your hopes or expectations.

realize^{복습}
[ríːəlàiz]

v. 깨닫다, 알아차리다; 실현하다, 달성하다
If you realize that something is true, you become aware of that fact or understand it.

partial[*]
[páːrʃəl]

a. 부분적인, 불완전한; ~을 매우 좋아하는 (partially ad. 부분적으로)
If something happens or exists partially, it happens or exists to some extent, but not completely.

rotten[*]
[ratn]

a. 썩은, 부패한; 형편없는, 끔찍한
If food, wood, or another substance is rotten, it has decayed and can no longer be used.

punk
[pʌŋk]

n. (불쏘시개로 쓰는) 썩은 나무; 불량한 남자, 불량 청소년 (punky a. 천천히 타는)
Punk is soft, crumbly wood that has been attacked by fungus, used as tinder.

smolder^{복습}
[smóuldər]

v. (서서히) 타다; (불만 등이) 들끓다; n. 연기
If something smolders, it burns slowly, producing smoke but not flames.

extent^{**}
[ikstént]

n. 정도, 규모; 크기
The extent of something is its length, area, or size.

disaster[*]
[dizǽstər]

n. 완전한 실패작; 참사, 재난; 엄청난 불행, 재앙
If you refer to something as a disaster, you are emphasizing that you think it is extremely bad or unacceptable.

blind^{복습}
[blaind]

v. 눈이 멀게 하다; (잠시) 앞이 안 보이게 하다; a. 눈이 먼; 눈치 채지 못하는
If something blinds you, it makes you unable to see, either for a short time or permanently.

shaft[*]
[ʃæft]

n. 화살대; (기다란) 손잡이; 수직 통로, 수갱
A shaft is a long thin piece of wood or metal that forms part of a spear, ax, golf club, or other object.

harden[*]
[haːrdn]

v. 굳다; (얼굴·목소리 등이) 굳어지다; 단호해지다
When something hardens or when you harden it, it becomes stiff or firm.

split^{복습}
[split]

v. (split-split) 나뉘다; 찢어지다, 쪼개지다; 분열되다; n. 분열; (길게 찢어진) 틈
If something splits or if you split it, it is divided into two or more parts.

130

fork**
[fɔːrk]

v. 갈라지다, 나뉘다; n. 포크; (도로 · 강 등의) 분기점 (forked a. 끝이 갈라진)
Something that divides into two parts and forms a 'Y' shape can be described as forked.

bare*
[bɛər]

a. 아무것도 안 덮인; 맨손의; 벌거벗은; 텅 빈; v. (신체의 일부를) 드러내다
A bare surface is not covered or decorated with anything.

figure^{복습}
[fígjər]

v. 생각하다, 중요하다; n. (멀리서 흐릿하게 보이는) 사람; 수치; (중요한) 인물
(figure for idiom ~의 대책을 세우다)
If you figure that something is the case, you think or guess that it is the case.

lace*
[leis]

n. (구두 등의) 끈; 레이스; v. 끈으로 묶다
Laces are thin pieces of material that are put through special holes in some types of clothing, especially shoes. The laces are tied together in order to tighten the clothing.

take care of^{복습}

idiom ~을 처리하다; ~을 돌보다
To take care of someone or something means to do what is necessary to deal with a person or situation.

cheek^{복습}
[ʧiːk]

n. 뺨, 볼; 엉덩이
Your cheeks are the sides of your face below your eyes.

hummock^{복습}
[hʌ́mək]

n. 작은 언덕
A hummock is a small raised area of ground, like a very small hill.

precise*
[prisáis]

a. 정확한, 정밀한; 엄밀한, 꼼꼼한
You use precise to emphasize that you are referring to an exact thing, rather than something vague.

instant^{복습}
[ínstənt]

n. 순간, 아주 짧은 동안; a. 즉각적인
An instant is an extremely short period of time.

splinter
[splíntər]

n. (나무 · 금속 · 유리 등의) 조각; v. 쪼개지다, 깨지다; 분열되다, 갈라지다
A splinter is a very thin, sharp piece of wood, glass, or other hard substance, which has broken off from a larger piece.

chip^{복습}
[ʧip]

n. 조각, 토막; 감자칩; v. 깨지다, 이가 빠지다; 잘게 썰다
A chip is a small piece of something or a small piece which has been broken off something.

forehead^{복습}
[fɔ́ːrhèd]

n. 이마
Your forehead is the area at the front of your head between your eyebrows and your hair.

slight^{복습}
[slait]

a. 약간의, 조금의; 작고 여윈 (slightly ad. 약간, 조금)
Slightly means to some degree but not to a very large degree.

stiff^{복습}
[stif]

a. 뻣뻣한; 결리는, 뻐근한; 경직된; 심한; ad. 몹시, 극심하게
Something that is stiff is firm or does not bend easily.

journal*
[dʒə́ːrnl]

n. 일기; 저널, 학술지
A journal is an account which you write of your daily activities.

slender^{복습}
[sléndər]

a. 가느다란; 날씬한, 호리호리한
If you describe something as slender, you mean that it is not very wide.

fluid 복습
[fluːid]

a. 부드러운, 우아한; 가변적인; n. 유체(流體), 유동체
Fluid movements or lines or designs are smooth and graceful.

surround**
[səráund]

v. 둘러싸다, 에워싸다; 포위하다
If a person or thing is surrounded by something, that thing is situated all around them.

virtual*
[və́ːrtʃuəl]

a. 사실상의; 가상의
You can use virtual to indicate that something is so nearly true that for most purposes it can be regarded as true.

infuriate
[infjúərièit]

v. 극도로 화나게 하다
If something or someone infuriates you, they make you extremely angry.

notice 복습
[nóutis]

v. 알아채다, 인지하다; 주의하다; n. 신경 씀, 주목, 알아챔
If you notice something or someone, you become aware of them.

refract
[rifrǽkt]

v. (빛을) 굴절시키다
When a ray of light or a sound wave refracts or is refracted, the path it follows bends at a particular point, for example when it enters water or glass.

biology*
[baiálədʒi]

n. 생물학; 생태
Biology is the science which is concerned with the study of living things.

aim 복습
[eim]

v. 겨누다; 목표하다; n. 겨냥, 조준; 목적
If you aim a weapon or object at something or someone, you point it toward them before firing or throwing it.

flurry 복습
[fláːri]

n. 질풍, 한 줄기의 바람; (잠시 한바탕 벌어지는) 소동
A flurry is a small swirling mass of something, especially snow or leaves, moved by sudden gusts of wind.

splash 복습
[splæʃ]

n. 첨벙 하는 소리; (어디에 떨어지는) 방울; v. 첨벙거리다; (물 등을) 끼얹다
A splash is the sound made when something hits water or falls into it.

tighten 복습
[taitn]

v. (더 단단히) 조이다; (더) 팽팽해지다; 더 엄격하게 하다
If a part of your body tightens, the muscles in it become tense and stiff, for example because you are angry or afraid.

swell 복습
[swel]

v. (마음이) 벅차다; 부풀다; (소리가) 더 커지다; n. 증가, 팽창
If you swell with a feeling, you are suddenly full of that feeling.

fashion**
[fǽʃən]

v. (손으로) 만들다; n. 방법, 방식; 유행(하는 스타일)
If you fashion an object or a work of art, you make it.

exult
[igzʌ́lt]

v. 기뻐서 어쩔 줄 모르다, 의기양양하다
If you exult in a triumph or success that you have had, you feel and show great happiness and pleasure because of it.

skin 복습
[skin]

n. (동물의) 껍질; 피부; 거죽, 외피; v. (동물의) 가죽을 벗기다; (피부가) 까지다
An animal skin is skin which has been removed from a dead animal. Skins are used to make things such as coats and rugs.

132

flaky
[fléiki]

a. 얇게 벗겨지는; 괴짜인; 뭘 잘 잊어먹는
Something that is flaky breaks easily into small thin pieces or tends to come off in small thin pieces.

moist*
[mɔist]

a. 촉촉한
Something that is moist is slightly wet.

tender^{복습}
[téndər]

a. 연한; 따가운; 상냥한, 다정한
Meat or other food that is tender is easy to cut or chew.

mash
[mæʃ]

v. 으깨다; n. (부드럽게) 으깬 음식
If you mash food that is solid but soft, you crush it so that it forms a soft mass.

tongue^{복습}
[tʌŋ]

n. 혀; 말버릇
Your tongue is the soft movable part inside your mouth which you use for tasting, eating, and speaking.

steam^{복습}
[sti:m]

v. 김을 내뿜다; 화내다, 발끈하다; n. 김, 증기; 추진력
If something steams, it gives off steam.

scrap*
[skræp]

n. (pl.) 남은 음식; 폐품; (종이 · 옷감 등의) 조각; v. 폐기하다, 버리다
Scraps are pieces of unwanted food which are thrown away or given to animals.

bait*
[beit]

n. 미끼; v. 미끼를 놓다; (일부러) 화를 돋우다
Bait is food which you put on a hook or in a trap in order to catch fish or animals.

feast*
[fi:st]

n. 진수성찬; 연회, 잔치; v. 맘껏 먹다
A feast is a large and special meal.

celebrate**
[séləbrèit]

v. 기념하다, 축하하다 (celebration n. 축하)
The celebration of something is praise and appreciation which is given to it.

stomach^{복습}
[stʌ́mək]

n. 위(胃), 복부, 배
Your stomach is the organ inside your body where food is digested before it moves into the intestines.

grease^{복습}
[gri:s]

n. 기름, 지방; v. 기름을 바르다
Grease is animal fat that is produced by cooking meat. You can use grease for cooking.

smear^{복습}
[smiə:r]

v. 마구 바르다; 더럽히다; n. 얼룩, 자국
If you smear a surface with an oily or sticky substance or smear the substance onto the surface, you spread a layer of the substance over the surface.

rescue*
[réskju:]

v. 구하다, 구출하다; n. 구출, 구조, 구제
If you rescue someone, you get them out of a dangerous or unpleasant situation.

survive^{복습}
[sərváiv]

v. 살아남다, 생존하다
If a person or living thing survives in a dangerous situation such as an accident or an illness, they do not die.

Check Your Reading Speed

1분에 몇 단어를 읽는지 리딩 속도를 측정해보세요.

$$\frac{1,936 \text{ words}}{\text{reading time ( ) sec}} \times 60 = (\quad) \text{ WPM}$$

Build Your Vocabulary

disaster ^{복습}
[dizǽstər]

n. 엄청난 불행, 재앙; 완전한 실패작; 참사, 재난
Disaster is something which has very bad consequences for you.

snowball
[snóubɔ:l]

v. (문제 등이) 눈덩이처럼 커지다; n. 눈 뭉치
If something such as a project or campaign snowballs, it rapidly increases and grows.

humor ^{복습}
[hjú:mər]

n. 유머, (재치 있는) 농담; v. 비위를 맞춰 주다
You can refer to the amusing things that people say as their humor.

rectify
[réktəfài]

v. (잘못된 것을) 바로잡다
If you rectify something that is wrong, you change it so that it becomes correct or satisfactory.

sprain ^{복습}
[sprein]

v. (팔목·발목을) 삐다, 접지르다
If you sprain a joint such as your ankle or wrist, you accidentally damage it by twisting it or bending it violently.

heal ^{복습}
[hi:l]

v. 치유되다, 낫다; 치료하다, 고치다
When a broken bone or other injury heals or when something heals it, it becomes healthy and normal again.

refrigerator [*]
[rifrídʒərèitər]

n. 냉장고
A refrigerator is a large container which is kept cool inside, usually by electricity, so that the food and drink in it stays fresh.

incredible ^{복습}
[inkrédəbl]

a. 믿을 수 없는, 믿기 힘든 (incredibly ad. 믿을 수 없을 정도로, 엄청나게)
If you describe something or someone as incredible, you like them very much or are impressed by them, because they are extremely or unusually good.

starve ^{복습}
[sta:rv]

v. 굶주리다, 굶어죽다
If people starve, they suffer greatly from lack of food which sometimes leads to their death.

get around

idiom 돌아다니다
To get around means to be able to go to different places without difficulty, especially if you are old or ill.

vital [*]
[vaitl]

a. 필수적인; 생명 유지와 관련된; 활력이 넘치는
If you say that something is vital, you mean that it is necessary or very important.

134

drive ^{복습}
[draiv]

v. 만들다; 운전하다; 박아 넣다; 몰아가다; n. 드라이브; 충동, 욕구
The desire or feeling that drives a person to do something, especially something extreme, is the desire or feeling that causes them to do it.

creature **
[kríːʧər]

n. 생물, 생명체; 사람
You can refer to any living thing that is not a plant as a creature, especially when it is of an unknown or unfamiliar kind.

insect ^{복습}
[ínsekt]

n. 곤충
An insect is a small animal that has six legs. Most insects have wings. Ants, flies, butterflies, and beetles are all insects.

influence **
[ínfluəns]

n. 영향; 영향력; v. 영향을 주다
To have an influence on people or situations means to affect what they do or what happens.

smolder ^{복습}
[smóuldər]

v. (서서히) 타다; (불만 등이) 들끓다; n. 연기
If something smolders, it burns slowly, producing smoke but not flames.

shelter ^{복습}
[ʃéltər]

n. 대피처, 피신처; 피신; v. 피하다; 막아 주다, 보호하다
A shelter is a small building or covered place which is made to protect people from bad weather or danger.

be sound asleep

idiom 깊이 잠들어 있다
If someone is sound sleep, they are sleeping very deeply.

awaken ^{복습}
[əwéikən]

v. (잠에서) 깨다; (감정을) 불러일으키다
When you awaken, or when something or someone awakens you, you wake up.

unafraid
[ʌnəfréid]

a. 두려워하지 않는
If you are unafraid to do something, you are confident and not at all nervous about doing it.

coal ^{복습}
[koul]

n. 석탄
Coal is a hard black substance that is extracted from the ground and burned as fuel.

dig ^{복습}
[dig]

v. (구멍 등을) 파다; (무엇을 찾기 위해) 뒤지다; 찌르다; n. 쿡 찌르기
If people or animals dig, they make a hole in the ground or in a pile of earth, stones, or rubbish.

bury ^{복습}
[béri]

v. (땅에) 묻다; 뒤덮다; 감추다
To bury something means to put it into a hole in the ground and cover it up with earth.

sliver ^{복습}
[slívər]

n. (깨지거나 잘라 낸) 조각
A sliver of something is a small thin piece or amount of it.

faint ^{복습}
[feint]

a. 희미한, 약한; v. 실신하다, 기절하다; n. 실신, 기절
A faint sound, color, mark, feeling, or quality has very little strength or intensity.

bushy
[búʃi]

a. 숱이 많은; 무성한, 우거진
Bushy hair or fur is very thick.

tail ^{복습}
[teil]

n. (동물의) 꼬리; 끝부분; v. 미행하다
The tail of an animal, bird, or fish is the part extending beyond the end of its body.

stripe[*]
[straip]

n. 줄무늬; v. 줄무늬를 넣다
A stripe is a long line which is a different color from the areas next to it.

tiny ^{복습}
[táini]

a. 아주 작은
Something or someone that is tiny is extremely small.

fragment[*]
[frǽgmənt]

n. 조각, 파편; v. 산산이 부수다
A fragment of something is a small piece or part of it.

shell ^{복습}
[ʃel]

n. 껍데기; 포탄; 뼈대, 외부 구조; v. 껍질을 까다
The shell of a nut or egg is the hard covering which surrounds it.

replace^{**}
[ripléis]

v. 대신하다, 대체하다; 교체하다
If one thing or person replaces another, the first is used or acts instead of the second.

grab ^{복습}
[græb]

v. (와락 · 단단히) 붙잡다; 급히 ~하다; n. 와락 잡아채려고 함
If you grab something, you take it or pick it up suddenly and roughly.

handful ^{복습}
[hǽndfùl]

n. 줌, 움큼; 몇 안 되는 수
A handful of something is the amount of it that you can hold in your hand.

silly ^{복습}
[sili]

a. 어리석은, 바보 같은; 우스꽝스러운; n. 바보
If you say that someone or something is silly, you mean that they are foolish, childish, or ridiculous.

snap ^{복습}
[snæp]

v. 급히 움직이다; 딱 소리 내다; 딱 부러지다; (동물이) 물려고 하다; n. 탁 하는 소리
If you snap something into a particular position, or if it snaps into that position, it moves quickly into that position, with a sharp sound.

rear ^{복습}
[riər]

a. 뒤쪽의; n. 궁둥이; 뒤쪽; v. 앞다리를 들어올리며 서다
Your rear is the part of your body that you sit on.

curve ^{복습}
[kəːrv]

v. 곡선으로 나아가다, 곡선을 이루다; n. 커브, 곡선
If something curves, or if someone or something curves it, it has the shape of a curve.

spray[*]
[sprei]

v. 뿌리다; (작은 것을 아주 많이) 뿌리다; n. 물보라; 분무기; 뿌리기
If you spray a liquid somewhere or if it sprays somewhere, drops of the liquid cover a place or shower someone.

confine[*]
[kənfáin]

n. (pl.) 한계, 범위; v. 넣다, 가두다; 국한시키다
The confines of a place is the borders or edges of that place.

devastate
[dévəstèit]

v. 완전히 파괴하다; (사람에게) 엄청난 충격을 주다 (devastating a. 대단히 파괴적인)
If you describe something as devastating, you are emphasizing that it is very harmful or damaging.

sulfurous
[sʌ́lfjərəs]

a. 유황과 같은
Sulfurous air or places contain sulfur or smell of sulfur.

rotten^{복습}
[ratn]

a. 썩은, 부패한; 형편없는, 끔찍한
If food, wood, or another substance is rotten, it has decayed and can no longer be used.

odor^{복습}
[óudər]

n. (불쾌한) 냄새, 악취
An odor is a particular and distinctive smell.

stink
[stiŋk]

v. (고약한) 냄새가 나다, 악취가 풍기다; 수상쩍다; n. 악취
(stinking a. 악취가 나는, 냄새가 고약한)
You use stinking to describe something that is unpleasant or bad.

corrosive
[kəróusiv]

a. 부식성의; (정신적으로) 좀먹는
A corrosive substance is able to destroy solid materials by a chemical reaction.

sear
[siər]

v. (강한 통증 등이) 후끈 치밀다, 화끈거리게 하다; 그슬다
If something sears a part of your body, it causes a painful burning feeling there.

blind^{복습}
[blaind]

v. (잠시) 앞이 안 보이게 하다; 눈이 멀게 하다; a. 눈이 먼; 눈치 채지 못하는
If something blinds you, it makes you unable to see, either for a short time or permanently.

claw^{복습}
[klɔː]

v. 헤치며 나아가다; (손톱 · 발톱으로) 할퀴다; n. (동물 · 새의) 발톱
If you claw your way somewhere, you move there with great difficulty, trying desperately to find things to hold on to.

shore^{복습}
[ʃɔːr]

n. 기슭, 해안, 호숫가
The shores or the shore of a sea, lake, or wide river is the land along the edge of it.

stumble^{복습}
[stʌmbl]

v. 비틀거리다; 발을 헛디디다; (말 · 글 읽기를 하다가) 더듬거리다
If you stumble, you put your foot down awkwardly while you are walking or running and nearly fall over.

trip^{복습}
[trip]

v. 발을 헛디디다; ~를 넘어뜨리다; n. 여행; 발을 헛디딤
If you trip when you are walking, you knock your foot against something and fall or nearly fall.

scramble^{복습}
[skræmbl]

v. 재빨리 움직이다; 허둥지둥 해내다; n. (힘들게) 기어가기; 서로 밀치기
If you scramble to a different place or position, you move there in a hurried, awkward way.

back and forth^{복습}

idiom 여기저기에, 왔다갔다; 좌우로; 앞뒤로
If someone moves back and forth, they repeatedly move in one direction and then in the opposite direction.

slash^{복습}
[slæʃ]

v. 긋다, 베다; 대폭 줄이다; n. (칼 등으로) 긋기
If you slash something, you make a long, deep cut in it.

cartoon[*]
[ka:rtúːn]

n. 만화 영화, 만화
A cartoon is a humorous drawing or series of drawings in a newspaper or magazine.

joke^{복습}
[dʒouk]

v. 농담하다; 농담 삼아 말하다; n. 농담; 웃음거리
If you joke, you tell someone something that is not true in order to amuse yourself.

lifetime*
[láiftàim]

n. 평생, 일생, 생애
A lifetime is the length of time that someone is alive.

permanent**
[pə́:rmənənt]

a. 영구적인; 오래가는 (permanently ad. 영원히)
Something that is permanent lasts for ever.

impair
[impέər]

v. 손상시키다
If something impairs something such as an ability or the way something works, it damages it or makes it worse.

last**
[læst]

v. (특정한 시간 동안) 계속되다; 견디다, 버티다; 오래가다; ad. 맨 끝에, 마지막에
If an event, situation, or problem lasts for a particular length of time, it continues to exist or happen for that length of time.

lick**
[lik]

v. 핥다; 핥아먹다; n. 한 번 핥기, 핥아먹기
When people or animals lick something, they move their tongue across its surface.

thrash
[θræʃ]

v. 몸부림치다; 마구 때리다; n. 때림, 패배시킴
If someone thrashes about, or thrashes their arms or legs about, they move in a wild or violent way, often hitting against something.

carp
[ka:rp]

n. [동물] 잉어
A carp is a kind of fish that lives in lakes and rivers.

set about

idiom ~을 시작하다
If you set about doing something such as a task or an activity, you begin it, especially with energy or enthusiasm.

go on**

idiom (어떤 상황이) 계속되다; 말을 계속하다; 자자, 어서
To go on something means to continue an activity without stopping.

shortcut
[ʃɔ́:rtkʌ̀t]

n. 손쉬운 방법; 지름길
A shortcut is a method of achieving something more quickly or more easily than if you use the usual methods.

improve**
[imprú:v]

v. 개선하다, 향상시키다
If something improves or if you improve it, it gets better.

pine**
[pain]

n. 소나무
A pine tree or a pine is a tall tree which has very thin, sharp leaves and a fresh smell. Pine trees have leaves all year round.

fasten*
[fǽsn]

v. 고정시키다; 매다, 채우다; (단단히) 잠그다
If you fasten one thing to another, you attach the first thing to the second, for example with a piece of string or tape.

wedge*
[wedʒ]

v. (좁은 틈 사이에) 끼워 넣다; 고정시키다; n. 분열의 원인; 쐐기
If you wedge something somewhere, you fit it there tightly.

weave**
[wi:v]

v. (wove–woven) (옷감 등을) 짜다; 이리저리 빠져 나가다; n. 엮어서 만든 것; (직물을) 짜는 법
If you weave something such as a basket, you make it by crossing long plant stems or fibers over and under each other.

branch**
[brænʧ]

n. 나뭇가지; 지사, 분점; v. 갈라지다, 나뉘다
The branches of a tree are the parts that grow out from its trunk and have leaves, flowers, or fruit growing on them.

138

satisfied ^{복습}
[sǽtisfàid]

a. 만족하는, 흡족해하는; 납득하는
If you are satisfied with something, you are happy because you have got what you wanted or needed.

fist *
[fist]

n. 주먹
Your hand is referred to as your fist when you have bent your fingers in toward the palm in order to hit someone, to make an angry gesture, or to hold something.

judge ^{복습}
[dʒʌdʒ]

v. 판단하다; 심판을 보다; 짐작하다; n. 판사; 심판, 심사위원
If you judge something or someone, you form an opinion about them after you have examined the evidence or thought carefully about them.

spot ^{복습}
[spat]

n. (특정한) 곳; (작은) 점; v. 발견하다, 찾다, 알아채다
You can refer to a particular place as a spot.

mesh
[meʃ]

n. 그물망, 철망; v. 딱 들어맞다; 맞물리다
Mesh is material like a net made from wire, thread, or plastic.

hinge *
[hindʒ]

n. (문·뚜껑 등의) 경첩
A hinge is a piece of metal, wood, or plastic that is used to join a door to its frame or to join two things together so that one of them can swing freely.

method **
[méθəd]

n. 방법; 체계성
A method is a particular way of doing something.

hook ^{복습}
[huk]

v. 갈고리로 잠그다; (낚싯바늘로) 낚다; n. (낚시) 바늘; (갈)고리
If you hook one thing to another, you attach it there using a hook.

relative ^{복습}
[rélətiv]

a. 비교적인; 상대적인; 관계가 있는; n. 친척 (relatively ad. 비교적)
Relatively means to a certain degree, especially when compared with other things of the same kind.

structure **
[strʌ́kʧər]

n. 구조물, 건축물; 구조; v. 조직하다, 구조화하다
A structure is something that has been built.

filter *
[fíltər]

v. 새어 들어오다; 여과하다, 거르다; n. 여과기
If light or sound filters into a place, it comes in weakly or slowly, either through a partly covered opening, or from a long distance away.

all in all

idiom 대체로
You use all in all to introduce a summary or general statement.

bathe ^{복습}
[beið]

v. (강·바다 등에서) 멱을 감다; (몸을) 씻다, 세척하다; (빛으로) 휩싸다
If you bathe in a sea, river, or lake, you swim, play, or wash yourself in it.

constant ^{복습}
[kánstənt]

a. 끊임없는; 거듭되는; 변함없는
You use constant to describe something that happens all the time or is always there.

lay up

idiom (병·부상으로) ~를 드러눕게 하다
If someone is laid up, they are unable to work or take part in an activity because they are ill, sick, or injured.

temporary[**] [témpərèri]
a. 일시적인, 임시의 (temporarily ad. 일시적으로, 임시로)
Something that is temporary lasts for only a limited time.

rock face [rák feis]
n. (수직으로 서 있는) 바위 표면
A rock face is a bare vertical surface of natural rock.

ledge[복습] [ledʒ]
n. 절벽에서 튀어나온 바위; (벽에서 튀어나온) 선반
A ledge is a piece of rock on the side of a cliff or mountain, which is in the shape of a narrow shelf.

storage[*] [stɔ́:ridʒ]
n. 저장고, 보관소; 저장
If you refer to the storage of something, you mean that it is kept in a special place until it is needed.

reachable [ri:tʃəbl]
a. 가 닿을 수 있는, 도달 가능한 (unreachable a. 도달할 수 없는)
If you describe someone or something as unreachable, they are unable to be reached or contacted.

ladder[*] [lǽdər]
n. 사다리
A ladder is a piece of equipment used for climbing up something or down from something. It consists of two long pieces of wood, metal, or rope with steps fixed between them.

fashion[복습] [fǽʃən]
v. (손으로) 만들다; n. 방법, 방식; 유행(하는 스타일)
If you fashion an object or a work of art, you make it.

hatchet[복습] [hǽtʃit]
n. 손도끼
A hatchet is a small ax that you can hold in one hand.

chop[복습] [tʃap]
v. (장작 같은 것을) 패다; 내려치다; n. 내리치기, 찍기
(chop off idiom ~을 (~에서) 잘라 내다)
If you chop something off, you remove it by cutting it with a sharp heavy tool.

drag[복습] [dræg]
v. 끌다, 끌고 가다; 힘들게 움직이다; n. 끌기, 당기기; 장애물
If you drag something, you pull it along the ground, often with difficulty.

prop[복습] [prap]
v. 떠받치다; n. (연극·영화에 쓰이는) 소품; 지주, 버팀목
If you prop an object on or against something, you support it by putting something underneath it or by resting it somewhere.

manure [mənjúər]
n. (동물의 배설물로 만든) 거름; v. 거름을 주다
Manure is animal faeces, sometimes mixed with chemicals, that is spread on the ground in order to make plants grow healthy and strong.

scrape[복습] [skreip]
v. (무엇을) 긁어내다; (상처가 나도록) 긁다; n. 긁기; 긁힌 상처
If you scrape something from a surface, you remove it, especially by pulling a sharp object over the surface.

snug[복습] [snʌg]
a. 꼭 맞는; 포근한, 아늑한
Something such as a piece of clothing that is snug fits very closely or tightly.

grease[복습] [gri:s]
v. 기름을 바르다; n. 기름, 지방
If you grease a part of a car, machine, or device, you put oily substance on it in order to make it work smoothly.

140

bearing *
[béəriŋ]

n. (기계의) 베어링; 관련, 영향; 태도, 자세
Bearings are small metal balls that are placed between moving parts of a machine in order to make them move smoothly and easily over each other.

salmon *
[sǽmən]

n. [동물] 연어
A salmon is a large silver-colored fish.

overnight *
[òuvərnáit]

a. 야간의; 하룻밤 동안의; ad. 밤사이에, 하룻밤 동안
If you describe something as overnight, you mean that you are working, travelling, or happening during the night.

waste 복습
[weist]

n. (pl.) 쓰레기, 폐기물; 낭비, 허비; v. 낭비하다; 헛되이 쓰다
Waste is material which has been used and is no longer wanted, for example because the valuable or useful part of it has been taken out.

dangle
[dǽŋgl]

v. (무엇을 들고) 달랑거리다; 매달리다
If something dangles from somewhere or if you dangle it somewhere, it hangs or swings loosely.

trap 복습
[træp]

v. 덫으로 잡다; (위험한 장소에) 가두다; 끌어모으다; n. 덫; 함정
If a person traps animals or birds, he or she catches them using traps.

pond 복습
[pand]

n. 연못
A pond is a small area of water that is smaller than a lake.

bluff 복습
[blʌf]

n. (바다나 강가의) 절벽; 허세, 엄포; v. 허세를 부리다, 엄포를 놓다
A bluff is a cliff or very steep bank by the sea or river.

pile 복습
[pail]

n. 무더기; 쌓아 놓은 것, 더미; v. (차곡차곡) 쌓다; 우르르 가다
A pile of things is a mass of them that is high in the middle and has sloping sides.

chunk *
[ʧʌŋk]

n. 덩어리; 상당히 많은 양; v. 덩어리로 나누다
Chunks of something are thick solid pieces of it.

splinter 복습
[splíntər]

n. (나무·금속·유리 등의) 조각; v. 쪼개지다, 깨지다; 분열되다, 갈라지다
A splinter is a very thin, sharp piece of wood, glass, or other hard substance, which has broken off from a larger piece.

hunk
[hʌŋk]

n. 큰 덩어리, 두꺼운 조각
A hunk of something is a large piece of it.

amount to

idiom 결과적으로 ~이 되다, ~에 해당하다
To amount to something means to be the same as it, or to have the same effect as it.

pen *
[pen]

n. (가축의) 우리, 펜; v. (동물·사람을 우리 등에) 가두다; (글 등을) 쓰다
A pen is a small area with a fence round it in which farm animals are kept for a short time.

come together 복습

idiom (하나로) 합치다
If two or more people or things come together, they form one group or one piece.

dart *
[da:rt]

v. 쏜살같이 움직이다; 흘깃 쳐다보다; n. (작은) 화살; 쏜살같이 달림
If a person or animal darts somewhere, they move there suddenly and quickly.

trash[*]
[træʃ]

n. 쓰레기; v. 부수다, 엉망으로 만들다; (필요 없는 것을) 버리다
Trash consists of unwanted things or waste material such as used paper, empty containers and bottles, and waste food.

prospect[**]
[práspekt]

n. (어떤 일이 있을) 가망, 가능성; 예상
If there is some prospect of something happening, there is a possibility that it will happen.

enclose[**]
[inklóuz]

v. (담·울타리 등으로) 두르다; 동봉하다 (enclosure n. 울타리를 친 장소)
An enclosure is an area of land that is surrounded by a wall or fence and that is used for a particular purpose.

fine[복습]
[fain]

a. 아주 가는; 질 높은, 좋은; 괜찮은; n. 벌금
Something that is fine is very delicate, narrow, or small.

yell[복습]
[jel]

v. 고함치다, 소리 지르다; n. 고함, 외침
If you yell, you shout loudly, usually because you are excited, angry, or in pain.

breakthrough
[bréikθrùː]

n. 돌파구
A breakthrough is an important development or achievement.

142

1. What did NOT make hunting foolbirds difficult?

   A. They blended in with their surroundings.

   B. They would suddenly explode into flight.

   C. They hid in incredibly small places.

   D. They stood completely still.

2. What was the secret to finding foolbirds?

   A. Looking for the outline of their body instead of their color

   B. Looking for the color of their feathers instead of their outline

   C. Listening for the sound of their feathers instead of their song

   D. Listening for the sound of their song instead of their feathers

3. What was part of Brian's strategy for catching foolbirds?

   A. He approached them with unpredictable movements.

   B. He approached them at an angle.

   C. He walked backward toward them.

   D. He walked straight toward them.

4. What caused the moose to attack him a second time?

   A. When he cried out, the sound of his voice frightened the moose.

   B. When he tried to get out of the lake, his movements made the moose upset.

   C. When he stepped on a lily pad root, the moose got angry.

   D. When he made eye contact with the moose, the moose felt threatened.

5. What did he think of the moose attack?

   A. He thought he had done a good job of defending himself.

   B. He felt like he had learned an important lesson.

   C. He sincerely regretted making the moose mad.

   D. He could not figure out why the moose had attacked him.

6. How did he react after the tornado was over?

   A. He was emotional about all the bad luck he had had.

   B. He got stressed by how dangerous nature was.

   C. He knew he was strong enough to move on.

   D. He wished the tornado had not destroyed so many things.

7. Why was he sad when he saw the plane sticking out of the water?

   A. He remembered that the pilot was still inside of the plane.

   B. He could not understand why the pilot had died and he had survived.

   C. He realized that the plane could not be repaired or flown again without a pilot.

   D. He thought about how much his life had changed since the flight.

1분에 몇 단어를 읽는지 리딩 속도를 측정해보세요.

$$\frac{2{,}204 \text{ words}}{\text{reading time (} \quad \text{) sec}} \times 60 = (\qquad) \text{ WPM}$$

Build Your Vocabulary

measure ^{복습}
[méʒər]

v. 측정하다; 판단하다; n. 조치, 정책; 척도
If you measure a quantity that can be expressed in numbers, such as the length of something, you discover it using a particular instrument or device, for example a ruler.

burn ^{복습}
[bəːrn]

v. (마음 등에) 새겨지다; 데다, (햇볕 등에) 타다; 불에 타다; 화끈거리다; n. 화상
To burn into means to implant something firmly in someone's head, brain, or memory.

mental ^{복습}
[mentl]

a. 마음의, 정신의; 정신병의
Mental means relating to the process of thinking.

journal ^{복습}
[dʒəːrnl]

n. 일기; 저널, 학술지
A journal is an account which you write of your daily activities.

camp ^{복습}
[kæmp]

n. 야영지; 수용소; 진영; v. 야영하다
A camp is an outdoor area with buildings, tents, or caravans where people stay on holiday.

crave ^{복습}
[kreiv]

v. 열망하다, 갈망하다; 간절히 원하다
If you crave something, you want to have it very much.

saliva ^{복습}
[səláivə]

n. 침, 타액
Saliva is the watery liquid that forms in your mouth and helps you to chew and digest food.

intent [*]
[intént]

a. 작정한; ~에 전념하는; 몰두하는; n. 의도
If you are intent on doing something, you are eager and determined to do it.

quarter ^{**}
[kwɔ́ːrtər]

n. 4분의 1; 구역; v. 4등분하다; 숙소를 제공하다
A quarter is one of four equal parts of something.

squirrel ^{복습}
[skwɔ́ːrəl]

n. [동물] 다람쥐
A squirrel is a small animal with a long furry tail.

chatter ^{복습}
[ʃǽtər]

v. 재잘거리다; 수다를 떨다; n. 수다, 재잘거림; 딱딱거리는 소리
When birds or animals chatter, they make high-pitched noises.

swear ^{복습}
[swɛər]

v. 욕을 하다; 맹세하다
If someone swears, they use language that is considered to be rude or offensive, usually because they are angry.

limb ^{복습}
[lim]

n. (큰) 나뭇가지; (하나의) 팔, 다리
The limbs of a tree are its branches.

146

reddish ^{복습}
[rédiʃ]

a. 발그레한, 불그스름한
Reddish means slightly red in color.

fur ^{복습}
[fəːr]

n. (동물의) 털; 모피
Fur is the thick and usually soft hair that grows on the bodies of many mammals.

dawn ^{복습}
[dɔːn]

n. 새벽, 여명; v. 분명해지다, 이해되기 시작하다; 밝다
Dawn is the time of day when light first appears in the sky, just before the sun rises.

bound[*]
[baund]

v. 뛰어가다, 껑충껑충 달리다; 튀어오르다; a. ~할 가능성이 큰
If a person or animal bounds in a particular direction, they move quickly with large steps or jumps.

freeze ^{복습}
[friːz]

v. (두려움 등으로 몸이) 얼어붙다; 얼다; n. 얼어붙음; 동결; 한파
If someone who is moving freezes, they suddenly stop and become completely still and quiet.

spear ^{복습}
[spiər]

n. 창; v. (창 등으로) 찌르다; (물고기를) 작살로 잡다
A spear is a weapon consisting of a long pole with a sharp metal point attached to the end.

fool ^{복습}
[fuːl]

n. 바보; a. 바보 같은; v. 속이다, 기만하다
If you call someone a fool, you are indicating that you think they are not at all sensible and show a lack of good judgment.

exasperate ^{복습}
[igzǽspərèit]

v. 몹시 화나게 하다, 짜증나게 하다
If someone or something exasperates you, they annoy you and make you feel frustrated or upset.

insane[*]
[inséin]

a. 제정신이 아닌; 정신 이상의, 미친
If you describe a decision or action as insane, you think it is very foolish or excessive.

flock ^{복습}
[flak]

n. (동물의) 떼; (사람들) 무리; v. (많은 수가) 모이다; 떼 지어 가다
A flock of birds, sheep, or goats is a group of them.

camouflage
[kǽməflàːʒ]

n. 위장; 속임수; v. 위장하다, 감추다
Camouflage is the way in which some animals are colored and shaped so that they cannot easily be seen in their natural surroundings.

lean ^{복습}
[liːn]

v. ~에 기대다; 기울이다, (몸을) 숙이다; a. 군살이 없는, 호리호리한
When you lean in a particular direction, you bend your body in that direction.

clump ^{복습}
[klʌmp]

n. 수풀; 무리, 무더기; v. 무리를 짓다, 함께 모이다
If you lean on or against someone or something, you rest against them so that they partly support your weight.

explode ^{복습}
[iksplóud]

v. 갑자기 ~하다; 폭발하다; (강한 감정을) 터뜨리다
To explode means to move very quickly.

deafening
[défəniŋ]

a. 귀청이 터질 듯한, 귀가 먹먹한
A deafening noise is a very loud noise.

flight ^{복습}
[flait]

n. 비행; 탈출, 도피; 항공기; 계단, 층계
A flight of birds is a group of them flying together.

figure out [복습]   idiom ~을 이해하다, 알아내다; 계산하다, 산출하다
If you figure out someone or something, you come to understand them by thinking carefully.

locate *   v. ~의 정확한 위치를 찾아내다; (특정 위치에) 두다
[lóukeit]   If you locate something or someone, you find out where they are.

blend in   idiom (주위 환경에) 섞여들다; 조화를 이루다
If something blends in with something else or with its surroundings, it looks similar to it or them, or matches well.

dumb *   a. 멍청한, 바보 같은; 말을 못 하는
[dʌm]   If you say that something is dumb, you think that it is silly and annoying.

insulting *   a. 모욕적인
[insʌ́ltiŋ]   Something that is insulting is rude or offensive.

fright [복습]   n. 놀람, 두려움
[frait]   Fright is a sudden feeling of fear, especially the fear that you feel when something unpleasant surprises you.

memorable   a. 기억할 만한
[mémərəbl]   Something that is memorable is worth remembering or likely to be remembered, because it is special or very enjoyable.

pitch   n. 송진; (감정 · 활동의) 정도; 음의 높이; v. 내던지다; (소리 · 음을 특정한 높이로) 내다
[pitʃ]   (pitchy a. 끈끈한)
Pitch is a resin derived from the sap of various coniferous trees, as the pines.

stump *   n. (나무의) 그루터기; 남은 부분; v. 당황하게 하다; 쿵쿵거리며 걷다
[stʌmp]   A stump is a small part of something that remains when the rest of it has been removed or broken off.

blow [복습]   v. 폭파하다; (바람 · 입김에) 날리다; (입으로) 불다; n. 세게 때림, 강타; 충격
[blou]   To blow something out, off, or away means to remove or destroy it violently with an explosion.

set out [복습]   idiom (일 · 과제 등에) 착수하다; (여행을) 시작하다
If you set out, you start an activity with a particular aim.

halfway [복습]   ad. (거리 · 시간상으로) 가운데쯤에; 부분적으로, 불완전하게
[hǽfwèi]   Halfway means in the middle of a place or between two points, at an equal distance from each of them.

give up   idiom 포기하다; 그만두다; 단념하다
If you give up, you stop trying to do something, usually because it is too difficult.

work out [복습]   idiom ~을 해결하다; ~을 계획해 내다
If you work things out, you solve problems by considering the facts.

sarcasm   n. 빈정댐, 비꼼
[sá:rkæzm]   Sarcasm is speech or writing which actually means the opposite of what it seems to say. Sarcasm is usually intended to mock or insult someone.

148

fry *
[frai]

v. (기름에) 굽다, 튀기다
When you fry food, you cook it in a pan that contains hot fat or oil.

catch one's eye 복습
idiom 눈에 띄다; 눈길을 끌다
If something catches your eye, you suddenly notice it.

land 복습
[lænd]

v. (땅·표면에) 내려앉다, 착륙하다; 놓다, 두다; n. 육지, 땅; 지역
When someone or something lands, they come down to the ground after moving through the air or falling.

pointed 복습
[pɔ́intid]

a. (끝이) 뾰족한; (말 등이) 날카로운
Something that is pointed has a point at one end.

streamlined
[strí:mlaind]

a. 유선형의, 날씬한
A streamlined vehicle, animal, or object has a shape that allows it to move quickly or efficiently through air or water.

bullet **
[búlit]

n. 총알
A bullet is a small piece of metal with a pointed or rounded end, which is fired out of a gun.

pear *
[pɛər]

n. (서양) 배
A pear is a sweet, juicy fruit which is narrow near its stalk, and wider and rounded at the bottom. Pears have white flesh and thin green or yellow skin.

feather 복습
[féðər]

n. (새의) 털, 깃털; v. 깃털로 덮다
A bird's feathers are the soft covering on its body. Each feather consists of a lot of smooth hairs on each side of a thin stiff center.

outline *
[áutlàin]

n. 윤곽; v. 윤곽을 보여주다; 개요를 서술하다
The outline of something is its general shape, especially when it cannot be clearly seen.

flop
[flap]

v. ~을 떨어뜨리다; 퍼덕거리다; 털썩 주저앉다; n. 실패작
If something flops onto something else, it falls there heavily or untidily.

stabilize
[stéibəlàiz]

v. 안정시키다; 고정시키다
If something stabilizes, or is stabilized, it becomes stable.

twig 복습
[twig]

n. (나무의) 잔가지
A twig is a very small thin branch that grows out from a main branch of a tree or bush.

distance 복습
[dístəns]

n. 거리; 먼 곳; v. (~에) 관여하지 않다
The distance between two points or places is the amount of space between them.

prong 복습
[prɔːŋ]

n. (뾰족하게 나뉘어져 있는) 갈래
The prongs of something such as a fork are the long, thin pointed parts.

amaze 복습
[əméiz]

v. (대단히) 놀라게 하다; 경악하게 하다 (amazingly ad. 놀랄 만큼, 굉장하게)
You say that something is amazing when it is very surprising and makes you feel pleasure, approval, or wonder.

angle ^{복습}
[ǽŋgl]

n. 기울기; 각도, 각; 관점; v. 비스듬히 움직이다
An angle is the difference in direction between two lines or surfaces. Angles are measured in degrees.

thrust ^{복습}
[θrʌst]

v. 찌르다; (거칠게) 밀다; n. 추진력; 찌르기
If you thrust something or someone somewhere, you push or move them there quickly with a lot of force.

lunge ^{복습}
[lʌndʒ]

v. 달려들다, 돌진하다; n. 돌진
If you lunge in a particular direction, you move in that direction suddenly and clumsily.

come close

idiom 거의 ~할 뻔하다
If you come close to do something, you almost achieve it or do it.

flutter [*]
[flʌ́tər]

v. (날개를) 파닥이다; 훨훨 날아가다; (가볍게) 흔들다; n. 흔들림; 소동, 혼란
If something light such as a small bird or a piece of paper flutters somewhere, it moves through the air with small quick movements.

trot ^{복습}
[trat]

v. 빨리 걷다; 총총걸음을 걷다; n. 속보, 빠른 걸음
If you trot somewhere, you move fairly fast at a speed between walking and running, taking small quick steps.

glow ^{복습}
[glou]

v. 빛나다, 타다; (얼굴이) 상기되다; n. (은은한) 불빛; 홍조
If something glows, it produces a dull, steady light.

neat ^{복습}
[ni:t]

a. 깔끔한; 정돈된, 단정한; 뛰어난
A neat place, thing, or person is tidy and smart, and has everything in the correct place.

bake ^{복습}
[beik]

v. (음식을) 굽다; (열로) 굽다
If you bake, you spend some time preparing and mixing together ingredients to make bread, cakes, pies, or other food which is cooked in the oven.

get rid of

idiom ~을 처리하다, 없애다
When you get rid of something that you do not want or do not like, you take action so that you no longer have it or suffer from it.

come off

idiom 떼어낼 수 있다
If something such as dirt or paint comes off something, it is removed by washing or rubbing.

pluck ^{복습}
[plʌk]

v. (잡아 당겨) 빼내다; (기타 등의 현을) 뜯다
If you pluck something from somewhere, you take it between your fingers and pull it sharply from where it is.

fragile [*]
[frǽdʒəl]

a. 부서지기 쉬운; 섬세한
Something that is fragile is easily broken or damaged.

peel ^{복습}
[pi:l]

v. (과일 · 채소 등의) 껍질을 벗기다; 껍질이 벗겨지다; n. 껍질
When you peel fruit or vegetables, you remove their skins.

immediate ^{복습}
[imí:diət]

a. 즉각적인; 당면한; 아주 가까이에 있는 (immediately ad. 즉시, 즉각)
If something happens immediately, it happens without any delay.

raw^{복습}
[rɔː]

a. 익히지 않은; 가공되지 않은; 다듬어지지 않은
Raw food is food that is eaten uncooked, that has not yet been cooked, or that has not been cooked enough.

odor^{복습}
[óudər]

n. (불쾌한) 냄새, 악취
An odor is a particular and distinctive smell.

dung
[dʌŋ]

n. (큰 동물의) 똥
Dung is faeces from animals, especially from large animals such as cattle and horses.

coil[*]
[kɔil]

n. 고리; 전선; v. (고리 모양으로) 감다, 휘감다
A coil of rope or wire is a length of it that has been wound into a series of loops.

throw up^{복습}

idiom ~을 토하다; ~을 두드러지게 하다
If you throw up, you bring food you have eaten back out of your mouth.

hunger^{복습}
[hʌ́ŋgər]

n. 배고픔; 굶주림; 갈망
Hunger is the feeling of weakness or discomfort that you get when you need something to eat.

overcome^{복습}
[ouvərkʌ́m]

v. (overcame–overcome) 극복하다; 꼼짝 못하게 되다, 압도당하다
If you overcome a problem or a feeling, you successfully deal with it and control it.

breast^{**}
[brest]

n. (새·동물의) 가슴살; 가슴
You can refer to piece of meat that is cut from the front of a bird or lamb as breast.

feed^{복습}
[fiːd]

v. 먹이를 주다; 공급하다; 먹여 살리다; n. (동물의) 먹이
If you feed a person or animal, you give them food to eat and sometimes actually put it in their mouths.

stiff^{복습}
[stif]

a. 뻣뻣한; 결리는, 뻐근한; 경직된; 심한; ad. 몹시, 극심하게
Something that is stiff is firm or does not bend easily.

band[*]
[bænd]

v. 줄무늬를 두르다; 묶다; n. 무리, 일행; 띠, 끈 (banded a. 줄무늬 모양의)
If something is banded, it has one or more bands on it, often of a different color which contrasts with the main color.

speckle^{복습}
[spekl]

n. 작은 반점 (specked a. 작은 반점들이 있는, 얼룩덜룩한)
A speckled surface is covered with small marks, spots, or shapes.

tear^{복습}
[tɛər]

① v. 찢다, 뜯다; 뜯어 내다; n. 찢어진 곳, 구멍 ② n. 눈물
If a person or animal tears at something, they pull it violently and try to break it into pieces.

increase^{복습}
[inkríːs]

v. (양·수·가치 등이) 증가하다, 인상되다, 늘다; n. 증가
If something increases or you increase it, it becomes greater in number, level, or amount.

magical[*]
[mǽdʒikəl]

a. 마술적인, 마술에 실린 (것한); 홀홀한 아주 멋진 (magically ad. 신비하게)
Something that is magical seems to use magic or to be able to produce magic.

flame ^{복습}
[fleim]

n. 불길, 불꽃; 격정; v. 활활 타오르다; 시뻘게지다
A flame is a hot bright stream of burning gas that comes from something that is burning.

ignite ^{복습}
[ignáit]

v. 불을 붙이다, 점화하다
When you ignite something or when it ignites, it starts burning or explodes.

proper ^{복습}
[prápər]

a. 적절한, 제대로 된; 올바른, 정당한 (properly ad. 제대로, 적절히)
The proper thing is the one that is correct or most suitable.

drip ^{복습}
[drip]

v. (액체가) 뚝뚝 흐르다; 가득 담고 있다; n. (액체가) 뚝뚝 떨어짐
When liquid drips somewhere, or you drip it somewhere, it falls in individual small drops.

rotate *
[róuteit]

v. 회전하다; 교대로 하다
When something rotates or when you rotate it, it turns with a circular movement.

fork ^{복습}
[fɔ:rk]

v. 갈라지다, 나뉘다; n. 포크; (도로 · 강 등의) 분기점 (forked a. 끝이 갈라진)
Something that divides into two parts and forms a 'Y' shape can be described as forked.

method ^{복습}
[méθəd]

n. 방법; 체계성
A method is a particular way of doing something.

patient ^{복습}
[péiʃənt]

a. 참을성 있는, 인내심 있는; n. 환자 (patience n. 인내심)
If you have patience, you are able to stay calm and not get annoyed, for example when something takes a long time, or when someone is not doing what you want them to do.

settle ^{복습}
[setl]

v. 자리를 잡다; 진정되다; (서서히) 가라앉다; 결정하다
If you settle yourself somewhere or settle somewhere, you sit down or make yourself comfortable.

chew ^{복습}
[ʧu:]

v. (음식을) 씹다; 물어뜯다, 깨물다; 심사숙고하다; n. 씹기, 깨물기
When you chew food, you use your teeth to break it up in your mouth so that it becomes easier to swallow.

bite ^{복습}
[bait]

n. 한 입; (짐승 · 곤충에게) 물린 상처; 물기; v. (곤충 · 뱀 등이) 물다; 베어 물다
A bite of something, especially food, is the action of biting it.

1분에 몇 단어를 읽는지 리딩 속도를 측정해보세요.

$$\frac{3,157 \text{ words}}{\text{reading time ( ) sec}} \times 60 = (\quad) \text{ WPM}$$

Build Your Vocabulary

arrow ^{복습}
[ǽrou]

n. 화살; 화살표
An arrow is a long thin weapon which is sharp and pointed at one end and which often has feathers at the other end. An arrow is shot from a bow.

thread ^{복습}
[θred]

n. 실; (가느다란) 줄기; v. (실 등을) 꿰다
Thread or a thread is a long very thin piece of a material such as cotton, nylon, or silk, especially one that is used in sewing.

tatter ^{복습}
[tǽtər]

v. 갈가리 찢다; n. (pl.) 넝마, 누더기 (tattered a. 낡을 대로 낡은, 누더기가 된)
If something such as clothing or a book is tattered, it is damaged or torn, especially because it has been used a lot over a long period of time.

pitch ^{복습}
[pitʃ]

n. 송진; (감정 · 활동의) 정도; 음의 높이; v. 내던지다; (소리 · 음을 특정한 높이로) 내다
Pitch is a resin derived from the sap of various coniferous trees, as the pines.

stump ^{복습}
[stʌmp]

n. (나무의) 그루터기; 남은 부분; v. 당황하게 하다; 쿵쿵거리며 걷다
A stump is a small part of something that remains when the rest of it has been removed or broken off.

sliver ^{복습}
[slívər]

n. (깨지거나 잘라 낸) 조각
A sliver of something is a small thin piece or amount of it.

feather ^{복습}
[féðər]

n. (새의) 털, 깃털; v. 깃털로 덮다
A bird's feathers are the soft covering on its body. Each feather consists of a lot of smooth hairs on each side of a thin stiff center.

shaft ^{복습}
[ʃæft]

n. 화살대; (기다란) 손잡이; 수직 통로, 수갱
A shaft is a long thin piece of wood or metal that forms part of a spear, ax, golf club, or other object.

accurate ^{★★}
[ǽkjurət]

a. 정확한; 정밀한 (accurately ad. 정확히)
An accurate weapon or throw reaches the exact point or target that it was intended to reach.

skin ^{복습}
[skin]

v. (동물의) 가죽을 벗기다; (피부가) 까지다; n. 피부; (동물의) 껍질, 가죽, 외피
If you skin a dead animal, you remove its skin.

meat ^{복습}
[mi:t]

n. 고기
Meat is flesh taken from a dead animal that people cook and eat.

strip ^{복습}
[strip]

n. 가느다란 조각; v. (물건을) 다 뜯어내다; 옷을 벗다
A strip of something such as paper, cloth, or food is a long, narrow piece of it.

stand ^{복습}
[stænd]

n. 수목, 관목; 가판대, 좌판; v. 서다; (어떤 위치에) 세우다
A stand is a group of growing plants of a specified kind, especially trees.

nut [*]
[nʌt]

n. 견과; 너트; 괴짜, 미친 사람
The firm shelled fruit of some trees and bushes are called nuts. Some nuts can be eaten.

brush ^{복습}
[brʌʃ]

n. 덤불, 잡목 숲; 붓; 솔; v. (솔이나 손으로) 털다; 솔질을 하다; ~을 스치다
Brush is an area of rough open land covered with small bushes and trees. You also use brush to refer to the bushes and trees on this land.

bush ^{복습}
[buʃ]

n. 관목, 덤불; 우거진 것
A bush is a large plant which is smaller than a tree and has a lot of branches.

stickler
[stíklər]

n. 까다로운 사람
If you are a stickler for something, you always demand or require it.

pod
[pad]

n. (콩이 들어 있는) 꼬투리
A pod is a seed container that grows on plants such as peas or beans.

ripe ^{복습}
[raip]

a. 익은, 여문
Ripe fruit or grain is fully grown and ready to eat.

stem ^{복습}
[stem]

n. 줄기, 대
The stem of a plant is the thin, upright part on which the flowers and leaves grow.

pause ^{복습}
[pɔːz]

v. (말·일을 하다가) 잠시 멈추다; 정지시키다; n. (말·행동 등의) 멈춤
If you pause while you are doing something, you stop for a short period and then continue.

cricket [*]
[kríkit]

n. [곤충] 귀뚜라미
A cricket is a small jumping insect that produces short, loud sounds by rubbing its wings together.

sign ^{***}
[sain]

n. 신호, 표시; 기색, 흔적; 표지판, 간판; v. 서명하다; 신호를 보내다
A sign is a movement of your arms, hands, or head which is intended to have a particular meaning.

alarm [*]
[əláːrm]

n. 불안, 공포; 경보 장치; v. 불안하게 하다; 경보장치를 달다
Alarm is a feeling of fear or anxiety that something unpleasant or dangerous might happen.

perfect ^{***}
[pə́ːrfikt]

v. 완벽하게 하다; a. 완벽한
If you perfect something, you improve it so that it becomes as good as it can possibly be.

method ^{복습}
[méθəd]

n. 방법; 체계성
A method is a particular way of doing something.

bare ^{복습}
[bɛər]

a. 맨손의; 벌거벗은; 아무것도 안 덮인; 텅 빈; v. (신체의 일부를) 드러내다
If someone does something with their bare hands, they do it without using any weapons or tools.

attitude^{**}
[ǽtitjùːd]

n. 자세; (정신적인) 태도, 사고방식; 반항적인 태도
An attitude is the position of your body.

bow ^{복습}
[bou]

① n. 활 ② n. 절, (고개 숙여 하는) 인사; v. (허리를 굽혀) 절하다
A bow is a weapon for shooting arrows which consists of a long piece of curved wood with a string attached to both its ends.

release^{복습}
[rilíːs]

v. 놓아 주다; 풀다; (감정을) 발산하다; n. 풀어 줌; 발표, 공개
If you release someone or something, you stop holding them.

pouch ^{복습}
[pauʧ]

n. 주머니; (캥거루 같은 동물의) 새끼 주머니
A pouch is a flexible container like a small bag.

sleeve ^{복습}
[sliːv]

n. (옷의) 소매, 소맷자락
The sleeves of a coat, shirt, or other item of clothing are the parts that cover your arms.

tie^{**}
[tai]

v. 묶다; 결부시키다; n. 끈; 유대
If you tie two things together or tie them, you fasten them together with a knot.

aim ^{복습}
[eim]

v. 겨누다; 목표하다; n. 겨냥, 조준; 목적
If you aim a weapon or object at something or someone, you point it toward them before firing or throwing it.

jerk ^{복습}
[dʒɔːrk]

v. 홱 움직이다; n. 얼간이; 홱 움직임
If you jerk something or someone in a particular direction, or they jerk in a particular direction, they move a short distance very suddenly and quickly.

breast ^{복습}
[brest]

n. 가슴; (새·동물의) 가슴살
A bird's breast is the front part of its body.

debate^{**}
[dibéit]

v. 곰곰이 생각하다; 논의하다; n. 토론, 토의; 논쟁, 논란
If you debate whether to do something or what to do, you think or talk about possible courses of action before deciding exactly what you are going to do.

string ^{복습}
[striŋ]

n. 줄; (악기의) 현; 일련; v. 묶다, 매달다; (실 등에) 꿰다
String is thin rope made of twisted threads, used for tying things together or tying up parcels.

flurry ^{복습}
[flɔ́ːri]

n. 질풍, 한 줄기의 바람; (잠시 한바탕 벌어지는) 소동
A flurry is a small swirling mass of something, especially snow or leaves, moved by sudden gusts of wind.

strike ^{복습}
[straik]

v. (struck−struck/stricken) (세게) 치다, 부딪치다; (생각 등이) 갑자기 떠오르다; n. 공격; 치기, 때리기
If you strike someone or something, you deliberately hit them.

flop ^{복습}
[flap]

v. 퍼덕거리다; ~을 떨어뜨리다, 털썩 주저앉다; n. 실패작
To flop means to move or hang in a loose, heavy, and uncontrolled way.

slam^{복습}
[slæm]

v. 세게 치다, 놓다; 쾅 닫다; n. 쾅 하고 놓기; 탕 하는 소리
If you slam something down, you put it there quickly and with great force.

retrieve
[ritríːv]

v. 되찾아오다, 회수하다; 수습하다
If you retrieve something, you get it back from the place where you left it.

kneel^{복습}
[niːl]

v. 무릎을 꿇다
When you kneel, you bend your legs so that your knees are touching the ground.

edge^{복습}
[edʒ]

n. 끝, 가장자리; 우위; v. 조금씩 움직이다; 테두리를 두르다
The edge of something is the place or line where it stops, or the part of it that is furthest from the middle.

weapon^{복습}
[wépən]

n. 무기, 흉기
A weapon is an object such as a gun, a knife, or a missile, which is used to kill or hurt people in a fight or a war.

dip[*]
[dip]

v. (액체에) 살짝 담그다; 내려가다; n. (잠깐 하는) 수영; (보통 일시적인) 하락
If you dip something in a liquid, you put it into the liquid for a short time, so that only part of it is covered, and take it out again.

detach[*]
[ditǽʃ]

v. 분리하다, 떼어놓다
If one thing detaches from another, it becomes separated from it.

runaway
[rʌ́nəwei]

a. 제멋대로 가는, 제어가 안 되는, 고삐 풀린; 달아난, 가출한
A runaway vehicle or animal is moving forward quickly, and its driver or rider has lost control of it.

horn[*]
[hɔːrn]

n. (양·소 등의) 뿔; (차량의) 경적
The horns of an animal such as a cow or deer are the hard pointed things that grow from its head.

forehead^{복습}
[fɔ́ːrhèd]

n. 이마
Your forehead is the area at the front of your head between your eyebrows and your hair.

lung^{복습}
[lʌŋ]

n. 폐, 허파
Your lungs are the two organs inside your chest which fill with air when you breathe in.

mud^{복습}
[mʌd]

n. 진흙, 진창
Mud is a sticky mixture of earth and water.

insane^{복습}
[inséin]

a. 제정신이 아닌; 정신 이상의, 미친
If you describe a decision or action as insane, you think it is very foolish or excessive.

boss
[bɔːs]

n. (동·식물) 돌기, 혹; 상관, 상사; v. ~를 쥐고 흔들다
Boss can refer to a stuck out part or body of animals.

muck^{복습}
[mʌk]

n. 진흙, 진창; 배설물
Muck is dirt or some other unpleasant substance.

156

sputter ^{복습}
[spʌ́tər]

v. (엔진·불길 등이) 펑펑 하는 소리를 내다; 식식거리며 말하다
If something such as an engine or a flame sputters, it works or burns in an uneven way and makes a series of soft popping sounds.

surface ^{복습}
[sə́:rfis]

n. 표면, 지면, 수면; 외관; v. 수면으로 올라오다; (갑자기) 나타나다
The surface of something is the flat top part of it or the outside of it.

suck ^{복습}
[sʌk]

v. 빨아 먹다; (특정한 방향으로) 빨아들이다; n. 빨기, 빨아 먹기
If you suck something, you hold it in your mouth and pull at it with the muscles in your cheeks and tongue, for example in order to get liquid out of it.

panic ^{복습}
[pǽnik]

n. 극심한 공포, 공황; 허둥지둥함; v. 어쩔 줄 모르다, 공황 상태에 빠지다
Panic is a very strong feeling of anxiety or fear, which makes you act without thinking carefully.

wipe ^{복습}
[waip]

v. (먼지·물기 등을) 닦다; 지우다; n. 닦기
If you wipe something, you rub its surface to remove dirt or liquid from it.

sideways ^{복습}
[sáidwèiz]

ad. 옆으로; 옆에서
Sideways means in a direction to the left or right, not forward or backward.

lily pad
[líli pæd]

n. (물 위에 뜨는) 수련의 잎
A lily pad is the large round leaf of a water lily that floats on water.

root ^{**}
[ru:t]

n. (식물의) 뿌리; (문제의) 근원; v. (식물이) 뿌리를 내리다
The roots of a plant are the parts of it that grow under the ground.

crawl ^{복습}
[krɔ:l]

v. 기어가다; 우글거리다; n. 기어가기
When you crawl, you move forward on your hands and knees.

charge ^{**}
[ʧa:rdʒ]

v. 돌격하다; 급히 가다, 달려가다; (요금·값을) 청구하다; n. 요금; 책임, 담당
If you charge toward someone or something, you move quickly and aggressively toward them.

hoof [*]
[huf]

n. (pl. hooves) 발굽; 발굽 소리
The hooves of an animal such as a horse are the hard lower parts of its feet.

hammer ^{복습}
[hǽmər]

v. 쿵쿵 치다; 망치로 치다; n. 망치, 해머
If you hammer something, you hit or kick it very hard.

fist ^{복습}
[fist]

n. 주먹
Your hand is referred to as your fist when you have bent your fingers in toward the palm in order to hit someone, to make an angry gesture, or to hold something.

rib [*]
[rib]

n. 갈비(뼈), 늑골; 늑재
Your ribs are the 12 pairs of curved bones that surround your chest.

hunch
[hʌnʧ]

v. (등을) 구부리다; n. 예감
If you hunch forward, you raise your shoulders, put your head down, and lean forward, often because you are cold, ill, or unhappy.

pretend [pritɛ́nd]
v. ~인 척하다. ~인 것처럼 굴다; ~라고 가장하다
If you pretend that something is the case, you act in a way that is intended to make people believe that it is the case, although in fact it is not.

bank [bæŋk]
n. 둑; 은행; v. (비행기 · 차를) 좌우로 기울이다; 땔감을 쌓아 올리다
A bank is a sloping raised land, especially along the sides of a river.

injure [índʒər]
v. 부상을 입히다; (평판 · 자존심 등을) 해치다
If you injure a person or animal, you damage some part of their body.

knee [ni:]
n. 무릎; v. 무릎으로 치다
Your knee is the place where your leg bends.

take stock
idiom 꼼꼼히 살펴보다; 재고 조사를 하다
If you take stock, you pause to think about all the aspects of a situation or event before deciding what to do next.

jab [dʒæb]
v. (쿡) 찌르다; n. 비난; (쿡) 찌르기; (권투에서) 잽
If you jab one thing into another, you push it there with a quick, sudden movement and with a lot of force.

wrench [rentʃ]
v. (발목 · 어깨를) 삐다; 확 비틀다; (가슴을) 쓰라리게 하다; n. 확 비틂
If you wrench one of your joints, you twist it and injure it.

shoreline [[ʃɔ́:rlàin]
n. 해안선
A shoreline is the edge of a sea, lake, or wide river.

shallow [ʃǽlou]
a. 얕은; 피상적인; n. (pl.) (강 · 바다의) 얕은 곳
A shallow container, hole, or area of water measures only a short distance from the top to the bottom.

sight [sait]
n. 시야; 광경, 모습; 보기, 봄; v. 갑자기 보다
A sight is something that you see.

wade [weid]
v. (물 · 진흙 속을 힘겹게) 헤치며 걷다
If you wade through something that makes it difficult to walk, usually water or mud, you walk through it.

mess [mes]
v. 엉망으로 만들다; n. (지저분하고) 엉망인 상태; (많은 문제로) 엉망인 상황
If you mess up something, you make it dirty or untidy.

madness [mǽdnis]
n. 광기; 어리석은 행동
Madness is the state of being mentally ill, or unable to behave in a reasonable way.

grateful** [gréitfəl]
a. 고마워하는, 감사하는
If you are grateful for something that someone has given you or done for you, you have warm, friendly feelings toward them and wish to thank them.

glow [glou]
v. 빛나다, 타다; (얼굴이) 상기되다; n. (은은한) 불빛; 홍조
If something glows, it produces a dull, steady light.

nearby* [niərbái]
ad. 인근에, 가까운 곳에
If something is nearby, it is only a short distance away.

158

doze ^{복습}
[douz]

v. 깜빡 잠이 들다, 졸다; n. 잠깐 잠, 낮잠
When you doze, you sleep lightly or for a short period, especially during the daytime.

roar ^{복습}
[rɔːr]

v. 웅웅거리다; 고함치다; 굉음을 내며 질주하다; n. 함성; 울부짖는 듯한 소리
If something roars, it makes a very loud noise.

thunder ^{복습}
[θʌ́ndər]

n. 천둥; 천둥 같은 소리; v. 우르릉거리다; 천둥이 치다; 쏜살같이 보내다
Thunder is the loud noise that you hear from the sky after a flash of lightning, especially during a storm.

grimace ^{복습}
[grímɔs]

v. 얼굴을 찡그리다; n. 찡그린 표정
If you grimace, you twist your face in an ugly way because you are annoyed, disgusted, or in pain.

tighten ^{복습}
[taitn]

v. (더 단단히) 조이다; (더) 팽팽해지다; 더 엄격하게 하다
If a part of your body tightens, the muscles in it become tense and stiff, for example because you are angry or afraid.

mystery ^{**}
[místəri]

n. 신비스러운 사람, 것; 수수께끼, 미스터리
A mystery person or thing is one whose identity or nature is not known.

spirit ^{복습}
[spírit]

n. 영혼; (pl.) 기분, 마음; 태도
A spirit is a ghost or supernatural being.

comfort ^{복습}
[kʌ́mfərt]

n. 위로, 위안; 안락, 편안; v. 위로하다, 위안하다
Comfort is what you feel when worries or unhappiness stop.

cheer ^{**}
[tʃiər]

n. 쾌활함, 생기; 환호(성), 응원; v. 환호성을 지르다, 환호하다
Cheer can refer to a feeling of happiness.

peg [*]
[peg]

n. 못, 핀; 말뚝; v. 고정하다; (수준을) 정하다
A peg is a small hook or knob that is attached to a wall or door and is used for hanging things on.

bough [*]
[bau]

n. (나무의 큰) 가지
A bough is a large branch of a tree.

threat ^{**}
[θret]

n. 위협적인 존재; 위험; 협박
A threat to a person or thing is a danger that something unpleasant might happen to them.

restless [*]
[réstlis]

a. 불안한; 가만히 못 있는
If you have a restless night, you do not sleep properly and when you wake up you feel tired and uncomfortable.

belly ^{복습}
[béli]

n. 배, 복부
The belly of a person or animal is their stomach or abdomen.

tornado
[tɔːrnéidou]

n. 회오리바람, 토네이도
A tornado is a violent wind storm consisting of a tall column of air which spins round very fast and causes a lot of damage.

opening ^{복습}
[óupəniŋ]

n. (사람 등이 지나가거나 할 수 있는) 틈; 첫 부분; (시합을 쓸 수 있는) 빈자리; a. 첫, 시작 부분의
An opening is a hole or empty space through which things or people can pass.

force^{복습}
[fɔːrs]

n. 힘; 군대; 작용력; 영향력; v. 억지로 ~하다; ~를 강요하다
Force is the power or strength which something has.

spray^{복습}
[sprei]

v. (작은 것을 아주 많이) 뿌리다; 뿌리다; n. 물보라; 분무기; 뿌리기
If a lot of small things spray somewhere or if something sprays them, they are scattered somewhere with a lot of force.

spark^{복습}
[spaːrk]

n. 불꽃, 불똥; (전류의) 스파크; v. 촉발시키다; 불꽃을 일으키다
A spark is a tiny bright piece of burning material that flies up from something that is burning.

hesitate^{복습}
[hézətèit]

v. 망설이다, 주저하다; 거리끼다
If you hesitate, you do not speak or act for a short time, usually because you are uncertain, embarrassed, or worried about what you are going to say or do.

momentary^{복습}
[móuməntèri]

a. 순간적인, 잠깐의 (momentarily ad. 잠깐)
Momentarily means for a short time.

massive^{복습}
[mǽsiv]

a. (육중하면서) 거대한; 엄청나게 심각한
Something that is massive is very large in size, quantity, or extent.

whip^{복습}
[hwip]

v. 격렬하게 움직이다; 휙 빼내다; n. 채찍
If something, for example the wind, whips something, it strikes it sharply.

rag[*]
[ræg]

n. 해진 천
A rag is a piece of old cloth which you can use to clean or wipe things.

rip^{복습}
[rip]

v. (재빨리·거칠게) 떼어 내다, 뜯어 내다; (갑자기) 찢다; n. (길게) 찢어진 곳
When something rips or when you rip it, you tear it forcefully with your hands or with a tool such as a knife.

tool^{복습}
[tuːl]

n. 도구, 연장; 수단
A tool is any instrument or simple piece of equipment that you hold in your hands and use to do a particular kind of work.

gust
[gʌst]

n. 세찬 바람, 돌풍; v. (갑자기) 몰아치다
A gust is a short, strong, sudden rush of wind.

slip[*]
[slip]

v. 슬며시 가다; 미끄러지다; (옷 등을) 재빨리 벗다; n. (작은) 실수; 미끄러짐
If you slip somewhere, you go there quickly and quietly.

pray^{**}
[prei]

v. 기도하다, 빌다; 간절히 바라다 (prayer n. 기도문)
When people pray, they speak to God in order to give thanks or to ask for his help.

wave^{복습}
[weiv]

n. 물결; (열·소리·빛 등의) ―파; (감정·움직임의) 파도; (팔·손·몸을) 흔들기; v. (손·팔을) 흔들다; 손짓하다
A wave is a raised mass of water on the surface of water, especially the sea, which is caused by the wind or by tides making the surface of the water rise and fall.

spout
[spaut]

n. (액체의) 분출; (주전자 등의) 주둥이; v. (액체를) 내뿜다
A spout of liquid is a long stream of it which is coming out of something very forcefully.

160

column*
[kάləm]

n. 기둥 모양의 것; 기둥; (신문 · 잡지의) 정기 기고란
A column is something that has a tall narrow shape.

opposite복습
[ápəzit]

a. (정)반대의; 건너편의; 맞은편의; prep. 맞은편에
Opposite is used to describe things of the same kind which are completely different in a particular way.

rapid**
[rǽpid]

a. (속도가) 빠른; (행동이) 민첩한 (rapidly ad. 빠르게, 신속히)
A rapid movement is one that is very fast.

crash복습
[kræʃ]

v. 충돌하다; 부딪치다; 굉음을 내다; n. (자동차 · 항공기) 사고; 요란한 소리
If a moving vehicle crashes or if the driver crashes it, it hits something and is damaged or destroyed.

emphasize**
[émfəsàiz]

v. 강조하다; 힘주어 말하다
To emphasize something means to indicate that it is particularly important or true, or to draw special attention to it.

mosquito복습
[məskíːtou]

n. [곤충] 모기
Mosquitos are small flying insects which bite people and animals in order to suck their blood.

protective*
[prətéktiv]

a. 보호용의; 보호하려고 하는
Protective means designed or intended to protect something or someone from harm.

nostril복습
[nάstrəl]

n. 콧구멍
Your nostrils are the two openings at the end of your nose.

clog복습
[klag]

v. 막다; 움직임을 방해하다
When something clogs a hole or place, it blocks it so that nothing can pass through.

swarm복습
[swɔːrm]

n. (곤충의) 떼, 무리; 군중; v. 무리를 지어 다니다; 많이 모여들다
A swarm of bees or other insects is a large group of them flying together.

downpour
[dáunpɔːr]

n. 폭우
A downpour is a sudden and unexpected heavy fall of rain.

batter복습
[bǽtər]

v. 두드리다, 때리다, 구타하다; n. (야구에서) 타자
To batter someone means to hit them many times, using fists or a heavy object.

overhang복습
[òuvərhǽŋ]

n. 돌출부; v. 돌출하다, 쑥 나오다
An overhang is the part of something that sticks out over and above something else.

wrap복습
[ræp]

v. 둘러싸다; (무엇의 둘레를) 두르다; 포장하다; n. 포장지; 랩
If someone wraps their arms, fingers, or legs around something, they put them firmly around it.

insect복습
[ínsekt]

n. 곤충
An insect is a small animal that has six legs. Most insects have wings. Ants, flies, butterflies, and beetles are all insects.

slap복습
[slæp]

v. (손바닥으로) 철썩 때리다; 탁석 놓다; n. 철썩 때리기, 치기
If you slap someone, you hit them with the palm of your hand.

back to square one
idiom 원점으로 되돌아가다
If you are back to square one, you have to start dealing with something from the beginning again because the way you were dealing with it has failed.

flip^{복습}
[flip]
n. 톡 던지기; 회전; v. 홱 뒤집다, 휙 젖히다; 툭 던지다
A flip is an occasion when something turns over quickly or repeatedly.

coin^{복습}
[kɔin]
n. 동전; v. (새로운 낱말 · 어구를) 만들다
A coin is a small piece of metal which is used as money.

spit^{복습}
[spit]
v. (침 · 음식 등을) 뱉다; n. 침; (침 등을) 뱉기
If you spit liquid or food somewhere, you force a small amount of it out of your mouth.

count^{***}
[kaunt]
v. 중요하다; 간주하다; 인정하다; (수를) 세다; n. 셈, 계산; 수치
If something or someone counts for something or counts, they are important or valuable.

cold snap
[kóuld snæp]
n. 일시적 한파
A cold snap is a short period of cold and icy weather.

damp^{복습}
[dæmp]
a. 축축한; n. 축축한 곳
Something that is damp is slightly wet.

tongue^{복습}
[tʌŋ]
n. 혀; 말버릇
Your tongue is the soft movable part inside your mouth which you use for tasting, eating, and speaking.

bellow
[bélou]
v. (우렁찬 소리로) 고함치다; 크게 울리다; n. 울부짖는 소리; 고함소리
If someone bellows, they shout angrily in a loud, deep voice.

stretch^{복습}
[streʧ]
v. 기지개를 켜다; (팔 · 다리를) 뻗다; 펼쳐지다; n. (길게) 뻗은 구간; 기간
When you stretch, you put your arms or legs out straight and tighten your muscles.

unduly
[ʌndú:li]
ad. 지나치게, 과도하게
If you say that something does not happen or is not done unduly, you mean that it does not happen or is not done to an excessive or unnecessary extent.

rinse[*]
[rins]
v. 씻어 내다; 헹구다; n. (물에) 씻기, 헹구기
When you rinse something, you wash it in clean water in order to remove dirt or soap from it.

bait^{복습}
[beit]
n. 미끼; v. 미끼를 놓다; (일부러) 화를 돋우다
Bait is food which you put on a hook or in a trap in order to catch fish or animals.

scatter^{복습}
[skǽtər]
v. 흩뿌리다; 황급히 흩어지다; n. 흩뿌리기; 소수, 소량
If you scatter things over an area, you throw or drop them so that they spread all over the area.

jam^{복습}
[dʒæm]
v. 밀어 넣다; 움직이지 못하게 되다; n. 교통 체증; 혼잡; 잼
If you jam something somewhere, you push or put it there roughly.

driftwood^{복습}
[dríftwud]

n. 유목(流木)
Driftwood is wood which has been carried onto the shore by the motion of the sea or a river, or which is still floating on the water.

log^{복습}
[lɔːg]

n. 통나무
A log is a piece of a thick branch or of the trunk of a tree that has been cut so that it can be used for fuel or for making things.

precious^{복습}
[préʃəs]

a. 소중한; 귀중한, 값비싼; ad. 정말 거의 없는
If something is precious to you, you regard it as important and do not want to lose it.

intact
[intǽkt]

a. (하나도 손상되지 않고) 온전한, 전혀 다치지 않은
Something that is intact is complete and has not been damaged or changed.

pilot^{복습}
[páilət]

n. 조종사, 비행사
A pilot is a person who is trained to fly an aircraft.

shiver[*]
[ʃívər]

n. (추위·두려움 등으로 인한) 전율; 몸서리; 오한; v. (몸을) 떨다
A shiver is the act of shaking slightly because you are frightened, cold, or ill.

weight^{복습}
[weit]

n. 무거운 것; 무게, 체중
You can refer to a heavy object as a weight, especially when you have to lift it.

religious^{**}
[rilídʒəs]

a. 종교의, 종교적인; 독실한, 신앙심이 깊은
You use religious to describe things that are connected with religion or with one particular religion.

concentrate^{복습}
[kánsəntrèit]

v. (정신을) 집중하다; (한 곳에) 모으다; n. 농축물
If you concentrate on something, or concentrate your mind on it, you give all your attention to it.

1. What did Brian assume when he first thought about the survival pack?
   A. He assumed the pack had been ripped to pieces.
   B. He assumed the pack had floated out of the plane.
   C. He assumed the pack was full of money.
   D. He assumed the pack contained useful gear.

2. How did he build a raft?
   A. With logs that were long and smooth
   B. With logs that had limbs sticking out of them
   C. With rope made from thin pieces of birchwood
   D. With rope made from his shoelaces

3. Why was it difficult to push the raft?
   A. The raft did not move forward easily.
   B. The raft did not float well on the lake.
   C. The raft was fragile and could fall apart easily.
   D. The raft was too small to control well.

4. What did he discover when he hit the aluminum covering of the plane?
   A. The aluminum had small holes in it.
   B. The aluminum had strange marks on it.
   C. The aluminum was thin and weak.
   D. The aluminum was thick and firm.

5. How did he react when he dropped the hatchet in the water?

  A. He was shocked at how quickly the hatchet sunk.

  B. He was frustrated that he had not been more careful.

  C. He was tempted to blame anyone but himself.

  D. He was ready to give up on getting into the plane.

6. Why didn't he throw away the chopped pieces of aluminum?

  A. He did not want to pollute the lake.

  B. He did not want to risk getting cut by them later in the water.

  C. He was afraid the fish might eat them.

  D. He figured he could make tools or bait out of them.

7. Why did he panic right after he got the survival pack?

  A. He saw part of the pilot's remains.

  B. He noticed that the pack was torn.

  C. He was running out of air underwater.

  D. He leg got caught between the seats of the plane.

$$\frac{2{,}809 \text{ words}}{\text{reading time ( ) sec}} \times 60 = (\quad) \text{ WPM}$$

Build Your Vocabulary

site^{복습}
[sait]

n. 위치, 장소; (사건 등의) 현장; 대지, 용지 (campsite n. 야영지)
A site is a piece of ground that is used for a particular purpose or where a particular thing happens.

wreckage
[rékidʒ]

n. 잔해
When something such as a plane, car, or building has been destroyed, you can refer to what remains as wreckage or the wreckage.

shelter^{복습}
[ʃéltər]

n. 대피처, 피신처; 피신; v. 피하다; 막아 주다, 보호하다
A shelter is a small building or covered place which is made to protect people from bad weather or danger.

rib^{복습}
[rib]

n. 갈비(뼈), 늑골; 늑재
Your ribs are the 12 pairs of curved bones that surround your chest.

bark^{복습}
[baːrk]

n. 나무껍질; v. (명령·질문 등을) 빽 내지르다; (개가) 짖다
Bark is the tough material that covers the outside of a tree.

nearby^{복습}
[nìərbái]

ad. 인근에, 가까운 곳에
If something is nearby, it is only a short distance away.

shred^{복습}
[ʃred]

v. (갈가리) 자르다, 찢다; n. (가늘고 작은) 조각; 아주 조금
If you shred something such as food or paper, you cut it or tear it into very small, narrow pieces.

nest^{복습}
[nest]

n. 둥지; 보금자리; v. 둥지를 틀다
A nest is a home that a group of insects or other creatures make in order to live in and give birth to their young in.

damp^{복습}
[dæmp]

a. 축축한; n. 축축한 곳
Something that is damp is slightly wet.

crackle^{복습}
[krækl]

v. 탁탁 소리를 내다; n. 탁탁 하는 소리
If something crackles, it makes a rapid series of short, harsh noises.

spirit^{복습}
[spírit]

n. (pl.) 기분, 마음; 영혼; 태도
Your spirits are your feelings at a particular time, especially feelings of happiness or unhappiness.

chase**
[tʃeis]

v. 뒤쫓다, 추적하다; 추구하다; n. 추적, 추격; 추구함
(chase away idiom ~을 쫓아내다)
If you chase away something, you get rid of something unpleasant.

incessant*
[insésnt]

a. 끊임없는, 쉴새없는
An incessant process or activity is one that continues without stopping.

search ^{복습}
[səːrtʃ]

v. 찾아보다, 수색하다; n. 찾기, 수색
If you search for something or someone, you look carefully for them.

virtual ^{복습}
[vɔ́ːrtʃuəl]

a. 사실상의; 가상의 (virtually ad. 사실상, 거의)
You can use virtually to indicate that something is so nearly true that for most purposes it can be regarded as true.

drive ^{복습}
[draiv]

v. 몰아가다; 운전하다; 만들다; 박아 넣다; n. 드라이브, 자동차 여행; 충동, 욕구
If the wind, rain, or snow drives in a particular direction, it moves with great force in that direction.

locate ^{복습}
[lóukeit]

v. ~의 정확한 위치를 찾아내다; (특정 위치에) 두다
If you locate something or someone, you find out where they are.

evergreen ^{복습}
[évərgriːn]

n. 상록수, 늘푸른나무
An evergreen is a tree or bush which has green leaves all the year round.

branch ^{복습}
[bræntʃ]

n. 나뭇가지; 지사, 분점; v. 갈라지다, 나뉘다
The branches of a tree are the parts that grow out from its trunk and have leaves, flowers, or fruit growing on them.

muscle ^{복습}
[mʌsl]

n. 근육
A muscle is a piece of tissue inside your body which connects two bones and which you use when you make a movement.

set about ^{복습}

idiom ~을 시작하다
If you set about doing something such as a task or an activity, you begin it, especially with energy or enthusiasm.

square away ^{복습}

idiom ~을 정리하다
If you square away something, you do the things necessary to complete it.

ridge ^{복습}
[ridʒ]

n. 산등성이, 산마루; v. (표면을) 이랑처럼 만들다
A ridge is a long, narrow piece of raised land.

section **
[sékʃən]

n. 부분; 구역; (조직의) 부서; v. 구분하다, 구획하다
A section of something is one of the parts into which it is divided or from which it is formed.

weave ^{복습}
[wiːv]

n. 엮어서 만든 것; (직물을) 짜는 법; v. 이리저리 빠져 나가다; (옷감 등을) 짜다
A particular weave is the way in which the threads are arranged in a cloth or carpet.

intact ^{복습}
[intǽkt]

a. (하나도 손상되지 않고) 온전한, 전혀 다치지 않은
Something that is intact is complete and has not been damaged or changed.

injure ^{복습}
[índʒər]

v. 부상을 입히다; (평판 · 자존심 등을) 해치다
If you injure a person or animal, you damage some part of their body.

drag ^{복습}
[dræg]

v. 끌다, 끌고 가다; 힘들게 움직이다; n. 끌기, 당기기; 장애물
If you drag something, you pull it along the ground, often with difficulty.

crude ^{복습}
[kru:d]

a. 대충 만든; 대충의, 대강의 (crudely ad. 조잡하게, 투박하게)
If you describe an object that someone has made as crude, you mean that it has been made in a very simple way or from very simple parts.

improve ^{복습}
[imprú:v]

v. 개선하다, 향상시키다
If something improves or if you improve it, it gets better.

pine ^{복습}
[pain]

n. 소나무
A pine tree or a pine is a tall tree which has very thin, sharp leaves and a fresh smell. Pine trees have leaves all year round.

bough ^{복습}
[bau]

n. (나무의 큰) 가지
A bough is a large branch of a tree.

storm **
[stɔ:rm]

n. 폭풍, 폭풍우; v. 쿵쾅대며 가다, 뛰쳐나가다; 기습하다
A storm is very bad weather, with heavy rain, strong winds, and often thunder and lightning.

massive ^{복습}
[mǽsiv]

a. (육중하면서) 거대한; 엄청나게 심각한
Something that is massive is very large in size, quantity, or extent.

meat ^{복습}
[mi:t]

n. 고기
Meat is flesh taken from a dead animal that people cook and eat.

grind *
[graind]

v. (곡식 등을 잘게) 갈다; 문지르다; 괴롭히다; n. (기계의) 삐걱거리는 소리
(meatgrinder n. 고기 가는 기계)
A meatgrinder is a machine which cuts meat into very small pieces by forcing it through very small holes.

twist ^{복습}
[twist]

v. 휘다, 구부리다; (고개 · 몸 등을) 돌리다; n. 돌리기; (고개 · 몸 등을) 돌리기
If you twist something, you turn it to make a spiral shape, for example by turning the two ends of it in opposite directions.

snap ^{복습}
[snæp]

v. 딱 부러지다; 급히 움직이다; 딱 소리 내다; (동물이) 물려고 하다; n. 탁 하는 소리
If something snaps or if you snap it, it breaks suddenly, usually with a sharp cracking noise.

sideways ^{복습}
[sáidwèiz]

ad. 옆으로; 옆에서
Sideways means in a direction to the left or right, not forward or backward.

litter *
[lítər]

v. 흐트러져 어지럽히다; (쓰레기 등을) 버리다; n. 쓰레기; 어질러져 있는 것들
(littered with idiom ~로 어질러진, ~이 흩어진)
If a number of things litter a place, they are scattered untidily around it or over it.

limb ^{복습}
[lim]

n. (큰) 나뭇가지; (하나의) 팔, 다리
The limbs of a tree are its branches.

treetop
[trí:tɔp]

n. 나무 꼭대기, 나무 끝
The treetops are the top branches of the trees in a wood or forest.

spice *
[spais]

n. 양념, 향신료; 흥취, 묘미; v. 양념을 치다 (spicy a. 향긋한, 향기로운)
Spicy food is strongly flavored with spices.

sap
[sæp]

n. 수액(樹液); v. 약화시키다, 차츰 무너뜨리다
Sap is the watery liquid in plants and trees.

exhaust*
[igzɔ́ːst]

v. 기진맥진하게 하다; 다 써 버리다; n. (자동차 등의) 배기가스
(exhausted a. 기진맥진한)
If something exhausts you, it makes you so tired, either physically or mentally, that you have no energy left.

spear 복습
[spiər]

n. 창; v. (창 등으로) 찌르다; (물고기를) 작살로 잡다
A spear is a weapon consisting of a long pole with a sharp metal point attached to the end.

bow 복습
[bou]

① n. 활 ② n. 절, (고개 숙여 하는) 인사; v. (허리를 굽혀) 절하다
A bow is a weapon for shooting arrows which consists of a long piece of curved wood with a string attached to both its ends.

refine*
[rifáin]

v. 개선하다, 개량하다; 정제하다
If something such as a process, theory, or machine is refined, it is improved by having small changes made to it.

sane*
[sein]

a. 분별 있는; 제정신의, 정신이 온전한 (sanity n. 분별)
If there is sanity in a situation or activity, there is a purpose and a regular pattern, rather than confusion and worry.

insane 복습
[inséin]

a. 제정신이 아닌; 정신 이상의, 미친
If you describe a decision or action as insane, you think it is very foolish or excessive.

curve 복습
[kəːrv]

v. 곡선으로 나아가다, 곡선을 이루다; n. 커브, 곡선
If something curves, or if someone or something curves it, it has the shape of a curve.

tail 복습
[teil]

n. 끝부분; (동물의) 꼬리; v. 미행하다
You can use tail to refer to the end or back of something, especially something long and thin.

survive 복습
[sərváiv]

v. 살아남다, 생존하다 (survival n. 생존)
If you refer to the survival of something or someone, you mean that they manage to continue or exist in spite of difficult circumstances.

pack 복습
[pæk]

n. 꾸러미; 무리; v. (짐을) 싸다; (사람 · 물건으로) 가득 채우다
A pack of things is a collection of them that is sold or given together in a box or bag.

doze 복습
[douz]

v. 깜빡 잠이 들다, 졸다; n. 잠깐 잠, 낮잠
When you doze, you sleep lightly or for a short period, especially during the daytime.

gear 복습
[giər]

n. (특정 활동에 필요한) 장비; 기어
The gear involved in a particular activity is the equipment or special clothing that you use.

heal 복습
[hiːl]

v. 치유되다, 낫다; 치료하다, 고치다
When a broken bone or other injury heals or when something heals it, it becomes healthy and normal again.

chipper
[tʃípər]

a. 명랑 쾌활한
Chipper means cheerful and lively.

sink ^{복습}
[siŋk]

v. (sank-sunk) 가라앉다, 빠지다; 박다; (구멍을) 파다; n. (부엌의) 개수대
If a boat sinks or if someone or something sinks it, it disappears below the surface of a mass of water.

pen ^{복습}
[pen]

n. (가축의) 우리, 펜; v. (동물 · 사람을 우리 등에) 가두다; (글 등을) 쓰다
A pen is a small area with a fence round it in which farm animals are kept for a short time.

tiny ^{복습}
[táini]

a. 아주 작은
Something or someone that is tiny is extremely small.

bait ^{복습}
[beit]

n. 미끼; v. 미끼를 놓다; (일부러) 화를 돋우다
Bait is food which you put on a hook or in a trap in order to catch fish or animals.

patient ^{복습}
[péiʃənt]

a. 참을성 있는, 인내심 있는; n. 환자 (impatience n. 성급함; 조급)
Impatience is the feeling of being annoyed by someone's mistakes or because you have to wait.

at hand

idiom (시간 · 거리상으로) 가까이에 있는
If something is at hand, near at hand, or close at hand, it is very near in place or time.

stomach ^{복습}
[stʌ́mək]

n. 위(胃), 복부, 배
Your stomach is the organ inside your body where food is digested before it moves into the intestines.

shrink ^{복습}
[ʃriŋk]

v. 줄어들다; (놀람 · 충격으로) 움츠러들다 (shrunken a. 쪼그라든)
Someone or something that is shrunken has become smaller than they used to be.

signal ^{복습}
[sígnəl]

n. 신호; 징조; v. 암시하다; (동작 · 소리로) 신호를 보내다
A signal is a gesture, sound, or action which is intended to give a particular message to the person who sees or hears it.

savage [*]
[sǽvidʒ]

a. 야만적인, 흉포한; (비판 등이) 맹렬한; n. 포악한 사람; v. 흉포하게 공격하다
(savagely ad. 사납게)
Someone or something that is savage is extremely cruel, violent, and uncontrolled.

pointed ^{복습}
[póintid]

a. (끝이) 뾰족한; (말 등이) 날카로운
Something that is pointed has a point at one end.

wedge ^{복습}
[wedʒ]

n. 쐐기; 분열의 원인; v. (좁은 틈 사이에) 끼워 넣다; 고정시키다
A wedge is an object with one pointed edge and one thick edge, which you put under a door to keep it firmly in position.

spread ^{복습}
[spred]

v. 펴다; (넓은 범위에 걸쳐) 펼쳐지다; 퍼지다, 확산되다; n. 확산, 전파
If you spread something somewhere, you open it out or arrange it over a place or surface, so that all of it can be seen or used easily.

pond ^{복습}
[pand]

n. 연못
A pond is a small area of water that is smaller than a lake.

flick ^{복습}
[flik]

v. 튀기다; 털다; 잽싸게 움직이다; n. 재빨리 움직임
If you flick something away, or off something else, you remove it with a quick movement of your hand or finger.

170

motion ^{복습}
[móuʃən]

n. 동작, 몸짓; 운동, 움직임; v. (손 · 머리로) 몸짓을 해 보이다
A motion is an action, gesture, or movement.

wrist ^{복습}
[rist]

n. 손목
Your wrist is the part of your body between your hand and your arm which bends when you move your hand.

pin ^{복습}
[pin]

v. (핀으로) 고정시키다; 꼼짝 못하게 하다; n. 핀
If you pin something on or to something, you attach it with a pin.

neat ^{복습}
[ni:t]

a. 정돈된, 단정한; 깔끔한; 뛰어난 (neatly ad. 깔끔하게)
A neat place, thing, or person is tidy and smart, and has everything in the correct place.

flatten *
[flǽtn]

v. 납작해지다; (건물 · 나무 등을) 깨부수다
If you flatten something or if it flattens, it becomes flat or flatter.

hatchet ^{복습}
[hǽtʃit]

n. 손도끼
A hatchet is a small ax that you can hold in one hand.

sharpen ^{복습}
[ʃáːrpən]

v. (날카롭게) 갈다; (기량 등을) 갈고 닦다; 더 강렬해지다
If you sharpen an object, you make its edge very thin or you make its end pointed.

peg
[peg]

n. 못, 핀; 말뚝; v. 고정하다; (수준을) 정하다
A peg is a small hook or knob that is attached to a wall or door and is used for hanging things on.

crack ^{복습}
[kræk]

n. (좁은) 틈; 날카로운 소리; 금; v. 갈라지다; 깨지다, 부서지다
A crack is a very narrow gap between two things, or between two parts of a thing.

prop ^{복습}
[prap]

v. 떠받치다; n. (연극 · 영화에 쓰이는) 소품; 지주, 버팀목
If you prop an object on or against something, you support it by putting something underneath it or by resting it somewhere.

coal ^{복습}
[koul]

n. 석탄
Coal is a hard black substance that is extracted from the ground and burned as fuel.

hiss ^{복습}
[his]

v. 쉿 하는 소리를 내다; (화난 어조로) 낮게 말하다; n. 쉭쉭거리는 소리
To hiss means to make a sound like a long 's.'

steam ^{복습}
[sti:m]

v. 김을 내뿜다; 화내다, 발끈하다; n. 김, 증기; 추진력
If something steams, it gives off steam.

loosen ^{복습}
[lu:sn]

v. 느슨하게 하다; 풀다; (통제 · 구속 등을) 완화하다
If you loosen something that is stretched across something else, you make it less stretched or tight.

raft *
[ræft]

n. 뗏목
A raft is a floating platform made from large pieces of wood or other materials tied together.

paddle *
[pǽdl]

v. 물장구를 치다; 노를 젓다; n. (짧은) 노
If you paddle in the water, you swim slowly by moving your arms or legs gently through the water.

tie ^{복습}
[tai]

v. 묶다; 결부시키다; n. 끈; 유대
If you tie two things together or tie them, you fasten them together with a knot.

base^{***}
[beis]

n. 근거지; (사물의) 맨 아래 부분; 기초, 토대
Your base is the main place where you work, stay, or live.

rip ^{복습}
[rip]

v. (갑자기) 찢다; (재빨리 · 거칠게) 떼어 내다, 뜯어 내다; n. (길게) 찢어진 곳
When something rips or when you rip it, you tear it forcefully with your hands or with a tool such as a knife.

operate^{**}
[ápərèit]

v. (군사) 작전을 벌이다; 운용하다, 가동시키다; 영업하다
If military forces are operating in a particular region, they are in that place in order to carry out their orders.

rueful ^{복습}
[rúːfəl]

a. 후회하는, 유감스러워하는 (ruefully ad. 유감스러운 듯이)
If someone is rueful, they feel or express regret or sorrow in af siet and gentle way.

log ^{복습}
[lɔːg]

n. 통나무
A log is a piece of a thick branch or of the trunk of a tree that has been cut so that it can be used for fuel or for making things.

shore ^{복습}
[ʃɔːr]

n. 기슭, 해안, 호숫가
The shores or the shore of a sea, lake, or wide river is the land along the edge of it.

driftwood ^{복습}
[dríftwud]

n. 유목(流木)
Driftwood is wood which has been carried onto the shore by the motion of the sea or a river, or which is still floating on the water.

toss[*]
[tɔːs]

v. (가볍게) 던지다; (고개를) 홱 쳐들다; n. 던지기
If you toss something somewhere, you throw it there lightly, often in a rather careless way.

scatter ^{복습}
[skǽtər]

v. 흩뿌리다; 황급히 흩어지다; n. 흩뿌리기; 소수, 소량
If you scatter things over an area, you throw or drop them so that they spread all over the area.

tornado ^{복습}
[tɔːrnéidou]

n. 회오리바람, 토네이도
A tornado is a violent wind storm consisting of a tall column of air which spins round very fast and causes a lot of damage.

crosspiece
[krɔ́ːspiːs]

n. 가로장, 가로대
A crosspiece is a piece placed across something.

nail ^{복습}
[neil]

n. 못; 손톱; 발톱; v. (못 같은 것으로) 고정시키다
A nail is a thin piece of metal with one pointed end and one flat end.

cross ^{복습}
[krɔːs]

v. 서로 겹치게 놓다; (가로질러) 건너다; a. 짜증난, 약간 화가 난; n. 십자 기호
Lines or roads that cross meet and go across each other.

stable[*]
[steibl]

a. 안정된, 안정적인; 차분한; n. 마구간
If an object is stable, it is firmly fixed in position and is not likely to move or fall.

platform *
[plǽtfɔːrm]

n. (장비 등을 올려놓는) 대(臺); 연단, 강단
A platform is a structure built for people to work and live on when drilling for oil or gas at sea, or when extracting it.

frustrate 복습
[frʌ́streit]

v. 좌절감을 주다, 불만스럽게 하다; 방해하다
If something frustrates you, it upsets or angers you because you are unable to do anything about the problems it creates.

momentary 복습
[móumǝntèri]

a. 순간적인, 잠깐의
Something that is momentary lasts for a very short period of time, for example for a few seconds or less.

temper **
[témpǝr]

n. (걸핏하면 화를 내는) 성질; v. 누그러뜨리다, 완화시키다
If you refer to someone's temper or say that they have a temper, you mean that they become angry very easily.

smooth 복습
[smuːð]

a. 매끈한; 부드러운; (소리가) 감미로운; v. 매끈하게 하다
A smooth surface has no roughness, lumps, or holes.

scan *
[skæn]

v. (유심히) 살피다; 훑어보다; 정밀 촬영하다; n. 정밀 검사
When you scan a place or group of people, you look at it carefully, usually because you are looking for something or someone.

edge 복습
[edʒ]

n. 끝, 가장자리; 우위; v. 조금씩 움직이다; 테두리를 두르다
The edge of something is the place or line where it stops, or the part of it that is furthest from the middle.

clutter
[klʌ́tǝr]

v. 어질러놓다; (어수선하게) 채우다; n. 잡동사니; 어수선함
If things or people clutter a place, they fill it in an untidy way.

pile 복습
[pail]

n. 무더기; 쌓아 놓은 것, 더미; v. (차곡차곡) 쌓다; 우르르 가다
A pile of things is a mass of them that is high in the middle and has sloping sides.

float 복습
[flout]

v. (물 위나 공중에서) 떠가다; (물에) 뜨다; n. 부표
Something that floats in or through the air hangs in it or moves slowly and gently through it.

realize 복습
[ríːǝlàiz]

v. 깨닫다, 알아차리다; 실현하다, 달성하다
If you realize that something is true, you become aware of that fact or understand it.

stymie
[stáimi]

v. (계획 등을) 방해하다, 좌절시키다
If you are stymied by something, you find it very difficult to take action or to continue what you are doing.

string 복습
[striŋ]

n. 줄; (악기의) 현; 일련; v. 묶다, 매달다; (실 등에) 꿰다 (bowstring n. 활시위)
String is thin rope made of twisted threads, used for tying things together or tying up parcels.

toe *
[tou]

n. 발가락
Your toes are the five movable parts at the end of each foot.

tatter 복습
[tǽtǝr]

v. 갈가리 찢다; n. (pl.) 넝마, 누더기 (tattered a. 낡을 대로 낡은, 누더기가 된)
If something such as clothing or a book is tattered, it is damaged or torn, especially because it has been used a lot over a long period of time.

pouch
[pauʧ]

n. 주머니; (캥거루 같은 동물의) 새끼 주머니
A pouch is a flexible container like a small bag.

strip
[strip]

n. 가느다란 조각; v. (물건을) 다 뜯어내다; 옷을 벗다
A strip of something such as paper, cloth, or food is a long, narrow piece of it.

pull***
[pul]

v. ~의 흉내를 내다; ~에 성공하다; 끌다, 당기다; n. 끌기
To pull a someone, especially someone famous, means to copy the way they speak or behave.

swing
[swiŋ]

v. 휙 움직이다; 휘두르다; 방향을 바꾸다; (전후 · 좌우로) 흔들다;
n. 흔들기; 휘두르기
If something swings in a particular direction or if you swing it in that direction, it moves in that direction with a smooth, curving movement.

slide
[slaid]

v. (slid-slid/slidden) 미끄러지듯이 움직이다; 슬며시 넣다; n. 떨어짐; 미끄러짐
When something slides somewhere or when you slide it there, it moves there smoothly over or against something.

figure
[fígjər]

v. 생각하다; 중요하다; n. (멀리서 흐릿하게 보이는) 사람; 수치; (중요한) 인물
If you figure that something is the case, you think or guess that it is the case.

barely
[béərli]

ad. 거의 ~아니게; 간신히, 가까스로
You use barely to say that something is only just true or only just the case.

scrape
[skreip]

v. (무엇을) 긁어내다; (상처가 나도록) 긁다; n. 긁기; 긁힌 상처
If you scrape something from a surface, you remove it, especially by pulling a sharp object over the surface.

endless
[éndlis]

a. 끝없는; 무한한, 한없는
If you say that something is endless, you mean that it is very large or lasts for a very long time, and it seems as if it will never stop.

visualize
[víʒuəlàiz]

v. 마음속에 그려 보다, 상상하다
If you visualize something, you imagine what it is like by forming a mental picture of it.

awful
[ɔ́:fəl]

a. 끔찍한, 지독한; (정도가) 대단한, 아주 심한
If you say that something is awful, you mean that it is extremely unpleasant, shocking, or bad.

commercial
[kəmɔ́:rʃəl]

n. (텔레비전 · 라디오의) 광고; a. 상업의; 상업적인
A commercial is an advertisement that is broadcast on television or radio.

unbelievable
[ʌnbilí:vəbl]

a. 믿기 어려울 정도인; 믿기 힘든
If you say that something is unbelievable, you are emphasizing that it is very good, impressive, intense, or extreme.

chill
[ʧil]

n. 냉기, 한기; 오싹한 느낌; v. 아주 춥게 하다; 오싹하게 하다
A chill is a feeling of being cold.

174

reverse*
[rivə́ːrs]

a. 반대의; v. 후진하다; (정반대로) 뒤바꾸다; n. (정)반대; (자동차의) 후진 기어
Reverse means opposite to what you expect or to what has just been described.

opposite^{복습}
[ápəzit]

a. (정)반대의; 건너편의; 맞은편의; prep. 맞은편에
Opposite is used to describe things of the same kind which are completely different in a particular way.

pronounce**
[prənáuns]

v. 표명하다, 선언하다; 발음하다 (pronounced a. 확연한; 단호한)
Something that is pronounced is very noticeable.

wisp
[wisp]

n. (연기 · 구름의) 줄기; (작고 가느다란 것의) 조각
A wisp of something such as smoke or cloud is an amount of it in a long thin shape.

vapor*
[véipər]

n. 증기, 수증기
Vapor consists of tiny drops of water or other liquids in the air, which appear as mist.

last^{복습}
[læst]

v. 오래가다; (특정한 시간 동안) 계속되다; 견디다, 버티다; ad. 맨 끝에, 마지막에
If something lasts for a particular length of time, it continues to be able to be used for that time, for example because there is some of it left or because it is in good enough condition.

wade^{복습}
[weid]

v. (물 · 진흙 속을 힘겹게) 헤치며 걷다
If you wade through something that makes it difficult to walk, usually water or mud, you walk through it.

set out^{복습}

idiom (일 · 과제 등에) 착수하다; (여행을) 시작하다
If you set out means you start an activity with a particular aim.

eddy^{복습}
[édi]

n. (공기 · 먼지 · 물의) 회오리; v. 회오리를 일으키다, 소용돌이치다
An eddy is a movement in water or in the air which goes round and round instead of flowing in one continuous direction.

breeze^{복습}
[briːz]

n. 산들바람, 미풍; 식은 죽 먹기; v. 경쾌하게 움직이다
A breeze is a gentle wind.

rivet^{복습}
[rívit]

n. 대갈못, 리벳; v. 대갈못으로 고정하다; (흥미 · 관심을) 고정시키다
A rivet is a short metal pin with a flat head which is used to fasten flat pieces of metal together.

wrinkle*
[ríŋkl]

v. 주름이 생기다; 주름을 잡다, 찡그리다; n. 주름
When someone's skin wrinkles or when something wrinkles it, lines start to form in it because the skin is getting old or damaged.

vertical*
[və́ːrtikəl]

a. 수직의, 세로의; 종적(縱的)인; n. 수직
Something that is vertical stands or points straight up.

stabilizer
[stéibəlàizər]

n. (배 · 비행기 등의) 안정 장치
A stabilizer is a device, mechanism, or chemical that makes something stable.

gap**
[gæp]

n. 간격, 틈; 공백; 격차
A gap is a space between two things or a hole in the middle of something solid.

hinge ^{복습}
[hindʒ]

n. (문·뚜껑 등의) 경첩

A hinge is a piece of metal, wood, or plastic that is used to join a door to its frame or to join two things together so that one of them can swing freely.

secure[*]
[sikjúər]

a. 안정감 있는, 단단한; 안심하는; 안전한; v. 얻어 내다; (단단히) 고정시키다

If an object is secure, it is fixed firmly in position.

rear ^{복습}
[riər]

n. 뒤쪽; 궁둥이; a. 뒤쪽의; v. 앞다리를 들어올리며 서다

The rear of something such as a building or vehicle is the back part of it.

cargo[*]
[káːrgou]

n. (선박·비행기의) 화물

The cargo of a ship or plane is the goods that it is carrying.

hatch[*]
[hætʃ]

n. (배·항공기의) 출입구; v. 부화하다; (계획 등을) 만들어 내다

A hatch is an opening in the deck of a ship, through which people or cargo can go. You can also refer to the door of this opening as a hatch.

underwater[*]
[ʌndərwɔ́ːtər]

a. 물속의, 수중의

Something that exists or happens underwater exists or happens below the surface of the sea, a river, or a lake.

dive ^{복습}
[daiv]

v. (물 속으로) 뛰어들다; 급강하하다; 급히 움직이다; n. (물 속으로) 뛰어들기

If you dive into some water, you jump in head-first with your arms held straight above your head.

trap ^{복습}
[træp]

v. (위험한 장소에) 가두다; 덫으로 잡다; 끌어모으다; n. 덫; 함정

If you are trapped somewhere, something falls onto you or blocks your way and prevents you from moving or escaping.

shudder[*]
[ʃʌ́dər]

v. (공포·추위 등으로) 몸을 떨다; 마구 흔들리다; n. 몸이 떨림, 전율; 크게 흔들림

If you shudder, you shake with fear, horror, or disgust, or because you are cold.

strap ^{복습}
[stræp]

v. 끈으로 묶다; 붕대를 감다; n. 끈, 줄, 띠

If you strap something somewhere, you fasten it there with a strap.

current ^{복습}
[kɔ́ːrənt]

n. (물·공기의) 흐름; 해류; 전류; a. 현재의, 지금의

A current is a steady and continuous flowing movement of some of the water in a river, lake, or sea.

bar^{**}
[baːr]

n. (초콜릿·비누 등 막대기 같은 것) 개; 술집, 바; 막대기 (모양의 것); v. 빗장을 지르다, 판자를 붙여 막다 (candy bar n. 초콜릿바)

A candy bar is a long, thin, sweet food, usually covered in chocolate.

murk ^{복습}
[məːrk]

a. 흐림, 어두컴컴함 (murky a. 흐린)

Murky water or fog is so dark and dirty that you cannot see through it.

obvious ^{복습}
[ábviəs]

a. 분명한, 확실한; 너무 빤한; 명백한

If something is obvious, it is easy to see or understand.

block^{***}
[blak]

v. 막다, 차단하다; 방해하다; n. 구역, 블록; 사각형 덩어리

If you block someone's way, you prevent them from going somewhere or entering a place by standing in front of them.

176

1분에 몇 단어를 읽는지 리딩 속도를 측정해보세요.

$$\frac{2{,}508 \text{ words}}{\text{reading time (} \quad \text{) sec}} \times 60 = (\qquad) \text{ WPM}$$

Build Your Vocabulary

stabilizer^{복습}
[stéibəlàizər]

n. (배 · 비행기 등의) 안정 장치
A stabilizer is a device, mechanism, or chemical that makes something stable.

slam^{복습}
[slæm]

v. 세게 치다, 놓다; 쾅 닫다; n. 쾅 하고 놓기; 탕 하는 소리
If you slam something down, you put it there quickly and with great force.

fist^{복습}
[fist]

n. 주먹
Your hand is referred to as your fist when you have bent your fingers in toward the palm in order to hit someone, to make an angry gesture, or to hold something.

blow^{복습}
[blou]

n. 세게 때림, 강타; 충격; v. (입으로) 불다; (바람 · 입김에) 날리다; 폭파하다
If someone receives a blow, they are hit with a fist or weapon.

bend^{복습}
[bend]

v. (bent–bent) 구부리다; (몸 · 머리를) 굽히다, 숙이다; n. (도로 · 강의) 굽이, 굽은 곳
If you bend something that is flat or straight, you use force to make it curved or to put an angle in it.

strike^{복습}
[straik]

v. (세게) 치다, 부딪치다; (생각 등이) 갑자기 떠오르다; n. 공격; 치기, 때리기
If you strike someone or something, you deliberately hit them.

skin^{복습}
[skin]

n. 거죽, 외피; 피부; (동물의) 껍질; v. (동물의) 가죽을 벗기다; (피부가) 까지다
A skin can refer to any outer covering.

skeleton[*]
[skélətn]

n. (건물 등의) 뼈대; 골격; 해골
The skeleton of something such as a building or a plan is its basic framework.

hatchet^{복습}
[hǽtʃit]

n. 손도끼
A hatchet is a small ax that you can hold in one hand.

hack
[hæk]

v. (마구 · 거칠게) 자르다, 난도질하다; (컴퓨터를) 해킹하다
If you hack something or hack at it, you cut it with strong, rough strokes using a sharp tool such as an ax or knife.

experimental[*]
[ikspèrəméntl]

a. 실험적인, 시험적인; 경험에 바탕을 둔
An experimental action is done in order to see what it is like, or what effects it has.

swing^{복습}
[swiŋ]

n. 흔들기; 휘두르기; v. 휙 움직이다; 휘두르다; 방향을 바꾸다; (전후 · 좌우로) 흔들다
A swing is an attempt to hit someone or something by making a smooth curving movement with your hand, a weapon, or a piece of sports equipment.

triangle*
[tráiæŋgl]

n. 삼각형 (triangular a. 삼각형의)
Something that is triangular is in the shape of a triangle.

cable*
[keibl]

n. 전선, 케이블; 굵은 밧줄
A cable is a thick wire, or a group of wires inside a rubber or plastic covering, which is used to carry electricity or electronic signals.

control^{복습}
[kəntróul]

n. 통제, 제어; (기계 · 차량의) 제어 장치; v. 지배하다; 조정하다
If you have control of something or someone, you are able to make them do what you want them to do.

frenzy
[frénzi]

n. 광분, 광란 (frenzied a. 광분한, 광란한)
Frenzied activities or actions are wild, excited, and uncontrolled.

opening^{복습}
[óupəniŋ]

n. (사람 등이 지나가거나 할 수 있는) 틈; 첫 부분; (사람을 쓸 수 있는) 빈자리;
a. 첫, 시작 부분의
An opening is a hole or empty space through which things or people can pass.

brace^{복습}
[breis]

n. 버팀대; 치아 교정기; v. (스스로) 대비를 하다; (몸에) 단단히 힘을 주다
A brace is a piece of wood or metal used for supporting an object so that it does not fall down.

bump^{복습}
[bʌmp]

v. (~에) 부딪치다; 덜컹거리며 가다; n. 쿵, 탁 (하는 소리)
If you bump into something or someone, you accidentally hit them while you are moving.

tool^{복습}
[tu:l]

n. 도구, 연장; 수단
A tool is any instrument or simple piece of equipment that you hold in your hands and use to do a particular kind of work.

weapon^{복습}
[wépən]

n. 무기, 흉기
A weapon is an object such as a gun, a knife, or a missile, which is used to kill or hurt people in a fight or a war.

yell^{복습}
[jel]

v. 고함치다, 소리 지르다; n. 고함, 외침
If you yell, you shout loudly, usually because you are excited, angry, or in pain.

choke**
[ʧouk]

v. 숨이 막히다; (목소리가) 잠기다; 채우다; n. 숨이 막힘
When you choke or when something chokes you, you cannot breathe properly or get enough air into your lungs.

snarl*
[sna:rl]

n. 으르렁거림; v. 으르렁거리다; 으르렁거리듯 말하다
A snarl is a deep, rough sound, usually made in anger.

rage^{복습}
[reidʒ]

n. 격렬한 분노; v. 맹위를 떨치다; 몹시 화를 내다
Rage is strong anger that is difficult to control.

careless**
[kéərlis]

a. 부주의한, 조심성 없는; 무심한 (carelessness n. 부주의, 경솔)
If you are careless, you do not pay enough attention to what you are doing, and so you make mistakes, or cause harm or damage.

178

raft ^{복습}
[ræft]

n. 뗏목
A raft is a floating platform made from large pieces of wood or other materials tied together.

stupidity[*]
[stju:pídəti]

n. 어리석음, 어리석은 짓
Stupidity is the behavior that shows a lack of good sense or judgement.

pity ^{복습}
[píti]

n. 연민, 동정; v. 애석해 하다; 불쌍해하다, 동정하다 (self−pity n. 자기 연민)
Self-pity is a feeling of unhappiness that you have about yourself and your problems, especially when this is unnecessary or greatly exaggerated.

dive ^{복습}
[daiv]

v. (물 속으로) 뛰어들다; 급강하하다; 급히 움직이다; n. (물 속으로) 뛰어들기
If you dive into some water, you jump in head-first with your arms held straight above your head.

gym^{**}
[dʒim]

n. (= gymnasium) 체육관; (= gymnastics) 체조, 체육
A gym is a club, building, or large room, usually containing special equipment, where people go to do physical exercise and get fit.

pool^{**}
[pu:l]

n. 수영장; 웅덩이; v. (자금 · 정보 등을) 모으다
A pool is the same as a swimming pool which is a large hole in the ground that has been made and filled with water so that people can swim in it.

exact ^{복습}
[igzǽkt]

a. 정확한; 꼼꼼한, 빈틈없는
Exact means correct in every detail.

anchor[*]
[ǽŋkər]

v. 고정시키다; 닻을 내리다, 정박하다; n. 닻; 정신적 지주
If you anchor an object somewhere, you fix it to something to prevent it moving from that place.

obvious ^{복습}
[ábviəs]

a. 분명한, 확실한; 너무 빤한; 명백한 (obviously ad. 분명히)
You use obviously to indicate that something is easily noticed, seen, or recognized.

angle ^{복습}
[ǽŋgl]

n. 기울기; 각도, 각; 관점; v. 비스듬히 움직이다
An angle is the difference in direction between two lines or surfaces. Angles are measured in degrees.

expand[*]
[ikspǽnd]

v. 확대시키다, 팽창시키다; 더 상세히 하다
If something expands or is expanded, it becomes larger.

swivel ^{복습}
[swívəl]

v. (몸 · 눈 · 고개를) 휙 돌리다; 돌리다, 회전시키다; n. 회전 고리
If you swivel in a particular direction, you turn suddenly in that direction.

thrust ^{복습}
[θrʌst]

n. 찌르기; 추진력; v. 찌르다; (거칠게) 밀다
A thrust is a quick hard push.

visible[*]
[vízəbl]

a. (눈에) 보이는, 알아볼 수 있는; 뚜렷한 (visibility n. 눈에 보이는 상태)
Visibility means how far or how clearly you can see in particular weather conditions.

claw ^{복습}
[klɔ:]

v. 헤치며 나아가다; (손톱 · 발톱으로) 할퀴다; n. (동물 · 새의) 발톱
If you claw your way somewhere, you move there with great difficulty, trying desperately to find things to hold on to.

pressure [préʃər]
n. 압력; 압박; 스트레스; v. 강요하다; 압력을 가하다
The pressure in a place or container is the force produced by the quantity of gas or liquid in that place or container.

pop [pap]
v. 펑 하는 소리가 나다; 불쑥 나타나다; 눈이 휘둥그레지다; n. 펑 (하는 소리); 탄산수
If something pops, it makes a short sharp sound.

run out of
idiom ~을 다 써버리다; ~이 없어지다
If you run out of something like money or time, you use up all of them.

explode [iksplóud]
v. 갑자기 ~하다; 폭발하다; (강한 감정을) 터뜨리다
To explode means to move very quickly.

surface [sɔ́:rfis]
n. 표면, 지면, 수면; 외관; v. 수면으로 올라오다; (갑자기) 나타나다
The surface of something is the flat top part of it or the outside of it.

whale [hweil]
n. [동물] 고래
Whales are very large mammals that live in the sea.

stale [steil]
a. 퀴퀴한, (좋지 못한) 냄새가 나는; 신선하지 않은
Stale air or a stale smells is unpleasant because it is no longer fresh.

wheeze [hwi:z]
v. (숨쉬기가 힘이 들어서) 쌕쌕거리다; n. 쌕쌕거리는 소리
If someone wheezes, they breathe with difficulty and make a whistling sound.

search [sə:rtʃ]
v. 찾아보다, 수색하다; n. 찾기, 수색
If you search for something or someone, you look carefully for them.

curse [kə:rs]
v. 욕설을 하다; 저주를 내리다; n. 저주; 욕설, 악담
If you curse someone, you say insulting things to them because you are angry with them.

dumb [dʌm]
a. 멍청한, 바보 같은; 말을 못 하는
If you say that something is dumb, you think that it is silly and annoying.

capacity [kəpǽsəti]
n. 용량; 수용력; 능력
The capacity of a container is its volume, or the amount of liquid it can hold, measured in units such as liters or gallons.

lungful [lʌ́ŋfùl]
n. (공기 · 연기 등을) 한 번에 들이마신 양
If someone takes a lungful of something such as fresh air or smoke, they breathe in deeply so that their lungs feel as if they are full of that thing.

wheel [hwi:l]
v. (반대 방향으로) 홱 돌다; (바퀴 달린 것을) 밀다; n. (자동차 등의) 핸들; 바퀴
If you wheel around, you turn around suddenly where you are standing, often because you are surprised, shocked, or angry.

arrow [ǽrou]
n. 화살; 화살표
An arrow is a long thin weapon which is sharp and pointed at one end and which often has feathers at the other end. An arrow is shot from a bow.

spring [spriŋ]
v. 튀다; (갑자기) 뛰어오르다; 휙 움직이다; n. 샘; 봄; 생기, 활기
If something springs in a particular direction, it moves suddenly and quickly.

180

propel
[prəpél]

v. 나아가게 하다; 몰고 가다
To propel something in a particular direction means to cause it to move in that direction.

rake 복습
[reik]

v. (손톱으로) 긁다; 갈퀴질을 하다; n. 갈퀴
To rake means to pull your fingers through or along something, for example your hair or skin.

paddle 복습
[pǽdl]

n. (짧은) 노; v. 물장구를 치다; 노를 젓다
A paddle is a short pole with a wide flat part at one end or at both ends. You hold it in your hands and use it as an oar to move a small boat through water.

mud 복습
[mʌd]

n. 진흙, 진창
Mud is a sticky mixture of earth and water.

trigger 복습
[trígəːr]

n. 폭파 장치; (총의) 방아쇠; v. 촉발시키다
The trigger of a bomb is the device which causes it to explode.

go off

idiom (경보기 등이) 울리다; 폭발하다
If something such as an alarm goes off, it starts making a noise as a signal or warning.

limit**
[límit]

v. 제한하다; 한정하다; n. 한계, 한도; 제한, 허용치
If you limit something, you prevent it from becoming greater than a particular amount or degree.

grab 복습
[græb]

n. 와락 잡아채려고 함; v. (와락 · 단단히) 붙잡다; 급히 ~하다
A grab is an attempt to take hold of something.

clutch*
[klʌʧ]

v. (꽉) 움켜잡다; n. 움켜쥠
If you clutch at something or clutch something, you hold it tightly, usually because you are afraid or anxious.

motion 복습
[móuʃən]

n. 동작, 몸짓; 운동, 움직임; v. (손 · 머리로) 몸짓을 해 보이다
A motion is an action, gesture, or movement.

lung 복습
[lʌŋ]

n. 폐, 허파
Your lungs are the two organs inside your chest which fill with air when you breathe in.

flash 복습
[flæʃ]

n. (잠깐) 반짝임; 갑자기 떠오름; v. (잠깐) 비치다; 휙 내보이다; 휙 움직이다
A flash is a sudden burst of light or of something shiny or bright.

chop 복습
[ʧap]

v. (장작 같은 것을) 패다; 내려치다; n. 내리치기, 찍기
If you chop something, you cut it into pieces with strong downward movements of a knife or an ax.

peel 복습
[piːl]

v. 껍질이 벗겨지다; (과일 · 채소 등의) 껍질을 벗기다; n. 껍질
If you peel off something that has been sticking to a surface or if it peels off, it comes away from the surface.

sign 복습
[sain]

n. 기색, 흔적; 신호, 표시; 표지판, 간판; v. 서명하다; 신호를 보내다
If there is a sign of something, there is something which shows that it exists or is happening.

substantial*
[səbstǽnʃəl]

a. (양 · 가치 · 중요성이) 상당한; 크고 튼튼한
Substantial means large in amount or degree.

poke ^{복습}
[pouk]

v. (손가락 등으로) 쿡 찌르다; 쑥 내밀다; n. (손가락 등으로) 찌르기
If you poke someone or something, you quickly push them with your finger or with a sharp object.

zipper
[zípər]

v. 지퍼로 잠그다; n. 지퍼
When you zipper something, you fasten it using a zipper.

jam ^{복습}
[dʒæm]

v. 밀어 넣다; 움직이지 못하게 되다; n. 교통 체증; 혼잡; 잼
If you jam something somewhere, you push or put it there roughly.

arrowhead
[ǽrouhed]

n. 화살촉
An arrowhead is the sharp, pointed part of an arrow.

lure ^{복습}
[luər]

n. 미끼; 유혹, 매력; v. 꾀다, 유혹하다
A lure is an object which is used to attract animals so that they can be caught.

cross ^{복습}
[krɔːs]

v. 서로 겹치게 놓다; (가로질러) 건너다; a. 짜증난, 약간 화가 난; n. 십자 기호
Lines or roads that cross meet and go across each other.

crisscross
[krískrɔ̀ːs]

v. 교차하다; 십자를 그리다; a. (많은 선이 교차하는) 십자형의
If two sets of lines or things crisscross, they cross over each other.

former
[fɔ́ːrmər]

n. 틀, 모형; 전자; a. 예전의; (둘 중에서) 전자의
A former can refer to a transverse strengthening part in an aircraft wing or fuselage.

awful ^{복습}
[ɔ́ːfəl]

a. 끔찍한, 지독한; (정도가) 대단한, 아주 심한
If you say that something is awful, you mean that it is extremely unpleasant, shocking, or bad.

tangle＊
[tǽŋgl]

v. 헝클어지다, 얽히다; n. (실·머리카락 등이) 엉킨 것; (혼란스럽게) 꼬인 상태
If something is tangled or tangles, it becomes twisted together in an untidy way.

wiggle ^{복습}
[wigl]

v. 꿈틀꿈틀 움직이다; n. 꿈틀꿈틀 움직이기
If you wiggle something or if it wiggles, it moves up and down or from side to side in small quick movements.

hold back ^{복습}

idiom ~을 저지하다; (감정을) 누르다; (진전·발전을) 저해하다
If you hold back someone or something, you prevent them from moving forward or from entering or leaving a place.

settle ^{복습}
[setl]

v. 자리를 잡다; 진정되다; (서서히) 가라앉다; 결정하다
If something settles or if you settle it, it sinks slowly down and becomes still.

reconsider
[rìːkənsídər]

v. 재고하다; 다시 생각하다
If you reconsider a decision or opinion, you think about it and try to decide whether it should be changed.

hammer ^{복습}
[hǽmər]

v. 쿵쿵 치다; 망치로 치다; n. 망치, 해머
If you hammer something, you hit or kick it very hard.

solid ^{복습}
[sálid]

a. 단단한; 완전한; 확실한; 견고한, 속이 꽉 찬; n. 고체, 고형물
A substance that is solid is very hard or firm.

182

eel
[i:l]

v. (장어처럼) 꿈틀꿈틀 움직이다; n. [동물] 장어
If you eel through somewhere, you move with smooth twists and turns.

fabric^{복습}
[fǽbrik]

n. 직물, 천
Fabric is cloth or other material produced by weaving together cotton, nylon, wool, silk, or other threads.

bare^{복습}
[bɛər]

a. 벌거벗은; 맨손의; 아무것도 안 덮인; 텅 빈; v. (신체의 일부를) 드러내다
If a part of your body is bare, it is not covered by any clothing.

plate**
[pleit]

n. (금속) 판; 접시, 그릇; (자동차) 번호판; v. 판을 대다
A plate is a flat piece of metal, especially on machinery or a building.

underwater^{복습}
[ʌndərwɔ́:tər]

a. 물속의, 수중의
Something that exists or happens underwater exists or happens below the surface of the sea, a river, or a lake.

definite**
[défənit]

a. 확실한, 확고한; 분명한, 뚜렷한 (definitely ad. 확실히, 분명히)
You use definitely to emphasize that something is the case, or to emphasize the strength of your intention or opinion.

drive^{복습}
[draiv]

v. (drove–driven) 몰아가다; 운전하다; 만들다; 박아 넣다; n. 드라이브; 충동, 욕구
If the wind, rain, or snow drives in a particular direction, it moves with great force in that direction.

gulp^{복습}
[gʌlp]

n. 꿀꺽 마시기; v. 꿀꺽꿀꺽 삼키다; (숨을) 깊이 들이마시다
A gulp of air, food, or drink, is a large amount of it that you swallow at once.

tear^{복습}
[tɛər]

① v. (tore–torn) 찢다, 뜯다; 뜯어 내다; n. 찢어진 곳, 구멍 ② n. 눈물
If a person or animal tears at something, they pull it violently and try to break it into pieces.

loosen^{복습}
[lu:sn]

v. 느슨하게 하다; 풀다; (통제 · 구속 등을) 완화하다
If you loosen something that is stretched across something else, you make it less stretched or tight.

break free

idiom 떨쳐 풀다; 도망치다
If someone or something breaks free, they remove themselves from the place in which they have been trapped or become fixed.

leap*
[li:p]

v. (leapt/leaped–leapt/leaped) 뛰다, 뛰어오르다; (서둘러) ～하다; n. 높이뛰기, 도약; 급증
If you leap, you jump high in the air or jump a long distance.

pale**
[peil]

a. (색깔이) 옅은; 창백한, 핼쑥한; v. 창백해지다
If something is pale, it is very light in color or almost white.

nibble
[nibl]

v. 조금씩 물어뜯다, 갉아먹다; n. 조금씩 물어뜯기, 한 입 분량
When an animal nibbles something, it takes small bites of it quickly and repeatedly.

chew^{복습}
[tʃu:]

v. 물어뜯다, 깨물다; 심사숙고하다; (음식을) 씹다; n. 씹기, 깨물기
If a person or animal chews an object, they bite it with their teeth.

skull*
[skʌl]

n. 두개골, 해골
Your skull is the bony part of your head which encloses your brain.

wobble [wabl]	v. (불안정하게) 흔들리다; 뒤뚱거리며 가다; n. 흔들림, 떨림; (마음·자신감의) 동요 If something or someone wobbles, they make small movements from side to side, for example because they are unsteady.
horror^{복습} [hɔ́:rər]	n. 공포, 경악; ~의 참상 Horror is a feeling of great shock, fear, and worry caused by something extremely unpleasant.
jerk^{복습} [dʒə:rk]	v. 홱 움직이다; n. 얼간이; 홱 움직임 If you jerk something or someone in a particular direction, or they jerk in a particular direction, they move a short distance very suddenly and quickly.
instinct[*] [ínstiŋkt]	n. 본능; 직감 (instinctive a. 본능에 따른, 본능적인) An instinctive feeling, idea, or action is one that you have or do without thinking or reasoning.
cage[*] [keidʒ]	n. 새장; 우리; v. 우리에 가두다 (birdcage n. 새장) A birdcage is a structure of wire or metal bars in which birds are kept.
bracket [brǽkit]	n. 버팀대, 받침대; 괄호; v. 같은 범주로 보다 Brackets are pieces of metal, wood, or plastic that are fastened to a wall in order to support something such as a shelf.
heave[*] [hi:v]	v. (크게) 들썩거리다; (아주 무거운 것을) 들어올리다; n. 들어올리기; 들썩거림 If you heave, or if your stomach heaves, you vomit or feel sick.
gasp^{복습} [gæsp]	v. 헉 하고 숨을 쉬다; 숨을 제대로 못 쉬다; n. 헉 하는 소리를 냄 When you gasp, you take a short quick breath through your mouth, especially when you are surprised, shocked, or in pain.
shore^{복습} [ʃɔ:r]	n. 기슭, 해안, 호숫가 The shores or the shore of a sea, lake, or wide river is the land along the edge of it.
cough^{복습} [kɔ:f]	v. 기침하다; 털털거리다; (기침을 하여 무엇을) 토하다; n. 기침 When you cough, you force air out of your throat with a sudden, harsh noise.
breeze^{복습} [bri:z]	n. 산들바람, 미풍; 식은 죽 먹기; v. 경쾌하게 움직이다 A breeze is a gentle wind.
rearrange [ri:əréindʒ]	v. 재배열하다; 재조정하다 If you rearrange things, you change the way in which they are organized or ordered.
squeeze^{복습} [skwi:z]	v. (좁은 곳에) 비집고 들어가다; (꼭) 쥐다; n. (손으로 꼭) 쥐기 If you squeeze a person or thing somewhere or if they squeeze there, they manage to get through or into a small space.
tie^{복습} [tai]	v. 묶다; 결부시키다; n. 끈; 유대 If you tie two things together or tie them, you fasten them together with a knot.
bone tired [bòun táiərd]	a. 지칠 대로 지친 If you are bone tired, you are extremely tired.

184

chill ^{복습}
[ʧil]

v. 아주 춥게 하다; 오싹하게 하다; **n.** 냉기, 한기; 오싹한 느낌

When cold weather or something cold chills a person or a place, it makes that person or that place feel very cold.

make it ^{복습}

idiom 해내다; 가다; (힘든 경험 등을) 버텨 내다

If you make it, you succeed in a particular activity.

couple***
[kʌpl]

v. 연결하다; **n.** 두 사람; 커플

If you say that one thing produces a particular effect when it is coupled with another, you mean that the two things combine to produce that effect.

barely ^{복습}
[béərli]

ad. 거의 ~아니게; 간신히, 가까스로

You use barely to say that something is only just true or only just the case.

surge*
[sə:rdʒ]

v. (재빨리) 밀려들다; (강한 감정이) 휩싸다;
n. (갑자기) 밀려듦; (강한 감정이) 치밀어 오름

If a crowd of people surge forward, they suddenly move forward together.

slide ^{복습}
[slaid]

v. 미끄러지듯이 움직이다; 슬며시 넣다; **n.** 떨어짐; 미끄러짐

When something slides somewhere or when you slide it there, it moves there smoothly over or against something.

weed ^{복습}
[wi:d]

n. 잡초; **v.** 잡초를 뽑다

A weed is a wild plant that grows in gardens or fields of crops and prevents the plants that you want from growing properly.

bank ^{복습}
[bæŋk]

n. 둑; 은행; **v.** (비행기 · 차를) 좌우로 기울이다; 땔감을 쌓아 올리다

A bank is a sloping raised land, especially along the sides of a river.

crawl ^{복습}
[krɔ:l]

v. 기어가다; 우글거리다; **n.** 기어가기

When you crawl, you move forward on your hands and knees.

notice ^{복습}
[nóutis]

v. 알아채다, 인지하다; 주의하다; **n.** 신경 씀, 주목, 알아챔

If you notice something or someone, you become aware of them.

ashore*
[əʃɔ́:r]

ad. 해안으로, 물가에

Someone or something that comes ashore comes from the sea onto the shore.

drag ^{복습}
[dræg]

n. 끌기, 당기기; 장애물; **v.** 끌다, 끌고 가다; 힘들게 움직이다

If you drag something, you pull it along the ground, often with difficulty.

shoreline ^{복습}
[[ʃɔ́:rlàin]

n. 해안선

A shoreline is the edge of a sea, lake, or wide river.

stumble ^{복습}
[stʌmbl]

v. 비틀거리다; 발을 헛디디다; (말 · 글 읽기를 하다가) 더듬거리다

If you stumble, you put your foot down awkwardly while you are walking or running and nearly fall over.

knee ^{복습}
[ni:]

n. 무릎; **v.** 무릎으로 치다

Your knee is the place where your leg bends.

doorway ^{복습}
[dɔ́:rwèi]

n. 출입구

A doorway is a space in a wall where a door opens and closes.

chapter 19 & epilogue

1. Why did Brian feel strange when he held the rifle?

   A. The rifle could easily injure or kill him.

   B. The rifle was heavier than his other tools.

   C. The rifle put him above nature.

   D. The rifle seemed less powerful than he had imagined.

2. What did he think about the emergency transmitter?

   A. He thought it was worthless because it did not play music.

   B. He thought it was broken because it did not make a sound.

   C. He thought it was not working because it needed time to warm up.

   D. He thought it was not working because he was too far away from civilization.

3. What did he decide to do with the packages of food?

   A. He decided to save them all for an emergency.

   B. He decided to only eat a few of them each day.

   C. He decided to eat as many of them as he wanted that day.

   D. He decided to open all of them up and try them that day.

4. What did he do when he saw the plane landing?

   A. He ran to the plane because he was excited to be rescued.

   B. He walked slowly toward the plane because he was suspicious.

   C. He hid in his shelter because he was terrified of the plane.

   D. He sat still because he was so surprised to see the plane.

5. How did the pilot know Brian's location?

   A. He followed the signal from the emergency transmitter.

   B. He noticed smoke rising from the shelter.

   C. He smelled the food that Brian was cooking.

   D. He received directions from the Cree.

6. What is one thing that Brian did when he returned home?

   A. He looked up the types of food and animals he had seen.

   B. He ate enough food to regain most of his weight and body fat.

   C. He wrote a book about his experience in the wilderness.

   D. He went back to all his previous habits and ways of thinking.

7. What would have happened to him in winter if he had not been found?

   A. He would have discovered more food.

   B. He would have struggled to find food.

   C. He would have encountered fewer dangerous animals.

   D. He would have explored new places.

1분에 몇 단어를 읽는지 리딩 속도를 측정해보세요.

$$\frac{1{,}735 \text{ words}}{\text{reading time (} \quad \text{) sec}} \times 60 = (\quad) \text{ WPM}$$

Build Your Vocabulary

treasure**
[tréʒər]

n. 대단히 귀중한 것; 보물; v. 대단히 소중히 여기다
Treasures are valuable objects, especially works of art and items of historical value.

unbelievable^{복습}
[ʌnbilíːvəbl]

a. 믿기 어려울 정도인; 믿기 힘든
If you say that something is unbelievable, you are emphasizing that it is very good, impressive, intense, or extreme.

riches
[rítʃiz]

n. 부(富), 재물
Riches can refer to a large supply of something valuable.

content*
[kántent]

n. 내용물; 내용
The contents of a container such as a bottle, box, or room are the things that are inside it.

survive^{복습}
[sərváiv]

v. 살아남다, 생존하다 (survival n. 생존)
If you refer to the survival of something or someone, you mean that they manage to continue or exist in spite of difficult circumstances.

pack^{복습}
[pæk]

n. 꾸러미; 무리; v. (짐을) 싸다; (사람·물건으로) 가득 채우다
A pack of things is a collection of them that is sold or given together in a box or bag.

numb^{복습}
[nʌm]

a. 멍한; (신체 부위가) 감각이 없는; v. 감각이 없게 하다; 멍하게 만들다
If you are numb with shock, fear, or grief, you are so shocked, frightened, or upset that you cannot think clearly or feel any emotion.

exhaust^{복습}
[igzɔ́ːst]

v. 기진맥진하게 하다; 다 써 버리다; n. (자동차 등의) 배기가스
(exhaustion n. 탈진, 기진맥진)
Exhaustion is the state of being so tired that you have no energy left.

oblivious
[əblíviəs]

a. 의식하지 못하는, 안중에 없는
If you are oblivious to something or oblivious of it, you are not aware of it.

mosquito^{복습}
[məskíːtou]

n. [곤충] 모기
Mosquitos are small flying insects which bite people and animals in order to suck their blood.

false**
[fɔːls]

a. 틀린, 사실이 아닌; 잘못된, 거짓된
If something is false, it is incorrect, untrue, or mistaken.

dawn 복습
[dɔ:n]

n. 새벽, 여명; v. 분명해지다, 이해되기 시작하다; 밝다
Dawn is the time of day when light first appears in the sky, just before the sun rises.

awaken 복습
[əwéikən]

v. (잠에서) 깨다; (감정을) 불러일으키다
When you awaken, or when something or someone awakens you, you wake up.

instant 복습
[ínstənt]

a. 즉각적인; n. 순간, 아주 짧은 동안 (instantly ad. 즉각, 즉시)
You use instant to describe something that happens immediately.

dig 복습
[dig]

v. (무엇을 찾기 위해) 뒤지다; (구멍 등을) 파다; 찌르다; n. 쿡 찌르기
If you dig into something such as a deep container, you put your hand in it to search for something.

amaze 복습
[əméiz]

v. (대단히) 놀라게 하다; 경악하게 하다 (amazing a. 놀라운)
You say that something is amazing when it is very surprising and makes you feel pleasure, approval, or wonder.

roof 복습
[ru:f]

n. (터널 · 동굴 등의) 천장; 입천장; 지붕; v. 지붕을 씌우다
The roof of a building is the covering on top of it that protects the people and things inside from the weather.

pad *
[pæd]

n. 패드; 보호대; v. 소리 안 나게 걷다; 완충재를 대다
A pad is a fairly thick, flat piece of a material such as cloth or rubber. Pads are used, for example, to clean things, to protect things, or to change their shape.

pot **
[pat]

n. (둥글고 속이 깊은) 냄비, 솥; 병; v. (나무를) 화분에 심다
A pot is a deep round container used for cooking stews, soups, and other food.

fry 복습
[frai]

v. (기름에) 굽다, 튀기다
When you fry food, you cook it in a pan that contains hot fat or oil.

pan **
[pæn]

n. (손잡이가 달린 얕은) 냄비 (frying pan n. 프라이팬)
A frying pan is a flat metal pan with a long handle, in which you fry food.

fork 복습
[fɔ:rk]

n. 포크; (도로 · 강 등의) 분기점; v. 갈라지다, 나뉘다
A fork is a tool used for eating food which has a row of three or four long metal points at the end.

waterproof *
[wɔ́:tərpru:f]

a. 방수(防水)의; n. 방수복
Something which is waterproof does not let water pass through it.

container 복습
[kəntéinər]

n. 용기, 그릇; (화물 수송용) 컨테이너
A container is something such as a box or bottle that is used to hold or store things in.

sheath
[ʃi:θ]

n. 칼집; 싸개, 피복
A sheath is a covering for the blade of a knife.

compass 복습
[kʌ́mpəs]

n. 나침반; (pl.) (제도용) 컴퍼스; (도달 가능한) 범위
A compass is an instrument that you use for finding directions.

first-aid
[fɔ:rst-éid]

n. 응급 처치 (first-aid kit n. 구급상자)
First aid is simple medical treatment given as soon as possible to a person who is injured or who suddenly becomes ill.

kit*
[kit]

n. (도구 · 장비) 세트; 조립용품 세트
A kit is a group of items that are kept together, often in the same container, because they are all used for similar purposes.

bandage*
[bǽndidʒ]

n. 붕대; v. 붕대를 감다
A bandage is a long strip of cloth which is wrapped around a wounded part of someone's body to protect or support it.

tube복습
[tju:b]

n. 통; 관; 튜브
A tube of something such as paste is a long, thin container which you squeeze in order to force the paste out.

antiseptic
[æntəséptik]

n. 소독제; a. 소독이 되는
Antiseptic is a substance that kills germs and harmful bacteria.

paste*
[peist]

n. 연고; 반죽, 풀; v. 풀로 붙이다
Paste is a soft, wet, sticky mixture of a substance and a liquid, which can be spread easily.

scissors*
[sízərz]

n. 가위
Scissors are a small cutting tool with two sharp blades that are screwed together. You use scissors for cutting things such as paper and cloth.

cap**
[kæp]

n. 모자; 뚜껑; v. (~으로) 덮다
A cap is a soft, flat hat with a curved part at the front which is called a peak.

adjust**
[ədʒʌst]

v. 조정하다; 적응하다; (매무새 등을) 바로잡다 (adjustable a. 조절할 수 있는)
If something is adjustable, it can be changed to different positions or sizes.

immediate복습
[imí:diət]

a. 즉각적인; 당면한; 아주 가까이에 있는 (immediately ad. 즉시, 즉각)
If something happens immediately, it happens without any delay.

coil복습
[kɔil]

n. 고리; 전선; v. (고리 모양으로) 감다, 휘감다
A coil of rope or wire is a length of it that has been wound into a series of loops.

dozen복습
[dʌzn]

n. 12개; (pl.) 다수, 여러 개; 십여 개
If you have a dozen things, you have twelve of them.

lure복습
[luər]

n. 미끼; 유혹, 매력; v. 꾀다, 유혹하다
A lure is an object which is used to attract animals so that they can be caught.

hook복습
[huk]

n. (낚시) 바늘; (갈)고리; v. (낚싯바늘로) 낚다; 갈고리로 잠그다
A hook is a bent piece of metal or plastic that is used for catching or holding things, or for hanging things up.

sinker
[síŋkər]

n. (낚싯줄 · 그물에 매다는) 봉돌
A sinker is a weight attached to a fishing net or line to keep it under the water.

190

incredible ^{복습}
[inkrédəbl]

a. 믿을 수 없는, 믿기 힘든
If you describe something or someone as incredible, you like them very much or are impressed by them, because they are extremely or unusually good.

doorway ^{복습}
[dɔ́:rwèi]

n. 출입구
A doorway is a space in a wall where a door opens and closes.

puzzle [*]
[pʌzl]

v. 어리둥절하게 하다; n. 퍼즐; 수수께끼
If something puzzles you, you do not understand it and feel confused.

break off

idiom 분리되다, 갈라지다; 일을 멈추다 (broken-off a. 부서진, 떨어진)
If you break a piece off something, you remove it from the main part.

bulky
[bʌ́lki]

a. 부피가 큰; 덩치가 큰
Something that is bulky is large and heavy. Bulky things are often difficult to move or deal with.

stock ^{복습}
[stak]

n. (총의) 개머리판; 비축물, 저장품; 재고; v. 채우다, 갖추다
A stock is the support or handle of a tool, especially the part of a gun that rests against your shoulder.

rifle [*]
[raifl]

n. 라이플총, 소총; v. 샅샅이 뒤지다
A rifle is a gun with a long barrel.

rattle ^{복습}
[rætl]

v. 덜거덕거리다; 당황하게 하다; n. 덜컹거리는 소리
When something rattles or when you rattle it, it makes short sharp knocking sounds because it is being shaken or it keeps hitting against something hard.

butt
[bʌt]

n. (무기 · 도구의) 뭉툭한 끝 부분; 엉덩이; v. (머리로) 들이받다
The butt or the butt end of a weapon or tool is the thick end of its handle.

come off ^{복습}

idiom 떼어낼 수 있다
If something such as dirt or paint comes off something, it is removed by washing or rubbing.

barrel [*]
[bǽrəl]

n. (총의) 총열; (대형) 통; v. 쏜살같이 달리다
The barrel of a gun is the tube through which the bullet moves when the gun is fired.

magazine ^{***}
[mæɡəzíːn]

n. (총의) 탄창; 잡지
In an automatic gun, the magazine is the part that contains the bullets.

action ^{**}
[ǽkʃən]

n. (피아노 · 총 등의) 기계 장치; 행동, 조치
An action is the mechanism that makes a machine or instrument work.

assembly ^{**}
[əsémbli]

n. (차량 · 가구 등의) 조립; 의회
The assembly of a machine, device, or object is the process of fitting its different parts together.

clip ^{복습}
[klip]

n. 장전된 총알 한 세트; 핀, 클립; v. 핀으로 고정하다; 깎다, 자르다
A clip is a container that is fastened to a gun, from which bullets go into the gun to be fired.

shell [복습]
[ʃel]
n. 포탄; 껍데기; 뼈대, 외부 구조; v. 껍질을 까다
A shell is a weapon consisting of a metal container filled with explosives that can be fired from a large gun over long distances.

sporting*
[spɔ́:rtiŋ]
a. 스포츠의; 정정당당한
Sporting means relating to sports or used for sports.

screw**
[skru:]
v. 나사로 고정시키다; 돌려서 조이다; n. 나사
If you screw something somewhere or if it screws somewhere, you fix it in place by means of a screw or screws.

fire***
[faiər]
v. 발사하다; 해고하다; (엔진이) 점화되다; n. 화재, 불
If someone fires a gun or a bullet, or if they fire, a bullet is sent from a gun that they are using.

figure out [복습]
idiom ~을 이해하다, 알아내다; 계산하다, 산출하다
If you figure out someone or something, you come to understand them by thinking carefully.

put together
idiom 조립하다; (이것저것을 모아) 준비하다
To put something together means to make or prepare it by fitting or collecting parts together.

load***
[loud]
v. (탄환 등을) 재다; (짐·사람 등을) 싣다; 가득 안겨 주다; n. (많은 양의) 짐
When someone loads a weapon such as a gun, they put a bullet or missile in it so that it is ready to use.

bullet [복습]
[búlit]
n. 총알
A bullet is a small piece of metal with a pointed or rounded end, which is fired out of a gun.

remove [복습]
[rimú:v]
v. 없애다, 제거하다; (옷 등을) 벗다; 치우다, 내보내다
If you remove something from a place, you take it away.

fool [복습]
[fu:l]
n. 바보; a. 바보 같은; v. 속이다, 기만하다
If you call someone a fool, you are indicating that you think they are not at all sensible and show a lack of good judgment.

lean [복습]
[li:n]
v. ~에 기대다; 기울이다, (몸을) 숙이다; a. 군살이 없는, 호리호리한
If you lean on or against someone or something, you rest against them so that they partly support your weight.

deal [복습]
[di:l]
v. 처리하다; n. 많은; 거래, 합의; 대우, 처리
If you deal with something, you accept and control a difficult emotional situation so that you can start to live a normal life again despite it.

bark [복습]
[ba:rk]
n. 나무껍질; v. (명령·질문 등을) 빽 내지르다; (개가) 짖다
Bark is the tough material that covers the outside of a tree.

twig [복습]
[twig]
n. (나무의) 잔가지
A twig is a very small thin branch that grows out from a main branch of a tree or bush.

marvel*
[má:rvəl]
v. 경이로워하다, 경탄하다; n. 경이(로운 사람·것)
If you marvel at something, you express your great surprise, wonder, or admiration.

192

flame ^{복습}
[fleim]

n. 불길, 불꽃; 격정; v. 활활 타오르다; 시뻘게지다
A flame is a hot bright stream of burning gas that comes from something that is burning.

spark ^{복습}
[spa:rk]

n. 불꽃, 불똥; (전류의) 스파크; v. 촉발시키다; 불꽃을 일으키다
A spark is a tiny bright piece of burning material that flies up from something that is burning.

nest ^{복습}
[nest]

n. 둥지; 보금자리; v. 둥지를 틀다
A nest is a home that a group of insects or other creatures make in order to live in and give birth to their young in.

feed ^{복습}
[fi:d]

v. 공급하다; 먹이를 주다; 먹여 살리다; n. (동물의) 먹이
To feed something to a place, means to supply it to that place in a steady flow.

steady ^{복습}
[stédi]

a. 꾸준한; 흔들림 없는, 안정된; v. 진정되다; 가라앉히다
A steady situation continues or develops gradually without any interruptions and is not likely to change quickly.

roar ^{복습}
[ro:r]

n. 울부짖는 듯한 소리; 함성; v. 웅웅거리다; 고함치다; 굉음을 내며 질주하다
A roar is a loud, deep sound.

pitch ^{복습}
[piʧ]

n. 송진; (감정·활동의) 정도; 음의 높이; v. 내던지다; (소리·음을 특정한 높이로) 내다
Pitch is a resin derived from the sap of various coniferous trees, as the pines.

chunk ^{복습}
[ʧʌŋk]

n. 덩어리; 상당히 많은 양; v. 덩어리로 나누다
Chunks of something are thick solid pieces of it.

rummage
[rʌ́midʒ]

v. 뒤지다; n. 뒤지기
If you rummage through something, you search for something you want by moving things around in a careless or hurried way.

packet *
[pǽkit]

n. 통, 곽; 소포; 한 묶음
A packet is a small container in which a quantity of something is sold.

glory in

idiom ~을 대단히 기뻐하다
If you glory in something, you are very pleased or proud about it.

electronic **
[ilektránik]

a. 전자의, 전자 장비와 관련된
An electronic device has transistors or silicon chips which control and change the electric current passing through the device.

device ^{복습}
[diváis]

n. 장치, 기구; 폭발물; 방법
A device is an object that has been invented for a particular purpose, for example for recording or measuring something.

encase
[inkéis]

v. 감싸다, 둘러싸다
If a person or an object is encased in something, they are completely covered or surrounded by it.

surge ^{복습}
[sə:rdʒ]

n. (강한 감정이) 치밀어 오름; (갑자기) 밀려듦; v. (재빨리) 밀려들다; (강한 감정이) 휩싸다
A surge is a sudden large increase in something that has previously been steady, or has only increased or developed slowly.

receiver[*]
[risíːvər]

n. 수화기, 수신기; 받는 사람, 수취인
A receiver is the part of a radio or television that picks up signals and converts them into sound or pictures.

wire[**]
[waiər]

n. 전선, (전화기 등의) 선; 철사; v. 전선을 연결하다
A wire is a long thin piece of metal that is used to fasten things or to carry electric current.

spring[복습]
[spriŋ]

v. (sprang–sprung) 튀다; (갑자기) 뛰어오르다; 휙 움직이다; n. 샘; 봄; 생기, 활기
If something springs in a particular direction, it moves suddenly and quickly.

antenna[*]
[ænténə]

n. (통신) 안테나; (곤충의) 더듬이
An antenna is a device that sends and receives television or radio signals.

switch[복습]
[swiʧ]

n. 스위치; 전환; v. 전환하다, 바꾸다
A switch is a small control for an electrical device which you use to turn the device on or off.

emergency[복습]
[imə́ːrdʒənsi]

n. 비상
An emergency is an unexpected and difficult or dangerous situation, especially an accident, which happens suddenly and which requires quick action to deal with it.

transmitter[복습]
[trænsmítər]

n. 전송기, 송신기
A transmitter is a piece of equipment that is used for broadcasting television or radio programs.

back and forth[복습]

idiom 여기저기에, 왔다갔다; 좌우로; 앞뒤로
If someone moves back and forth, they repeatedly move in one direction and then in the opposite direction.

static[복습]
[stǽtik]

n. (수신기의) 잡음; 정전기; a. 고정된; 정지 상태의
If there is static on the radio or television, you hear a series of loud noises which spoils the sound.

ruin[복습]
[ruːin]

v. 엉망으로 만들다; 폐허로 만들다; n. 붕괴, 몰락; 파멸
To ruin something means to severely harm, damage, or spoil it.

crash[복습]
[kræʃ]

n. (자동차·항공기) 사고; 요란한 소리; v. 충돌하다; 부딪치다; 꽝음을 내다
A crash is an accident in which a moving vehicle hits something and is damaged or destroyed.

bar[복습]
[baːr]

n. (초콜릿·비누 등 막대기 같은 것) 개; 술집, 바; 막대기 (모양의 것);
v. 빗장을 지르다, 판자를 붙여 막다
A bar of something is a piece of it which is roughly rectangular.

bathe[복습]
[beið]

v. (강·바다 등에서) 멱을 감다; (몸을) 씻다, 세척하다; (빛으로) 휩싸다
If you bathe in a sea, river, or lake, you swim, play, or wash yourself in it.

regular[**]
[régjulər]

a. 규칙적인; 일반적인, 평범한; n. 단골손님, 고정 고객
(regularly ad. 규칙적으로)
Regular events happen often.

grime
[graim]

n. 때, 먼지; v. 더럽히다, 때묻게 하다
Grime is dirt which has collected on the surface of something.

194

frizz
[friz]

v. 곱슬곱슬하다; n. 곱슬곱슬한 머리
If your hair frizzes, it forms into small, crisp curls or little tufts.

matted^{복습}
[mǽtid]

a. 엉겨 붙은
If you describe someone's hair as matted, you mean that it has become a thick untidy mass, often because it is wet or dirty.

grease^{복습}
[gri:s]

n. 기름, 지방; v. 기름을 바르다
Grease is animal fat that is produced by cooking meat. You can use grease for cooking.

tangle^{복습}
[tǽŋgl]

v. 헝클어지다, 얽히다; n. (실 · 머리카락 등이) 엉킨 것; (혼란스럽게) 꼬인 상태
If something is tangled or tangles, it becomes twisted together in an untidy way.

clump^{복습}
[klʌmp]

v. 무리를 짓다, 함께 모이다; n. 무리, 무더기; 수풀
If things clump together, they gather together and form small groups or lumps.

mess^{복습}
[mes]

n. (지저분하고) 엉망인 상태; (많은 문제로) 엉망인 상황; v. 엉망으로 만들다
If you say that something is a mess or in a mess, you think that it is in an untidy state.

freeze^{복습}
[fri:z]

v. 얼다; (두려움 등으로 몸이) 얼어붙다; n. 얼어붙음; 동결; 한파
(freeze–dry v. (식품 등을) 동결 건조시키다)
Freeze-dried food has been preserved by a process of rapid freezing and drying.

quantity^{복습}
[kwántəti]

n. 양, 분량
Things that are produced or available in quantity are produced or available in large amounts.

package^{**}
[pǽkidʒ]

n. (포장용) 상자; 포장물; v. 포장하다
A package is a small container in which a quantity of something is sold.

dessert^{복습}
[dizə́:rt]

n. 디저트, 후식
Dessert is something sweet, such as fruit or a pudding, that you eat at the end of a meal.

count^{복습}
[kaunt]

v. (수를) 세다; 중요하다; 간주하다; 인정하다; n. 셈, 계산; 수치
When you count, you say all the numbers one after another up to a particular number.

stack^{복습}
[stæk]

n. 무더기, 더미; v. (깔끔하게 정돈하여) 쌓다
A stack of things is a pile of them.

go through^{복습}

idiom ~을 살펴보다; 거치다; ~을 겪다
If you go through something, you look at, check, or examine it closely and carefully, especially in order to find something.

feast^{복습}
[fi:st]

n. 진수성찬; 연회, 잔치; v. 맘껏 먹다
A feast is a large and special meal.

tangy^{복습}
[tǽŋi]

a. (맛이) 찌릿한, (냄새가) 톡 쏘는
A tangy flavor or smell is one that is sharp, especially a flavor like that of lemon juice or a smell like that of sea air.

tongue ^{복습}
[tʌŋ]

n. 혀; 말버릇
Your tongue is the soft movable part inside your mouth which you use for tasting, eating, and speaking.

tickle *
[tikl]

v. 간질이다; 재미있게 하다; n. (장난으로) 간지럽히기
If something tickles you or tickles, it causes an irritating feeling by lightly touching a part of your body.

slosh ^{복습}
[slaʃ]

v. 철벅거리다; (물 · 진창 속을) 철벅거리며 걷다
If a liquid sloshes around or if you slosh it around, it moves around in different directions.

swallow ^{복습}
[swálou]

v. (음식 등을) 삼키다; 집어삼키다; n. (음식 등을) 삼키기; [동물] 제비
If you swallow something, you cause it to go from your mouth down into your stomach.

spice ^{복습}
[spais]

n. 양념, 향신료; 흥취, 묘미; v. 양념을 치다
A spice is a part of a plant, or a powder made from that part, which you put in food to give it flavor.

precise ^{복습}
[prisáis]

a. 정확한, 정밀한; 엄밀한, 꼼꼼한
You use precise to emphasize that you are referring to an exact thing, rather than something vague.

tiny ^{복습}
[táini]

a. 아주 작은
Something or someone that is tiny is extremely small.

drone ^{복습}
[droun]

n. (낮게) 웅웅거리는 소리; 저음; v. 웅얼거리는 소리를 내다
A drone is a continuous low humming sound.

register ^{복습}
[rédʒistər]

v. 알아채다, 기억하다; (이름을) 등록하다; n. 기록부, 명부
If a piece of information does not register or if you do not register it, you do not really pay attention to it, and so you do not remember it or react to it.

ridge ^{복습}
[ridʒ]

n. 산등성이, 산마루; v. (표면을) 이랑처럼 만들다
A ridge is a long, narrow piece of raised land.

float ^{복습}
[flout]

n. 부표; v. (물 위나 공중에서) 떠가다; (물에) 뜨다
A float is a light object that is used to help someone or something float.

explode ^{복습}
[iksplóud]

v. 갑자기 ~하다; 폭발하다; (강한 감정을) 터뜨리다
To explode means to move very quickly.

tip ^{복습}
[tip]

v. 기울어지다, 젖혀지다; 살짝 건드리다; n. (뾰족한) 끝
If you tip an object or part of your body or if it tips, it moves into a sloping position with one end or side higher than the other.

tail ^{복습}
[teil]

n. 끝부분; (동물의) 꼬리; v. 미행하다
You can use tail to refer to the end or back of something, especially something long and thin.

glide ^{복습}
[glaid]

v. 활공하다; 미끄러지듯 움직이다; n. 미끄러지는 듯한 움직임
When birds or airplanes glide, they float on air currents.

settle^{복습}
[setl]

v. 자리를 잡다; 진정되다; (서서히) 가라앉다; 결정하다
If something settles or if you settle it, it sinks slowly down and becomes still.

spray^{복습}
[sprei]

n. 물보라; 분무기; 뿌리기; v. 뿌리다; (작은 것을 아주 많이) 뿌리다
Spray is a lot of small drops of water which are being thrown into the air.

taxi**
[tǽksi]

v. (비행기가 이륙 직전 · 착륙 직후에) 천천히 달리다; n. 택시
When an aircraft taxies along the ground, or when a pilot taxies a plane somewhere, it moves slowly along the ground.

bump^{복습}
[bʌmp]

v. (~에) 부딪치다; 덜컹거리며 가다; n. 쿵, 탁 (하는 소리)
If you bump into something or someone, you accidentally hit them while you are moving.

stare^{복습}
[stɛər]

v. 빤히 쳐다보다, 응시하다; n. 빤히 쳐다보기, 응시
If you stare at someone or something, you look at them for a long time.

pilot^{복습}
[páilət]

n. 조종사, 비행사
A pilot is a person who is trained to fly an aircraft.

hop*
[hap]

v. 깡충깡충 뛰다; 급히 움직이다; n. 깡충깡충 뛰기
If you hop, you move along by jumping on one foot.

trail off

idiom (목소리가) 차츰 잦아들다
If someone's speech trails off, it gradually becomes quieter and then stops.

cock*
[kak]

v. 몸을 뒤로 젖히다; 쫑긋 세우다; 높이 들다; n. [동물] 수탉
If you cock a part of your body such as your head or your eyes, you move it upward or in a particular direction.

quit^{복습}
[kwit]

v. (quit-quit) 그만하다; 떠나다
If you quit an activity or quit doing something, you stop doing it.

ragged*
[rǽgid]

a. 남루한, 초라한; (옷 등이) 누더기가 된, 다 해진
Someone who is ragged looks untidy and is wearing clothes that are old and torn.

burn^{복습}
[bəːrn]

v. 데다, (햇볕 등에) 타다; 불에 타다; 화끈거리다; (마음 등에) 새겨지다; n. 화상
If you burn part of your body, burn yourself, or are burnt, you are injured by fire or by something very hot.

cough^{복습}
[kɔːf]

v. 기침하다; 털털거리다; (기침을 하여 무엇을) 토하다; n. 기침
When you cough, you force air out of your throat with a sudden, harsh noise.

clear one's throat

idiom 목을 가다듬다; 헛기침하다
If you clear your throat, you cough once in order to make it easier to speak or to attract people's attention.

stew^{복습}
[stjuː]

n. 스튜; v. (음식을) 뭉근히 끓이다
A stew is a meal which you make by cooking meat and vegetables in liquid at a low temperature.

wave ^{복습}
[weiv]

v. (손 · 팔을) 흔들다; 손짓하다;

n. (열 · 소리 · 빛 등의) –파; 물결; (감정 · 움직임의) 파도; (팔 · 손 · 몸을) 흔들기

If you wave someone away or wave them on, you make a movement with your hand to indicate that they should move in a particular direction.

1분에 몇 단어를 읽는지 리딩 속도를 측정해보세요.

$$\frac{747 \text{ words}}{\text{reading time (\quad) sec}} \times 60 = (\quad) \text{ WPM}$$

Build Your Vocabulary

pilot^{복습}
[páilət]

n. 조종사, 비행사
A pilot is a person who is trained to fly an aircraft.

land^{복습}
[lænd]

v. (땅·표면에) 내려앉다, 착륙하다; 놓다, 두다; n. 육지, 땅; 지역
When someone or something lands, they come down to the ground after moving through the air or falling.

fur^{복습}
[fə:r]

n. 모피; (동물의) 털
Fur is the fur-covered skin of an animal that is used to make clothing or small carpets.

map^{**}
[mæp]

v. (배치·구조 등에 대한 정보를) 보여주다; 지도를 만들다; n. 지도
If you map something, you record in detail the spatial distribution of it.

trap^{복습}
[træp]

v. 덫으로 잡다; (위험한 장소에) 가두다; 끌어모으다; n. 덫; 함정
If a person traps animals or birds, he or she catches them using traps.

camp^{복습}
[kæmp]

n. 야영지; 수용소; 진영; v. 야영하다
A camp is an outdoor area with buildings, tents, or caravans where people stay on holiday.

unwitting
[ʌnwítiŋ]

a. 자신도 모르는 (unwittingly ad. 자신도 모르게)
If you describe a person or their actions as unwitting, you mean that the person does something or is involved in something without realizing it.

emergency^{복습}
[imə́:rdʒənsi]

n. 비상
An emergency is an unexpected and difficult or dangerous situation, especially an accident, which happens suddenly and which requires quick action to deal with it.

transmitter^{복습}
[trænsmítər]

n. 전송기, 송신기
A transmitter is a piece of equipment that is used for broadcasting television or radio programs.

regular^{복습}
[régjulər]

a. 규칙적인; 일반적인, 평범한; n. 단골손님, 고정 고객
Regular events happen often.

route^{**}
[ru:t]

n. 길, 경로; 방법; v. 보내다, 전송하다
A route is a way from one place to another.

rescue^{복습}
[réskju:]

v. 구하다, 구출하다; n. 구출, 구조, 구제
If you rescue someone, you get them out of a dangerous or unpleasant situation.

weight^{복습}
[weit]

n. 무게, 체중; 무거운 것
The weight of a person or thing is how heavy they are, measured in units such as kilograms, pounds, or tons.

virtual^{복습}
[vɔ́:rtʃuəl]

a. 사실상의; 가상의 (virtually ad. 사실상, 거의)
You can use virtually to indicate that something is so nearly true that for most purposes it can be regarded as true.

consume^{복습}
[kənsú:m]

v. 소모하다; (강렬한 감정이) 사로잡다; 먹다
To consume an amount of fuel, energy, or time means to use it up.

lean^{복습}
[li:n]

a. 군살이 없는, 호리호리한; v. 기울이다, (몸을) 숙이다; ~에 기대다
If you describe someone as lean, you mean that they are thin but look strong and healthy.

wiry
[wáiəri]

a. (여위지만) 강단 있는; 뻣뻣한
Someone who is wiry is rather thin but is also strong.

prove^{**}
[pru:v]

v. (~임이) 드러나다; 입증하다, 증명하다
If something proves to be true or to have a particular quality, it becomes clear after a period of time that it is true or has that quality.

permanent^{복습}
[pɔ́:rmənənt]

a. 영구적인; 오래가는
Something that is permanent lasts for ever.

immense[*]
[iméns]

a. 엄청난, 어마어마한 (immensely ad. 엄청나게, 대단히)
You use immensely to emphasize the degree or extent of a quality, feeling, or process.

last^{복습}
[læst]

v. (특정한 시간 동안) 계속되다; 오래가다; 견디다, 버티다; ad. 맨 끝에, 마지막에
If something lasts for a particular length of time, it continues to be able to be used for that time, for example because there is some of it left or because it is in good enough condition.

thoughtful[*]
[θɔ́:tfəl]

a. 생각에 잠긴; 사려 깊은
If you are thoughtful, you are quiet and serious because you are thinking about something.

grocery^{복습}
[gróusəri]

n. 식료 잡화점; (pl.) 식료 잡화류
A grocery or a grocery store is a grocer's shop.

stare^{복습}
[stɛər]

v. 빤히 쳐다보다, 응시하다; n. 빤히 쳐다보기, 응시
If you stare at someone or something, you look at them for a long time.

aisle[*]
[ail]

n. 통로
An aisle is a long narrow gap that people can walk along between rows of seats in a public building.

marvel^{복습}
[má:rvəl]

v. 경이로워하다, 경탄하다; n. 경이(로운 사람·것)
If you marvel at something, you express your great surprise, wonder, or admiration.

quantity^{복습}
[kwántəti]

n. 양, 분량
Things that are produced or available in quantity are produced or available in large amounts.

identify [복습]
[aidéntəfài]

v. (신원 등을) 확인하다; 찾다, 발견하다
If you can identify someone or something, you are able to recognize them or distinguish them from others.

game[***]
[geim]

n. 사냥감; 게임, 경기, 시합
Wild animals or birds that are hunted for sport and sometimes cooked and eaten are referred to as game.

gut [복습]
[gʌt]

n. 소화관; 배; 직감; v. 내부를 파괴하다
The gut is the tube inside the body of a person or animal through which food passes while it is being digested.

term [복습]
[təːrm]

v. (이름·용어로) 칭하다; n. 용어, 말; 기간
If you say that something is termed a particular thing, you mean that that is what people call it or that is their opinion of it.

choke [복습]
[tʃouk]

n. 숨이 막힘; v. 숨이 막히다; (목소리가) 잠기다; 채우다
A choke is an act or the sound of a person or animal having difficulty in breathing.

nut [복습]
[nʌt]

n. 견과; 너트; 괴짜, 미친 사람
The firm shelled fruit of some trees and bushes are called nuts. Some nuts can be eaten.

bush [복습]
[buʃ]

n. 관목, 덤불; 우거진 것
A bush is a large plant which is smaller than a tree and has a lot of branches.

fool [복습]
[fuːl]

n. 바보; a. 바보 같은; v. 속이다, 기만하다
If you call someone a fool, you are indicating that you think they are not at all sensible and show a lack of good judgment.

ruff
[rʌf]

n. (새나 짐승의) 목둘레 깃털, 목털; 주름 깃 (ruffed a. 목털이 있는)
A ruff is a thick band of feathers or fur round the neck of a bird or animal.

hen[*]
[hen]

n. (새의) 암컷; 암탉
The female of any bird can be referred to as a hen.

stupidity [복습]
[stjuːpídəti]

n. 어리석음, 어리석은 짓
Stupidity is the behavior that shows a lack of good sense or judgement.

turtle [복습]
[təːrtl]

n. [동물] (바다) 거북
A turtle is a large reptile which has a thick shell covering its body and which lives in the sea most of the time.

snap [복습]
[snæp]

v. (동물이) 물려고 하다; 급히 움직이다; 딱 소리 내다; 딱 부러지다; n. 탁 하는 소리
If an animal such as a dog snaps at you, it opens and shuts its jaws quickly near you, as if it were going to bite you.

bother [복습]
[báðər]

v. 신경 쓰이게 하다; 귀찮게 하다, 귀찮게 말을 걸다; 신경 쓰다; n. 성가심
If something bothers you, or if you bother about it, it worries, annoys, or upsets you.

government [복습]
[gʌ́vərnmənt]

n. 정부, 정권; 행정, 통치
The government of a country is the group of people who are responsible for governing it.

epilogue

201

recover**
[rikʌ́vər]

v. 되찾다; 회복되다; (의식 등을) 되찾다
If you recover something that has been lost or stolen, you find it or get it back.

site^{복습}
[sait]

n. 위치, 장소; (사건 등의) 현장; 대지, 용지 (campsite n. 야영지)
A site is a piece of ground that is used for a particular purpose or where a particular thing happens.

shelter^{복습}
[ʃéltər]

n. 대피처, 피신처; 피신; v. 피하다; 막아 주다, 보호하다
A shelter is a small building or covered place which is made to protect people from bad weather or danger.

brief^{복습}
[bri:f]

a. (시간이) 짧은; 간단한; v. ~에게 보고하다
Something that is brief lasts for only a short time.

press^{복습}
[pres]

n. 언론; v. 누르다; (무엇에) 바짝 대다; 꾹 밀어 넣다
Journalists are referred to as the press.

make much of

idiom ~을 중시하다
To make much of someone or something means to give a lot of importance to them.

network**
[nétwə̀:rk]

n. (라디오 · 텔레비전의) 방송망; 망; 관계; v. 통신망을 연결하다
A radio or television network is a company or group of companies that broadcasts radio or television programmes throughout an area.

furor
[fjúərɔ:r]

n. (일시적인) 열중, 열광
A furor is a sudden expression of excitement or anger by a lot of people, especially in reaction to something.

adventure**
[ædvénʧər]

n. 모험; 모험심
If someone has an adventure, they become involved in an unusual, exciting, and rather dangerous journey or series of events.

turn out^{복습}

idiom ~인 것으로 드러나다; 되어 가다; 나타나다
If things turn out, they are discovered or they prove to be the case finally and surprisingly.

dreamer
[drí:mər]

n. 몽상가; 꿈을 꾸는 사람
If you describe someone as a dreamer, you mean that they spend a lot of time thinking about and planning for things that they would like to happen but which are improbable or impractical.

trigger^{복습}
[trígə:r]

v. 촉발시키다; n. (총의) 방아쇠; 폭파 장치
If something triggers an event or situation, it causes it to begin to happen or exist.

nightmare*
[náitmɛər]

n. 악몽; 아주 끔찍한 일
A nightmare is a very frightening dream.

frighten^{복습}
[fraitn]

v. 겁먹게 하다, 놀라게 하다 (frightening a. 무서운)
If something is frightening, it makes you feel afraid, anxious, or nervous.

awaken^{복습}
[əwéikən]

v. (잠에서) 깨다; (감정을) 불러일으키다
When you awaken, or when something or someone awakens you, you wake up.

predict[*]
[pridíkt]

v. 예측하다, 예견하다 (prediction n. 예측, 예견)
If you make a prediction about something, you say what you think will happen.

effective[복습]
[iféktiv]

a. 효과적인; 시행되는 (ineffective a. 효과적이지 못한)
If you say that something is ineffective, you mean that it has no effect on a process or situation.

note[***]
[nout]

v. ~에 주목하다; 언급하다; n. 음, 음표; (pl.) 필기, 기록
If you tell someone to note something, you are drawing their attention to it.

force[복습]
[fɔ:rs]

v. 억지로 ~하다; ~를 강요하다; n. 군대; 작용력; 힘; 영향력
If a situation or event forces you to do something, it makes it necessary for you to do something that you would not otherwise have done.

rough[복습]
[rʌf]

a. 힘든, 골치 아픈; 매끈하지 않은, 거친; (행동이) 거친; 개략적인
If you say that someone has had a rough time, you mean that they have had some difficult or unpleasant experiences.

freeze[복습]
[fri:z]

v. (froze-frozen) 얼다; (두려움 등으로 몸이) 얼어붙다; n. 얼어붙음; 동결; 한파
If a liquid or a substance containing a liquid freezes, or if something freezes it, it becomes solid because of low temperatures.

seeming
[sí:miŋ]

a. 외견상의, 겉보기의 (seemingly ad. 외견상으로, 겉보기에는)
If something is seemingly the case, you mean that it appears to be the case, even though it may not really be so.

plentiful[*]
[pléntifəl]

a. 풍부한
Things that are plentiful exist in such large amounts or numbers that there is enough for people's wants or needs.

brush[복습]
[brʌʃ]

n. 덤불, 잡목 숲; 붓; 솔; v. (솔이나 손으로) 털다; 솔질을 하다; ~을 스치다
Brush is an area of rough open land covered with small bushes and trees. You also use brush to refer to the bushes and trees on this land.

scarce[*]
[skɛərs]

a. 부족한, 드문; ad. 겨우, 간신히; 거의 ~없다
If something is scarce, there is not enough of it.

existent
[igzístənt]

a. 실제로 존재하는, 현존하는 (nonexistent a. 존재하지 않는)
If you say that something is nonexistent, you mean that it does not exist when you feel that it should.

predator
[prédətər]

n. 포식자, 포식 동물; 약탈자
A predator is an animal that kills and eats other animals.

sweep[**]
[swi:p]

v. 휩쓸고 가다; (빗자루로) 쓸다; 훑다; n. 쓸기, 비질하기
If something sweeps from one place to another, it moves there extremely quickly.

wipe[복습]
[waip]

v. 지우다; (먼지 · 물기 등을) 닦다; n. 닦기
(wipe out idiom ~을 완전히 없애 버리다)
To wipe out means to destroy something completely or cause something to be completely lost.

amaze^{복습}
[əméiz]

v. (대단히) 놀라게 하다; 경악하게 하다 (amazing a. 놀라운)
You say that something is amazing when it is very surprising and makes you feel pleasure, approval, or wonder.

local**
[lóukəl]

a. 지역의, 현지의; n. 주민, 현지인
Local means existing in or belonging to the area where you live, or to the area that you are talking about.

population**
[pàpjuléiʃən]

n. [생태] 개체군; 인구; (모든) 주민
If you refer to a particular type of population in a country or area, you are referring to all the people or animals of that type there.

initial^{복습}
[iníʃəl]

a. 처음의, 초기의; n. 이름의 첫 글자
You use initial to describe something that happens at the beginning of a process.

rapid^{복습}
[rǽpid]

a. (속도가) 빠른; (행동이) 민첩한 (rapidly ad. 빠르게, 신속히)
A rapid movement is one that is very fast.

eventually**
[ivénʧuəli]

ad. 결국, 마침내
Eventually means at the end of a situation or process or as the final result of it.

career**
[kəríər]

n. 경력, 이력
Your career is the part of your life that you spend working.

real estate
[ríːəl estèit]

n. 부동산 중개업; 부동산
Real estate businesses or real estate agents sell houses, buildings, and land.

come close^{복습}

idiom 거의 ~할 뻔하다
If you come close to do something, you almost achieve it or do it.

204

수고하셨습니다!

드디어 끝까지 다 읽으셨군요! 축하드립니다! 여러분은 이 책을 통해 총 42,328개의 단어를 읽으셨고, 1,500개 이상의 어휘와 표현들을 익히셨습니다. 이 책에 나온 어휘는 다른 원서를 읽을 때에도 빈번히 만날 수 있는 필수 어휘들입니다. 이 책을 읽었던 경험은 비슷한 수준의 다른 원서들을 읽을 때 큰 도움이 될 것입니다. 이제 자신의 상황에 맞게 원서를 반복해서 읽거나, 오디오북을 들어 볼 수 있습니다. 혹은 비슷한 수준의 다른 원서를 찾아 읽는 것도 좋습니다. 일단 원서를 완독한 뒤에 어떻게 계속 영어 공부를 이어갈 수 있을지, 도움말을 꼼꼼히 살펴보고 각자 상황에 맞게 적용해 보세요!

리딩(Reading)을 확실하게 다지고 싶다면? 반복해서 읽어 보세요!

리딩 실력을 탄탄하게 다지고 싶다면, 같은 원서를 2~3번 반복해서 읽을 것을 권합니다. 같은 책을 여러 번 읽으면 지루할 것 같지만, 꼭 그렇지도 않습니다. 반복해서 읽을 때 처음과 주안점을 다르게 두면, 전혀 다른 느낌으로 재미있게 읽을 수 있습니다.

처음 원서를 읽을 때는 생소한 단어들과 스토리로 인해 읽으면서 곧바로 이해하기가 매우 힘들 수 있습니다. 전체 맥락을 잡고 읽어도 약간 버거운 느낌이지요. 하지만 반복해서 읽기 시작하면 달라집니다. 일단 내용을 파악한 상황이기 때문에 문장 구조나 어휘의 활용에 더 집중하게 되고, 조금 더 깊이 있게 읽을 수 있습니다. 좋은 표현과 문장을 수집하고 메모할 만한 여유도 생기게 되지요. 어휘도 많이 익숙해졌기 때문에 리딩 속도에도 탄력이 붙습니다. 처음 읽을 때는 '내용'에서 재미를 느꼈다면, 반복해서 읽을 때에는 '영어'에서 재미를 느끼게 되는 것입니다. 따라서 리딩 실력을 더욱 확고하게 다지고자 한다면, 같은 책을 2~3회 정도 반복해서 읽을 것을 권해 드립니다.

리스닝(Listening) 실력을 늘리고 싶다면?
귀를 통해서 읽어 보세요!

많은 영어 학습자들이 '리스닝이 안 돼서 문제'라고 한탄합니다. 그리고 리스닝 실력을 늘리는 방법으로 무슨 뜻인지 몰라도 반복해서 듣는 '무작정 듣기'를 선택합니다. 하지만 뜻도 모르면서 무작정 듣는 일에는 엄청난 인내력이 필요합니다. 그래서 대부분 며칠 시도하다가 포기해 버리고 말지요.

따라서 모르는 내용을 무작정 듣는 것보다는 어느 정도 알고 있는 내용을 반복해서 듣는 것이 더 효과적인 듣기 방법입니다. 그리고 이런 방식의 듣기에 활용할 수 있는 가장 좋은 교재가 오디오북입니다.

리스닝 실력을 향상하고 싶다면, 이 책에서 제공하는 오디오북을 이용해서 듣는 연습을 해 보세요. 활용법은 간단합니다. 일단 책을 한 번 완독했다면, 오디오북을 통해 다시 들어 보는 것입니다. 휴대 기기에 넣어 시간이 날 때 틈틈이 듣는 것도 좋고, 책상에 앉아 눈으로는 텍스트를 보며 귀로 읽는 것도 좋습니다. 이미 읽었던 내용이라 이해하기가 훨씬 수월하고, 애매했던 발음들도 자연스럽게 교정할 수 있습니다. 또 성우의 목소리 연기를 듣다 보면 내용이 더욱 생동감 있게 다가와 이해도가 높아지는 효과도 거둘 수 있습니다.

반대로 듣기에 자신 있는 사람이라면, 책을 읽기 전에 처음부터 오디오북을 먼저 듣는 것도 좋은 방법입니다. 귀를 통해 책을 쭉 읽어보고, 이후에 다시 눈으로 책을 읽으면서 잘 들리지 않았던 부분들을 보충하는 것이지요.

중요한 것은 내용을 따라가면서, 내용에 푹 빠져서 반복해 들어야 한다는 것입니다. 이렇게 연습을 반복해서 눈으로 읽지 않은 책이라도 '귀를 통해' 읽을 수 있을 정도가 되면, 리스닝으로 고생하는 일은 거의 없을 것입니다.

 왼쪽의 QR 코드를 인식하여 정식 오디오북을 들어 보세요!
더불어 롱테일북스 홈페이지(www.longtailbooks.co.kr)에서도
오디오북 MP3 파일을 다운로드 받을 수 있습니다.

스피킹(Speaking)이 고민이라면? 소리 내어 읽어 보세요!

스피킹 역시 많은 학습자들이 고민하는 부분입니다. 스피킹이 고민이라면, 원서를 큰 소리로 읽는 낭독 훈련(Voice Reading)을 해 보세요! '소리 내어 읽는 것이 말하기에 정말로 도움이 될까?'라고 의아한 생각이 들 수도 있습니다. 하지만 인간의 두뇌 입장에서 봤을 때, 성대 구조를 활용해서 '발화'한 다는 점에서는 소리 내어 읽기와 말하기에 큰 차이가 없다고 합니다. 소리 내어 읽는 것은 '타인의 생각'을 전달하고, 직접 말하는 것은 '자신의 생각'을 전달한다는 차이가 있을 뿐, 머릿속에서 문장을 처리하고 조음기관(혀와 성대 등)을 움직여 의미를 만든다는 점에서 같은 과정인 것이지요. 따라서 소리 내어 읽는 연습을 꾸준히 하는 것은 스피킹 연습에 큰 도움이 됩니다.

소리 내어 읽기를 하는 방법은 간단합니다. 일단 오디오북을 들으면서 성우의 목소리를 최대한 따라 하며 같이 읽어 보세요. 발음뿐 아니라 억양, 어조, 느낌까지 완벽히 따라 한다고 생각하면서 소리 내어 읽습니다. 따라 읽는 것이 조금 익숙해지면, 옆의 누군가에게 이 책을 읽어 준다는 생각으로 소리 내어 계속 읽어 나갑니다. 한 번 눈과 귀로 읽었던 책이기 때문에 보다 수월하게 진행할 수 있고, 자연스럽게 어휘와 표현을 복습하는 효과도 거두게 됩니다. 또 이렇게 소리 내어 읽은 것을 녹음해서 들어 보면 스스로에게도 좋은 피드백이 됩니다.

최근 말하기가 강조되면서 소리 내어 읽기가 크게 각광을 받고 있기는 하지만, 그렇다고 소리 내어 읽기가 무조건 좋은 것만은 아닙니다. 책을 소리 내어 읽다 보면, 무의식적으로 속으로 발음을 하는 습관을 가지게 되어 리딩 속도 자체는 오히려 크게 떨어지는 현상이 발생할 수 있습니다. 따라서 빠른 리딩 속도가 중요한 수험생이나 고학력 학습자들에게는 소리 내어 읽기가 적절하지 않은 방법입니다. 효과가 좋다는 말만 믿고 무턱대고 따라 하기보다는 자신의 필요에 맞게 우선순위를 정하고 원서를 활용하는 것이 좋습니다.

라이팅(Writing)까지 욕심이 난다면? 요약하는 연습을 해 보세요!

원서를 라이팅 연습에 직접적으로 활용하는 데에는 한계가 있지만, 적절히 활용하면 원서도 유용한 라이팅 자료가 될 수 있습니다.

특히 책을 읽고 그 내용을 요약하는 연습은 큰 도움이 됩니다. 요약 훈련의 방식도 간단합니다. 원서를 읽고 그날 읽은 분량만큼 혹은 책을 다 읽고 전체 내용을 기반으로, 책 내용을 한번 요약하고 나의 느낌을 영어로 적어보는 것입니다.

이때 그 책에 나왔던 단어와 표현을 최대한 활용하여 요약하는 것이 중요합니다. 영어 표현력은 결국 얼마나 다양한 어휘로 많은 표현을 해 보았느냐가 좌우하게 됩니다. 이런 면에서 내가 읽은 책을, 그 책에 나온 문장과 어휘로 다시 표현해 보는 것은 매우 효율적인 방법입니다. 책에 나온 어휘와 표현을 단순히 읽고 무슨 말인지 아는 정도가 아니라, 실제로 직접 활용해서 쓸 수 있을 만큼 확실하게 익히게 되는 것이지요. 여기에 첨삭까지 받을 수 있는 방법이 있다면 금상첨화입니다.

이러한 '표현하기' 연습은 스피킹 훈련에도 그대로 적용될 수 있습니다. 책을 읽고 그 내용을 3분 안에 다른 사람에게 영어로 말하는 연습을 해 보세요. 순발력과 표현력을 기르는 좋은 훈련이 될 것입니다.

꾸준히 원서를 읽고 싶다면? 뉴베리 수상작을 계속 읽어 보세요!

뉴베리 상이 세계 최고 권위의 아동 문학상인 만큼, 그 수상작들은 확실히 완성도를 검증받은 작품이라고 할 수 있습니다. 특히 '쉬운 어휘로 쓰인 깊이 있는 문장'으로 이루어졌다는 점이 영어 학습자들에게 큰 호응을 얻고 있습니다. 이렇게 '검증된 원서'를 꾸준히 읽는 것은 영어 실력 향상에 큰 도움이 됩니다.

아래에 수준별로 제시된 뉴베리 수상작 목록을 보며 적절한 책들을 찾아 계속 읽어 보세요. 꼭 뉴베리 수상작이 아니더라도 마음에 드는 작가의 다른 책을 읽어 보는 것 또한 아주 좋은 방법입니다.

• 영어 초보자도 쉽게 읽을 만한 아주 쉬운 수준. 소리 내어 읽기에도 아주 적합.
Sarah, Plain and Tall*(Medal, 8,331단어), The Hundred Penny Box (Honor, 5,878단어), The Hundred Dresses*(Honor, 7,329단어), My Father's Dragon (Honor, 7,682단어), 26 Fairmount Avenue (Honor, 6,737단어)

- 중 · 고등학생 정도 영어 학습자라면 쉽게 읽을 수 있는 수준. 소리 내어 읽기에도 비교적 적합한 편.

Because of Winn−Dixie★(Honor, 22,123단어), What Jamie Saw (Honor, 17,203단어), Charlotte's Web (Honor, 31,938단어), Dear Mr. Henshaw (Medal, 18,145단어), Missing May (Medal, 17,509단어)

- 대학생 정도 영어 학습자라면 무난한 수준. 소리 내어 읽기에 적합하지 않음.

Number The Stars★(Medal, 27,197단어), A Single Shard (Medal, 33,726단어), The Tale of Despereaux★(Medal, 32,375단어), Hatchet★(Medal, 42,328단어), Bridge to Terabithia (Medal, 32,888단어), A Fine White Dust (Honor, 19,022단어), Jennifer, Hecate, Macbeth, William McKinley and Me, Elizabeth (Honor, 23,266단어)

- 원서 완독 경험을 가진 학습자에게 적절한 수준. 소리 내어 읽기에 적합하지 않음.

The Giver★(Medal, 43,617단어), From the Mixed−Up Files of Mrs. Basil E. Frankweiler (Medal, 30,906단어), The View from Saturday (Medal, 42,685단어), Holes★(Medal, 47,079단어), Criss Cross (Medal, 48,221단어), Walk Two Moons (Medal, 59,400단어), The Graveyard Book (Medal, 67,380단어)

뉴베리 수상작과 뉴베리 수상 작가의 좋은 작품을 엄선한 「뉴베리 컬렉션」에도 위 목록에 있는 도서 중 상당수가 포함될 예정입니다.

★ 「뉴베리 컬렉션」으로 이미 출간된 도서

**어떤 책들이 출간되었는지 확인하려면, 지금 인터넷 서점에서
뉴베리 컬렉션을 검색해 보세요.**

뉴베리 수상작을 동영상 강의로 만나 보세요!

영어원서 전문 동영상 강의 사이트 영서당(yseodang.com)에서는 뉴베리 컬렉션 『Holes』, 『Because of Winn-Dixie』, 『The Miraculous Journey of Edward Tulane』, 『Wayside School 시리즈』 등의 동영상 강의를 제공하고 있습니다. 뉴베리 수상작이라는 최고의 영어 교재와 EBS 출신 인기 강사가 만난 명강의! 지금 사이트를 방문해서 무료 샘플 강의를 들어 보세요!

'스피드 리딩 카페'를 통해 원서 읽기 습관을 길러 보세요!

일상에서 영어를 한마디도 쓰지 않는 비영어권 국가에서 살고 있는 우리가 영어 환경에 가장 쉽고, 편하고, 부담 없이 노출되는 방법은 바로 '영어원서 읽기'입니다. 언제 어디서든 원서를 붙잡고 읽기만 하면 곧바로 영어를 접하는 환경이 만들어지기 때문이지요. 하루에 20분씩만 꾸준히 읽는다면, 1년에 무려 120시간 동안 영어에 노출될 수 있습니다. 이러한 이유 때문에 영어 교육 전문가들이 영어 원서 읽기를 추천하는 것이지요.
하지만 원서 읽기가 좋다는 것을 알아도 막상 꾸준히 읽는 것은 쉽지 않습니다. 그럴 때에는 13만 명 이상의 회원을 보유한 국내 최대 원서 읽기 동호회 〈스피드 리딩 카페〉(cafe.naver.com/readingtc)를 방문해 보세요.
원서별로 정리된 무료 PDF 단어장과 수준별 추천 원서 목록 등 유용한 자료는 물론, 뉴베리 수상작을 포함한 다양한 원서의 리뷰와 정보를 무료로 확인할 수 있습니다. 특히 함께 모여서 원서를 읽는 '북클럽'은 중간에 포기하지 않고 원서 읽기 습관을 기르는 데 큰 도움이 될 것입니다.

chapters 1 & 2

1.B   When he saw Brian look at him, the pilot seemed to open up a bit and he smiled. "Ever fly in the copilot's seat before?" He leaned over and lifted the headset off his right ear and put it on his temple, yelling to overcome the sound of the engine. Brian shook his head. He had never been in any kind of plane, never seen the cockpit of a plane except in films or on television. It was loud and confusing. "First time." "It's not as complicated as it looks. Good plane like this almost flies itself." The pilot shrugged. "Makes my job easy." He took Brian's left arm. "Here, put your hands on the controls, your feet on the rudder pedals, and I'll show you what I mean."

2. A   So this summer, this first summer when he was allowed to have "visitation rights" with his father, with the divorce only one month old, Brian was heading north.

3. C   Brian took the sack and opened the top. Inside there was a hatchet, the kind with a steel handle and a rubber handgrip. The head was in a stout leather case that had a brass—riveted belt loop. "It goes on your belt." His mother spoke now without looking at him. There were some farm trucks on the road now and she had to weave through them and watch traffic. "The man at the store said you could use it. You know. In the woods with your father."

4. B   Because it was a bush flight from a small airport there had been no security and the plane had been waiting, with the engine running when he arrived and he had grabbed his suitcase and pack bag and run for the plane without stopping to remove the hatchet. So it was still on his belt.

5. D   "Your signal is breaking up and I lost most of it. Understand . . . pilot . . . you can't fly. Correct? Over." Brian could barely hear him now, heard mostly noise and static. "That's right. I can't fly. The plane is flying now but I don't know how much longer. Over." ". . . lost signal. Your location please. Flight number . . . location . . . ver." "I don't know my flight number or location. I don't know anything. I told you that, over." He waited now, waited but there was nothing.

6. C   When the plane ran out of fuel it would go down. Period. Or he could pull

the throttle out and make it go down now. He had seen the pilot push the throttle in to increase speed. If he pulled the throttle back out, the engine would slow down and the plane would go down. Those were his choices. He could wait for the plane to run out of gas and fall or he could push the throttle in and make it happen sooner.

7. A   He did what he could, tightened his seatbelt, positioned himself, rehearsed mentally again and again what his procedure should be. When the plane ran out of gas he should hold the nose down and head for the nearest lake and try to fly the plane kind of onto the water. That's how he thought of it. Kind of fly the plane onto the water. And just before it hit he should pull back on the wheel and slow the plane down to reduce the impact.

chapters 3 & 4

1. C   Then a wild crashing sound, ripping of metal, and the plane rolled to the right and blew through the trees, out over the water and down, down to slam into the lake, skip once on water as hard as concrete, water that tore the windshield out and shattered the side windows, water that drove him back into the seat. Somebody was screaming, screaming as the plane drove down into the water. Someone screamed tight animal screams of fear and pain and he did not know that it was his sound, that he roared against the water that took him and the plane still deeper, down in the water.

2. B   His mother. She was sitting in a station wagon, a strange wagon. He saw her and she did not see him. Brian was going to wave or call out, but something stopped him. There was a man in the car. Short blond hair, the man had. Wearing some kind of white pullover tennis shirt.

3. A   Brian opened his eyes and screamed. For seconds he did not know where he was, only that the crash was still happening and he was going to die, and he screamed until his breath was gone. Then silence, filled with sobs as he pulled in air, half crying. How could it be so quiet? Moments ago there was nothing but noise, crashing and tearing, screaming, now quiet. Some birds were singing. How could birds be singing? His legs felt wet and he raised up on his hands and looked back down at them. They were in the lake. Strange. They went down into the water. He tried to move, but pain hammered into him and made his breath shorten into gasps and he stopped, his legs still in the water.

4. D   He was still in pain, all-over pain. His legs were cramped and drawn up, tight and aching, and his back hurt when he tried to move. Worst was a keening throb in his head that pulsed with every beat of his heart. It seemed that the whole crash had happened to his head. He rolled on his back and felt his sides and his legs, moving

things slowly. He rubbed his arms; nothing seemed to be shattered or even sprained all that badly. When he was nine he had plowed his small dirt bike into a parked car and broken his ankle, had to wear a cast for eight weeks, and there was nothing now like that. Nothing broken. Just battered around a bit.

5. A   Things seemed to go back and forth between reality and imagination—except that it was all reality. One second he seemed only to have imagined that there was a plane crash that he had fought out of the sinking plane and swum to shore; that it had all happened to some other person or in a movie playing in his mind. Then he would feel his clothes, wet and cold, and his forehead would slash a pain through his thoughts and he would know it was real, that it had really happened. But all in a haze, all in a haze-world.

6. B   And when the sun was fully up and heating him directly, bringing steam off of his wet clothes and bathing him with warmth, the mosquitoes and flies disappeared. Almost that suddenly. One minute he was sitting in the middle of a swarm; the next, they were gone and the sun was on him. Vampires, he thought. Apparently they didn't like the deep of night, perhaps because it was too cool, and they couldn't take the direct sunlight.

7. D   If the plane had come down a little to the left it would have hit the rocks and never made the lake. He would have been smashed. Destroyed. The word came. I would have been destroyed and torn and smashed. Driven into the rocks and destroyed. Luck, he thought. I have luck, I had good luck there. But he knew that was wrong. If he had had good luck his parents wouldn't have divorced because of the Secret and he wouldn't have been flying with a pilot who had a heart attack and he wouldn't be here where he had to have good luck to keep from being destroyed.

chapters 5 & 6

1. A   He stood, using the tree to pull himself up because there was still some pain and much stiffness, and looked down at the lake. It was water. But he did not know if he could drink it. Nobody had ever told him if you could or could not drink lakes.

2. D   With his mind opened and thoughts happening it all tried to come in with a rush, all of what had occurred and he could not take it. The whole thing turned into a confused jumble that made no sense. So he fought it down and tried to take one thing at a time. He had been flying north to visit his father for a couple of months, in the summer, and the pilot had had a heart attack and had died, and the plane had crashed somewhere in the Canadian north woods but he did not know how far they had flown or in what direction or where he was . . . Slow down, he thought. Slow down more. My name is

214

Brian Robeson and I am thirteen years old and I am alone in the north woods of Canada. All right, he thought, that's simple enough. I was flying to visit my father and the plane crashed and sank in a lake. There, keep it that way. Short thoughts.

3. C   Brian had once had an English teacher, a guy named Perpich, who was always talking about being positive, thinking positive, staying on top of things. That's how Perpich had put it—stay positive and stay on top of things. Brian thought of him now— wondered how to stay positive and stay on top of this. All Perpich would say is that I have to get motivated. He was always telling kids to get motivated.

4. D   Ahh, there it was—the moment when the pilot had his heart attack his right foot had jerked down on the rudder pedal and the plane had slewed sideways. What did that mean? Why did that keep coming into his thinking that way, nudging and pushing? It means, a voice in his thoughts said, that they might not be coming for you tonight or even tomorrow. When the pilot pushed the rudder pedal the plane had jerked to the side and assumed a new course. Brian could not remember how much it had pulled around, but it wouldn't have had to be much because after that, with the pilot dead, Brian had flown for hour after hour on the new course.

5. B   There were large things in the woods. There were wolves, he thought, and bears—other things. In the dark he would be in the open here, just sitting at the bottom of a tree. He looked around suddenly, felt the hair on the back of his neck go up. Things might be looking at him right now, waiting for him—waiting for dark so they could move in and take him. He fingered the hatchet at his belt. It was the only weapon he had, but it was something. He had to have some kind of shelter.

6. B   He wanted to stay near the lake because he thought the plane, even deep in the water, might show up to somebody flying over and he didn't want to diminish any chance he might have of being found.

7. A   He saw a robin, and some kind of sparrows, and a flock of reddish orange birds with thick beaks. Twenty or thirty of them were sitting in one of the pines. They made much noise and flew away ahead of him when he walked under the tree. He watched them fly, their color a bright slash in solid green, and in this way he found the berries. The birds landed in some taller willow type of undergrowth with wide leaves and started jumping and making noise. At first he was too far away to see what they were doing, but their color drew him and he moved toward them, keeping the lake in sight on his right, and when he got closer he saw they were eating berries.

chapters 7 & 8

1. D   It was still very early, only just past true dawn, and the water was so calm he

could see his reflection. It frightened him—the face was cut and bleeding, swollen and lumpy, the hair all matted, and on his forehead a cut had healed but left the hair stuck with blood and scab. His eyes were slits in the bites and he was—somehow—covered with dirt. He slapped the water with his hand to destroy the mirror. Ugly, he thought. Very, very ugly. And he was, at that moment, almost overcome with self-pity.

2. C   Back at the shelter the berries lay in a pile where he had dumped them when he grabbed his windbreaker—gut cherries he called them in his mind now—and he thought of eating some of them. Not such a crazy amount, as he had, which he felt brought on the sickness in the night— but just enough to stave off the hunger a bit.

3. A   If the bear had wanted you, his brain said, he would have taken you. It is something to understand, he thought, not something to run away from. The bear was eating berries. Not people. The bear made no move to hurt you, to threaten you. It stood to see you better, study you, then went on its way eating berries. It was a big bear, but it did not want you, did not want to cause you harm, and that is the thing to understand here.

4. C   Outside the rain poured down, but Brian lay back, drinking the syrup from the berries, dry and with the pain almost all gone, the stiffness also gone, his belly full and a good taste in his mouth. For the first time since the crash he was not thinking of himself, of his own life. Brian was wondering if the bear was as surprised as he to find another being in the berries.

5. D   His fingers gingerly touched a group of needles that had been driven through his pants and into the fleshy part of his calf. They were stiff and very sharp on the ends that stuck out, and he knew then what the attacker had been. A porcupine had stumbled into his shelter and when he had kicked it the thing had slapped him with its tail of quills.

6. B   He did not know how long it took, but later he looked back on this time of crying in the corner of the dark cave and thought of it as when he learned the most important rule of survival, which was that feeling sorry for yourself didn't work. It wasn't just that it was wrong to do, or that it was considered incorrect. It was more than that— it didn't work. When he sat alone in the darkness and cried and was done, was all done with it, nothing had changed. His leg still hurt, it was still dark, he was still alone and the self-pity had accomplished nothing.

7. C   The hatchet was still in his hand, and as he stretched and raised it over his head it caught the first rays of the morning sun. The first faint light hit the silver of the hatchet and it flashed a brilliant gold in the light. Like fire. That is it, he thought. What they were trying to tell me. Fire. The hatchet was the key to it all. When he threw the

hatchet at the porcupine in the cave and missed and hit the stone wall it had showered sparks, a golden shower of sparks in the dark, as golden with fire as the sun was now. The hatchet was the answer. That's what his father and Terry had been trying to tell him. Somehow he could get fire from the hatchet. The sparks would make fire.

chapters 9 & 10

1. B   The material had to be finer. There had to be a soft and incredibly fine nest for the sparks. I must make a home for the sparks, he thought. A perfect home or they won't stay, they won't make fire. He started ripping the bark, using his fingernails at first, and when that didn't work he used the sharp edge of the hatchet, cutting the bark in thin slivers, hairs so fine they were almost not there.

2. C   What did it take? You have to have fuel, he thought—and he had that. The bark was fuel. Oxygen—there had to be air. He needed to add air. He had to fan on it, blow on it. He made the nest ready again, held the hatchet backward, tensed, and struck four quick blows. Sparks came down and he leaned forward as fast as he could and blew. Too hard. There was a bright, almost intense glow, and then it was gone. He had blown it out. Another set of strikes, more sparks. He leaned and blew, but gently this time, holding back and aiming the stream of air from his mouth to hit the brightest spot. Five or six sparks had fallen in a tight mass of bark hair and Brian centered his efforts there. The sparks grew with his gentle breath.

3. D   If he kept the fire small it would be perfect and would keep anything like the porcupine from coming through the door again. A friend and a guard, he thought. So much from a little spark. A friend and a guard from a tiny spark.

4. A   Between trips he added small pieces to the fire to keep it going and on one of the trips to get wood he noticed an added advantage of the fire. When he was in the shade of the trees breaking limbs the mosquitoes swarmed on him, as usual, but when he came to the fire, or just near the shelter where the smoke eddied and swirled, the insects were gone.

5. C   Why would anything wild come up from the water to play in the sand? Not that way, animals weren't that way. They didn't waste time that way. It had come up from the water for a reason, a good reason, and he must try to understand the reason, he must change to fully understand the reason himself or he would not make it. It had come up from the water for a reason, and the reason, he thought, squatting, the reason had to do with the pile of sand. He brushed the top off gently with his hand but found only damp sand. Still, there must be a reason and he carefully kept scraping and digging until, about four inches down, he suddenly came into a small chamber in the cool-damp sand and

there lay eggs, many eggs, almost perfectly round eggs the size of table tennis balls, and he laughed then because he knew.

6. B   He looked out across the lake and brought the egg to his mouth and closed his eyes and sucked and squeezed the egg at the same time and swallowed as fast as he could. "Ecch . . ." It had a greasy, almost oily taste, but it was still an egg. His throat tried to throw it back up, his whole body seemed to convulse with it, but his stomach took it, held it, and demanded more. The second egg was easier, and by the third one he had no trouble at all—it just slid down. He ate six of them, could have easily eaten all of them and not been full, but a part of him said to hold back, save the rest.

7. D   He fought the hunger down again, controlled it. He would take them now and store them and save them and eat one a day, and he realized as he thought it that he had forgotten that they might come. The searchers. Surely, they would come before he could eat all the eggs at one a day. He had forgotten to think about them and that wasn't good. He had to keep thinking of them because if he forgot them and did not think of them they might forget about him. And he had to keep hoping.

chapters 11 & 12

1. C   He did not know when the change started, but it was there; when a sound came to him now he didn't just hear it but would know the sound. He would swing and look at it—a breaking twig, a movement of air—and know the sound as if he somehow could move his mind back down the wave of sound to the source. He could know what the sound was before he quite realized he had heard it. And when he saw something—a bird moving a wing inside a bush or a ripple on the water—he would truly see that thing, not just notice it as he used to notice things in the city. He would see all parts of it; see the whole wing, the feathers, see the color of the feathers, see the bush, and the size and shape and color of its leaves.

2. C   When the wood was done he decided to get a signal fire ready. He moved to the top of the rock ridge that comprised the bluff over his shelter and was pleased to find a large, flat stone area. More wood, he thought, moaning inwardly. He went back to the fallen trees and found more dead limbs, carrying them up on the rock until he had enough for a bonfire. Initially he had thought of making a signal fire every day but he couldn't—he would never be able to keep the wood supply going. So while he was working he decided to have the fire ready and if he heard an engine, or even thought he heard a plane engine, he would run up with a burning limb and set off the signal fire.

3. A   Sitting on one limb was a blue bird with a crest and sharp beak, a kingfisher— he thought of a picture he had seen once—which left the branch while he watched and

dove into the water. It emerged a split part of a second later. In its mouth was a small fish, wiggling silver in the sun. It took the fish to a limb, juggled it twice, and swallowed it whole. Fish. Of course, he thought. There were fish in the lake and they were food. And if a bird could do it . . . He scrambled down the side of the bluff and trotted to the edge of the lake, looking down into the water. Somehow it had never occurred to him to look inside the water—only at the surface.

4. B   He had worked on the fish spear until it had become more than just a tool. He'd spent hours and hours on it, and now it didn't work. He moved into the shallows and stood and the fish came to him. Just as before they swarmed around his legs, some of them almost six inches long, but no matter how he tried they were too fast.

5. A   He needed something to spring the spear forward, some way to make it move faster than the fish—some motive force. A string that snapped—or a bow. A bow and arrow. A thin, long arrow with the point in the water and the bow pulled back so that all he had to do was release the arrow . . . yes. That was it. He had to "invent" the bow and arrow—he almost laughed as he moved out of the water and put his shoes on.

6. D   The wood was hard and he didn't want to cause it to split so he took his time, took small chips and concentrated so hard that at first he didn't hear it. A persistent whine, like the insects only more steady with an edge of a roar to it, was in his ears and he chopped and cut and was thinking of a bow, how he would make a bow, how it would be when he shaped it with the hatchet and still the sound did not cut through until the limb was nearly off the tree and the whine was inside his head and he knew it then. A plane!

7. B   He stood on the bluff over the lake, his face cooking in the roaring bonfire, watching the clouds of ash and smoke going into the sky and thought—no, more than thought—he knew then that he would not get out of this place. Not now, not ever. That had been a search plane. He was sure of it. That must have been them and they had come as far off to the side of the flight plan as they thought they would have to come and then turned back. They did not see his smoke, did not hear the cry from his mind. They would not return. He would never leave now, never get out of here.

chapters 13 & 14

1. A   He had never seen a wolf and the size threw him—not as big as a bear but somehow seeming that large. The wolf claimed all that was below him as his own, took Brian as his own. Brian looked back and for a moment felt afraid because the wolf was so . . . so right. He knew Brian, knew him and owned him and chose not to do anything to him. But the fear moved then, moved away, and Brian knew the wolf for what it was— another part of the woods, another part of all of it. Brian relaxed the tension on the spear

in his hand, settled the bow in his other hand from where it had started to come up. He knew the wolf now, as the wolf knew him, and he nodded to it, nodded and smiled.

2. D   When the plane had come and gone it had put him down, gutted him and dropped him and left him with nothing. The rest of that first day he had gone down and down until dark. He had let the fire go out, had forgotten to eat even an egg, had let his brain take him down to where he was done, where he wanted to be done and done. To where he wanted to die. He had settled into the gray funk deeper and still deeper until finally, in the dark, he had gone up on the ridge and taken the hatchet and tried to end it by cutting himself.

3. A   Of course—he had forgotten that water refracts, bends light. He had learned that somewhere, in some class, maybe it was biology—he couldn't remember. But it did bend light and that meant the fish were not where they appeared to be. They were lower, just below, which meant he had to aim just under them. He would not forget his first hit. Not ever. A roundshaped fish, with golden sides, sides as gold as the sun, stopped in front of the arrow and he aimed just beneath it, at the bottom edge of the fish, and released the arrow and there was a bright flurry, a splash of gold in the water. He grabbed the arrow and raised it up and the fish was on the end, wiggling against the blue sky.

4. B   It had been a feast day, his first feast day, and a celebration of being alive and the new way he had of getting food. By the end of that day, when it became dark and he lay next to the fire with his stomach full of fish and grease from the meat smeared around his mouth, he could feel new hope building in him. Not hope that he would be rescued—that was gone. But hope in his knowledge. Hope in the fact that he could learn and survive and take care of himself.

5. C   Small mistakes could turn into disasters, funny little mistakes could snowball so that while you were still smiling at the humor you could find yourself looking at death. In the city if he made a mistake usually there was a way to rectify it, make it all right. If he fell on his bike and sprained a leg he could wait for it to heal; if he forgot something at the store he could find other food in the refrigerator. Now it was different, and all so quick, all so incredibly quick. If he sprained a leg here he might starve before he could get around again; if he missed while he was hunting or if the fish moved away he might starve. If he got sick, really sick so he couldn't move he might starve.

6. D   Food had to be protected. While he was in the lake trying to clear his eyes the skunk went ahead and dug up the rest of the turtle eggs and ate every one. Licked all the shells clean and couldn't have cared less that Brian was thrashing around in the water like a dying carp. The skunk had found food and was taking it and Brian was paying for a lesson.

220

7. B   He had made a good shelter and food shelf, but he had no food except for fish and the last of the berries. And the fish, as good as they still tasted then, were not something he could store. His mother had left some salmon out by mistake one time when they went on an overnight trip to Cape Hesper to visit relatives and when they got back the smell filled the whole house. There was no way to store fish. At least, he thought, no way to store them dead. But as he looked at the weave of his structure a thought came to him and he moved down to the water. He had been putting the waste from the fish back in the water and the food had attracted hundreds of new ones. "I wonder . . ." They seemed to come easily to the food, at least the small ones. He had no trouble now shooting them and had even speared one with his old fish spear now that he knew to aim low. He could dangle something in his fingers and they came right up to it. It might be possible, he thought, might just be possible to trap them. Make some kind of pond . . .

chapters 15 & 16

1. C   Then there were the foolbirds. They exasperated him to the point where they were close to driving him insane. The birds were everywhere, five and six in a flock, and their camouflage was so perfect that it was possible for Brian to sit and rest, leaning against a tree, with one of them standing right in front of him in a willow clump, two feet away—hidden—only to explode into deafening flight just when Brian least expected it. He just couldn't see them, couldn't figure out how to locate them before they flew, because they stood so perfectly still and blended in so perfectly well.

2. A   And that had been the secret. He had been looking for feathers, for the color of the bird, for a bird sitting there. He had to look for the outline instead, had to see the shape instead of the feathers or color, had to train his eyes to see the shape . . .

3. B   But in the end he found that if he saw the bird sitting and moved sideways toward it—not directly toward it but at an angle, back and forth—he could get close enough to put the spear point out ahead almost to the bird and thrust-lunge with it. He came close twice, and then, down along the lake not far from the beaver house he got his first meat.

4. B   Mud filled his eyes, his ears, the horn boss on the moose drove him deeper and deeper into the bottom muck, and suddenly it was over and he felt alone. He sputtered to the surface, sucking air and fighting panic, and when he wiped the mud and water out of his eyes and cleared them he saw the cow standing sideways to him, not ten feet away, calmly chewing on a lily pad root. She didn't appear to even see him, or didn't seem to care about him, and Brian turned carefully and began to swim-crawl out of the water. As soon

as he moved, the hair on her back went up and she charged him again, using her head and front hooves this time, slamming him back and down into the water, on his back this time, and he screamed the air out of his lungs and hammered on her head with his fists and filled his throat with water and she left again.

5. D   So insane, he thought, letting sleep cover the pain in his chest—such an insane attack for no reason and he fell asleep with his mind trying to make the moose have reason.

6. C   I might be hit but I'm not done. When the light comes I'll start to rebuild. I still have the hatchet and that's all I had in the first place.

7. A   There it was, sticking up out of the water. The tornado must have flipped the plane around somehow when it hit the lake, changed the position of the plane and raised the tail. Well, he thought. Well, just look at that. And at the same moment a cutting thought hit him. He thought of the pilot, still in the plane, and that brought a shiver and massive sadness that seemed to settle on him like a weight and he thought that he should say or do something for the pilot; some words but he didn't know any of the right words, the religious words.

chapters 17 & 18

1. D   Curving his body, he rested his head on his arm, and began to sleep when a picture came into his head. The tail of the plane sticking out of the water. There it was, the tail sticking up. And inside the plane, near the tail somewhere, was the survival pack. It must have survived the crash because the plane's main body was still intact. That was the picture—the tail sticking up and the survival pack inside—right there in his mind as he dozed. His eyes snapped opened. If I could get at the pack, he thought. Oh, if I could get at the pack. It probably had food and knives and matches. It might have a sleeping bag. It might have fishing gear. Oh, it must have so many wonderful things—if I could get at the pack and just get some of those things.

2. B   What he needed were logs with limbs sticking out, then he could cross the limbs of one log over the limbs of another and "weave" them together as he had done his wall, the food shelf cover, and the fish gate. He scanned the area above the beach and found four dry treetops that had been broken off by the storm. These had limbs and he dragged them down to his work area at the water's edge and fitted them together.

3. A   Pushing the raft, he figured, was about like trying to push an aircraft carrier. All the branches that stuck down into the water dragged and pulled and the logs themselves fought any forward motion and he hadn't gone twenty feet when he realized that it was going to be much harder than he thought to get the raft to the plane. It barely moved and

if he kept going this way he would just about reach the plane at dark.

4. C He slammed his fist against the body of the plane and to his complete surprise the aluminum covering gave easily under his blow. He hit it again, and once more it bent and gave and he found that even when he didn't strike it but just pushed, it still moved. It was really, he thought, very thin aluminum skin over a kind of skeleton and if it gave that easily he might be able to force his way through . . .

5. B For all this time, all the living and fighting, the hatchet had been everything— he had always worn it. Without the hatchet he had nothing—no fire, no tools, no weapons—he was nothing. The hatchet was, had been him. And he had dropped it. "Arrrgghhh!" He yelled it, choked on it, a snarl-cry of rage at his own carelessness.

6. D He started chopping again, cutting the aluminum away in small triangles, putting each one on the raft as he chopped—he could never throw anything away again, he thought—because they might be useful later. Bits of metal, fish arrowheads or lures, maybe.

7. A It was the survival bag. He pulled and tore at it to loosen it and just as it broke free and his heart leaped to feel it rise he looked up, above the bag. In the light coming through the side window, the pale green light from the water, he saw the pilot's head only it wasn't the pilot's head any longer. The fish. He'd never really thought of it, but the fish—the fish he had been eating all this time had to eat, too. They had been at the pilot all this time, almost two months, nibbling and chewing and all that remained was the not quite cleaned skull and when he looked up it wobbled loosely. Too much. Too much. His mind screamed in horror and he slammed back and was sick in the water, sick so that he choked on it and tried to breathe water and could have ended there, ended with the pilot where it almost ended when they first arrived except that his legs jerked.

chapter 19 & epilogue

1. C It was a strange feeling, holding the rifle. It somehow removed him from everything around him. Without the rifle he had to fit in, to be part of it all, to understand it and use it—the woods, all of it. With the rifle, suddenly, he didn't have to know; did not have to be afraid or understand. He didn't have to get close to a foolbird to kill it—didn't have to know how it would stand if he didn't look at it and moved off to the side.

2. B He turned the switch back and forth a few times but nothing happened—he couldn't even hear static—so, as with the rifle, he set it against the wall and went back to the bag. It was probably ruined in the crash, he thought.

3. C If I'm careful, he thought, they'll last as long as . . . as long as I need them to

last. If I'm careful.... No. Not yet. I won't be careful just yet. First I am going to have a feast. Right here and now I am going to cook up a feast and eat until I drop and then I'll be careful.

4. D   It passed directly over him, very low, tipped a wing sharply over the tail of the crashed plane in the lake, cut power, glided down the long part of the L of the lake, then turned and glided back, touching the water gently once, twice, and settling with a spray to taxi and stop with its floats gently bumping the beach in front of Brian's shelter. He had not moved. It had all happened so fast that he hadn't moved. He sat with the pot of orange drink still in his hand, staring at the plane, not quite understanding it yet; not quite knowing yet that it was over.

5. A   The pilot who landed so suddenly in the lake was a fur buyer mapping Cree trapping camps for future buying runs—drawn by Brian when he unwittingly turned on the emergency transmitter and left it going.

6. A   There were many questions in his mind about what he had seen and known, and he worked at research when he got back, identifying the game and berries. Gut cherries were termed choke cherries, and made good jelly. The nut bushes where the foolbirds hid were hazelnut bushes. The two kinds of rabbits were snowshoes and cottontails; the foolbirds were ruffed grouse (also called fool hens by trappers, for their stupidity); the small food fish were bluegills, sunfish and perch; the turtle eggs were laid by a snapping turtle, as he had thought; the wolves were timber wolves, which are not known to attack or bother people; the moose was a moose.

7. B   Predictions are, for the most part, ineffective; but it might be interesting to note that had Brian not been rescued when he was, had he been forced to go into hard fall, perhaps winter, it would have been very rough on him. When the lake froze he would have lost the fish, and when the snow got deep he would have had trouble moving at all. Game becomes seemingly plentiful in the fall (it's easier to see with the leaves off the brush) but in winter it gets scarce and sometimes simply nonexistent as predators (fox, lynx, wolf, owls, weasels, fisher, martin, northern coyote) sweep through areas and wipe things out.